Time and Globalization

T0347165

Both academic and popular representations of globalization, critical or celebratory, have tended to conceptualize it primarily in spatial terms, rather than simultaneously temporal ones. However, time, in both its ideational and material dimensions, has played an important role in mediating and shaping the directions, courses, and outcomes of globalization.

Focusing on the intersection of time and globalization, this book aims to create an interdisciplinary dialogue between the (largely separated) respective literatures on each of these themes. This dialogue will be of both theoretical and empirical significance, since many urgent issues of contemporary human affairs—from large epochal problems such as climate change, to everyday struggles with the dynamics of social acceleration—involve a complex interplay between temporality and globalization. A critical understanding of the relationship between time and globalization will not only facilitate innovative thinking about globalization; it will also foster our imagination of alternatives that may lead to more socially just and sustainable futures. This innovative collection illustrates the theoretical benefits of bridging time with globalization and also exemplifies the methodological strengths of engaging in cutting-edge, interdisciplinary scholarship to better understand the changing economic, social, political, cultural and ecological dynamics in this globalizing world.

This book was originally published as a special issue of the journal *Globalizations*.

Paul Huebener is Assistant Professor of English in the Centre for Humanities at Athabasca University, Canada. He is the author of *Timing Canada: The shifting politics of time in Canadian literary culture* (2015).

Susie O'Brien is Associate Professor in the Department of English and Cultural Studies at McMaster University, Canada. Her work has been published in *Canadian Literature, Postcolonial Text, Modern Fiction Studies, Cultural Critique, Interventions, Mosaic, South Atlantic Quarterly, The Review of Education, Pedagogy* and *Cultural Studies*.

Tony Porter is Professor of Political Science at McMaster University, Canada. His most recent books are *Transnational Financial Regulation after the Financial Crisis* (2014) and *Transnational Financial Associations and the Governance of Global Finance* (2013, with Heather McKeen-Edwards).

Liam Stockdale is a Postdoctoral Fellow at the Institute for Innovation and Excellence in Teaching and Learning, McMaster University, Canada. He is the author of *Taming an Uncertain Future: Temporality, Sovereignty, and the Politics of Anticipatory Governance* (2016).

Yanqiu Rachel Zhou is Associate Professor at the Institute on Globalization and the Human Condition and the School of Social Work, McMaster University, Canada. She has widely published in the fields of transnationalism, health, and social policy in edited books and in various peer-reviewed journals, including *Journal of Aging Studies, Health, Time and Society*, and *Social Science and Medicine.*

Time and Globalization

An interdisciplinary dialogue

Edited by
**Paul Huebener, Susie O'Brien, Tony Porter,
Liam Stockdale and Yanqiu Rachel Zhou**

Routledge
Taylor & Francis Group

LONDON AND NEW YORK

First published 2017 by Routledge

2 Park Square, Milton Park, Abingdon, Oxfordshire OX14 4RN
52 Vanderbilt Avenue, New York, NY 10017

Routledge is an imprint of the Taylor & Francis Group, an informa business

First issued in paperback 2018

British Library Cataloguing in Publication Data
A catalogue record for this book is available from the British Library

ISBN13: 978-1-138-29221-5 (hbk)
ISBN13: 978-0-367-14303-9 (pbk)

Typeset in Times New Roman
by RefineCatch Limited, Bungay, Suffolk

Publisher's Note
The publisher accepts responsibility for any inconsistencies that may have
arisen during the conversion of this book from journal articles to book chapters,
namely the possible inclusion of journal terminology.

Disclaimer
Every effort has been made to contact copyright holders for their permission to
reprint material in this book. The publishers would be grateful to hear from any
copyright holder who is not here acknowledged and will undertake to rectify
any errors or omissions in future editions of this book.

Contents

Citation Information

The chapters in this book were originally published in *Globalizations* volume 13, issue 3 (June 2016). When citing this material, please use the original page numbering for each article, as follows:

Chapter 7

'We Thought the World Was Makeable': Scenario Planning and Postcolonial Fiction
Susie O'Brien
Globalizations volume 13, issue 3 (June 2016) pp. 329–344

Chapter 8

Strategic Planning in the 'Empire of Speed'
Kamilla Petrick
Globalizations volume 13, issue 3 (June 2016) pp. 345–359

For any permission-related enquiries please visit:
http://www.tandfonline.com/page/help/permissions

Notes on Contributors

William D. Coleman is Professor of Political Science at the University of Waterloo and the Balsillie School of International Affairs, Canada. His research and teaching lie in the areas of globalization, global governance, and public policy.

Paul Huebener is Assistant Professor of English in the Centre for Humanities at Athabasca University, Canada. He is the author of *Timing Canada: The shifting politics of time in Canadian literary culture* (2015).

Dr Sabine LeBel is an adjunct professor at the University College Writing Centre and in the Arts, Culture, and Media Department at the University of Toronto, where she teaches a visual culture class and is developing a course on media and the environment.

Victor Li teaches in the Department of English and the Centre for Comparative Literature at the University of Toronto, Canada. His research focuses on contemporary literature and critical theory, the continuing influence of primitivism in Western culture, and postcolonial and globalization studies.

Cheryl Lousley is Associate Professor of English and Interdisciplinary Studies at Lakehead University Orillia, Canada, and the series editor of the Environmental Humanities book series with Wilfrid Laurier University Press.

Kamilla (Pietrzyk) Petrick completed her Ph.D. dissertation in 2013 on the topic of 'Fast Activism' and the alter-globalization movement in Canada, under the supervision of Dr Leo Panitch. Her work has appeared in *Fast Capitalism, Convergence, and Time & Society.*

Tony Porter is Professor of Political Science at McMaster University, Canada. His most recent books are *Transnational Financial Regulation after the Financial Crisis* (2014) and *Transnational Financial Associations and the Governance of Global Finance* (2013, with Heather McKeen-Edwards).

Liam Stockdale is a Postdoctoral Fellow at the Institute for Innovation and Excellence in Teaching and Learning, McMaster University, Canada. He is the author of *Taming an Uncertain Future: Temporality, Sovereignty, and the Politics of Anticipatory Governance* (2016).

Susie O'Brien is Associate Professor in the Department of English and Cultural Studies at McMaster University, Canada. Her work has been published in *Canadian Literature, Postcolonial Text, Modern Fiction Studies, Cultural Critique, Interventions, Mosaic, South Atlantic Quarterly, The Review of Education* and *Pedagogy and Cultural Studies.*

Yanqiu Rachel Zhou is Associate Professor at the Institute on Globalization and the Human Condition and the School of Social Work, McMaster University, Canada. She has widely published in the fields of transnationalism, health, and social policy in edited books and in various peer-reviewed journals, including *Journal of Aging Studies, Health, Time and Society,* and *Social Science and Medicine.*

INTRODUCTION

Exploring the Intersection of Time and Globalization

PAUL HUEBENER*, SUSIE O'BRIEN**, TONY PORTER**,
LIAM STOCKDALE** & YANQIU RACHEL ZHOU**

*Athabasca University, Athabasca, AB, Canada
**McMaster University, Hamilton, ON, Canada

Consider the following four contemporaneous yet diverse events:

- On 30 September 2014, Thomas Eric Duncan—a 42-year-old Liberian citizen who had traveled to Dallas, Texas to visit family—became the first person to be diagnosed with Ebola hemorrhagic fever in North America. By adding the USA to the list of countries with confirmed Ebola cases, Duncan's diagnosis and subsequent death exacerbated a simmering global panic over the potential worldwide transmission of the highly lethal disease, whose previous outbreaks had not spread significantly beyond their initial sites of emergence. It was subsequently revealed that the period between his initial infection and ultimate diagnosis saw Duncan travel thousands of kilometers across three continents while remaining unknown to either national or global public health authorities ('Retracing the steps of the Dallas Ebola patient', 2014).
- On 12 November 2014, US President Barack Obama and Chinese President Xi Jinping made a surprise announcement that their respective states—the world's two largest economies, energy consumers, and carbon emitters—had reached an agreement to jointly limit greenhouse gas emissions over the next two decades. Under the terms of the pact, the USA is required to reduce emissions to 26–28% below 2005 levels by 2025, while China pledged

1

for the first time to cap emissions growth and begin reductions by 2030 (White House, 2014). United Nations Framework Convention on Climate Change (UNFCCC) chief executive Christina Figueres favorably described the plan as an 'important pathway towards a better and more secure future for humankind' ('US and China strike deal on carbon cuts', 2014).

- On 4 January 2015, an American unmanned aerial vehicle—more commonly known as a drone—fired two missiles into a compound located in the Datta Khel sub-district of North Waziristan, near Pakistan's border with Afghanistan. The strike killed six suspected militants while wounding two others, and in so doing extended the US drone warfare campaign being waged across the Greater Middle East into its 13th year (Khan, 2015).
- In June 2014, the worldwide price of oil began a precipitous drop, ultimately falling 46% by December and significantly upending predictions about the trajectory of world commodity markets (Friedman, 2014). The decline fomented significant turmoil across the global economy by creating greater uncertainty about future economic trends and their intersection with geopolitical risks in areas of strategic energy importance (Giles, 2014).

Despite their broad substantive differences, each of these temporally concurrent incidents relates to a defining challenge of globalization—pandemic disease, climate change, transnational terrorism, and the centrality and volatility of fossil fuels in an increasingly integrated world economy. Perhaps less obviously, each is also notable for its representation of the interaction between *time* and globalization. For example, Thomas Eric Duncan used the established global mobility regime to travel from Monrovia to Dallas within the limited temporal window of Ebola's incubation period, thus globalizing the disease's reach to an extent not previously seen; the US–China climate agreement recognizes that the apparent benefits of economic globalization are incompatible with an uncertain environmental future exposed to the potentially catastrophic effects of major climatic changes; the American drone program uses the global range of drone technology to carry out targeted killings in the present to preclude those killed from posing any potential threat to the USA at some indefinite point in the future; and commodity futures markets are a central determinant of global oil prices, indicating that anticipatory speculation about the direction of the global economy was a crucial driver of the months-long decline.

That the interaction between time and globalization is crucial to each of these specific events and the broader challenges they represent suggests two points that serve as the impetus for this special issue. The first is that understanding the intersection of time and globalization is essential to thinking about the central problems of contemporary human conditions and experiences. Foregrounding this relationship can thus generate valuable and original analytical lenses through which to engage with the pressing social, political, economic, cultural, and ecological issues that characterize our current moment. The second point is that these two fundamental concepts of contemporary inquiry in the humanities and social sciences—globalization and time—cannot be adequately understood in isolation from one another. In other words, we cannot think seriously about globalization without thinking seriously about time; and conversely, we cannot adequately understand how time is perceived and experienced in the contemporary context without considering its relationship to the phenomena that constitute globalization.

A collective recognition of these two points inspired the guest editors of this special issue to found the Time and Globalization Working Project, based at McMaster University's Institute on Globalization and the Human Condition. This initiative began in November 2011 with a preliminary workshop that tentatively explored the intersection between time and globalization from an interdisciplinary perspective. A working paper forum collecting selected interventions from the workshop followed (Huebener, O'Brien, Porter, Stockdale, & Zhou, 2012), and after receiving a

Connection Grant from the Social Sciences and Humanities Research Council of Canada, the Project's steering committee set out to build a transnational network of scholars interested in exploring this theme in greater depth. This was realized through the convening of two subsequent workshops held at McMaster in October 2013 and September 2014, respectively, where preliminary and then revised versions of the papers collected here were among those presented and discussed by an international, multidisciplinary group of over 20 scholars.

In publishing this work, the aim is to introduce a selection of innovative meditations on the interaction between time and globalization into scholarly conversations across a variety of disciplines. In so doing, we hope in particular to highlight the analytical utility and critical potential of foregrounding temporal questions in the study of globalization. This collection of essays thus illustrates how taking the relationship between globalization and time seriously can enhance our understanding of each of these crucial concepts, both on their own terms and as they relate to some of the defining issues of the twenty-first-century world.

Building On and Going Beyond Existing Literatures

This special issue draws on and draws together themes from the rich and varied literatures on globalization and on time. Despite an overall dearth of engagement between the two literatures, there have been some important efforts to integrate time and globalization in some manner. For instance, the globalization literature has recognized that historically, timekeeping technologies played a key role in European intercontinental exploration and colonization (Sobel, 1995, p. 106). Precise timekeeping across global distances was thus spurred by, and in turn facilitated, the globalizing processes of exploration, cartography, resource exploitation, and colonization. What is more, globalization and colonization increasingly make visible the cultural and ideological aspects of time, as the imposition of Western forms of time reckoning such as clock time, along with narratives of progress and modernity, onto European colonies suggests that imperialism is as much a temporal process as it is a spatial one (Fabian, 1983). Other work has explored how the activation of international telegraph wires in the 1860s made the concept of global simultaneity more immediate, and 'the concept of a global "now" inserted itself into the average citizen's consciousness, at least in Western nations' (Dewdney, 2008, p. 64)—a development quickly followed by the invention of the space–time-collapsing telephone. The political and social significance of the creation of global time zones in the nineteenth century has also been insightfully analyzed by a number of globalization scholars (Barrows, 2011; Zerubavel, 1982). In analyses of our contemporary period, meanwhile, the link between globalization and the speed of communication is widely recognized (Hassan & Purser, 2007). Harvey's discussion of 'time–space compression', for example, links macro-historical shifts in capitalism to the search for 'new spaces within which capitalist production can proceed', as well as the accelerated turnover of production (1992, p. 183). Sassen (2000) has analyzed the interaction of slower national and faster global temporalities. Der Derian (1992), by contrast, has drawn on Paul Virilio's theoretical reflections on speed to analyze changes in international relations.

In analyzing the intersection of time and globalization, it is also useful to draw on insights from the broader literature on time, even if this literature often does not consider globalization in much depth. To the extent that it does, this is generally at a micro-sociological or implicitly national level, without specifying or analyzing its location in the larger world of cross-border relations. There have nonetheless been some notable contributions that inform our work, such as the sociological literature on the phenomenon of social acceleration, which has been the focus of especially fruitful analysis (Hassan & Purser, 2007; Rosa, 2013; Rosa & Scheuerman,

2009). Rosa's (2009) work in particular stands out, as he helpfully discusses efforts to measure social acceleration, as well as the drivers and political consequences of these changes.

Despite such diverse and valuable contributions, much more work is still needed to understand the interactions of time and globalization in the contemporary context. This is the challenge that we address in this special issue, as we aim to deepen our understanding of both concepts at a theoretical level while also directly engaging with some of the most urgent issues associated with globalization, such as financial and environmental crises, international aid, and the emergence and re-emergence of infectious diseases. It is particularly valuable to integrate understandings of how we imagine and experience changes in time and globalization at the most personal and planetary scales. Few changes are more centrally implicated in, and so freely range across, all aspects of human cultural and social life; and so our project has had an intensely interdisciplinary character from its start, which is reflected in the selection of articles included in this special collection.

This project is informed by a particular understanding of how to think about defining time. Felski (2000) has persuasively noted that time

> is a concept of enormous complexity, including questions of measurement, rhythm, synchronization, sequence, tempo and intensity. It spans the personal and the public, work and leisure, the instantaneous and the eternal, intimate relations and global structures, everyday life and conditions of extremity. It exists at many different levels and is experienced in radically divergent ways. (pp. 16–17)

Accordingly, it is our position that proposing any specific articulation of what we consider time to be would be counterproductive to the project at hand. Indeed, not only have two millennia of philosophic inquiry struggled to elucidate a clear ontology and phenomenology of time;[1] but attempting to do so here would work against the critical ethos that underpins this project, since it would serve to foreclose one of the key aspects of the terrain we are interested in exploring. In other words, the contextual variability of humanity's understanding and experience of time is one of the most interesting aspects of the contemporary intersection of temporality and globalization. Rather than addressing the ontology of time directly, therefore, we broadly concur with Allen (2008), who argues that

> time is defined in relation to the purposes it serves. Hence, we can never say what time is. Instead, we can only ask what kinds of worlds different forms of time make possible, and what interests are served by the creation of such worlds. (p. 217)

In this special issue, we are not interested in trying to 'say what time is'. Instead, we are interested in exploring the myriad worlds created by the myriad temporalities that are passively encountered and actively mobilized in the course of our ongoing experiences of globalization. We are also interested in the implications of interactions between time and globalization for our futures.

In preparing this collection, we have identified four important themes in analyzing the relationship between time and globalization, which challenge dominant understandings in key ways. The first, *chronopolitics*, is about the role of power in this relationship, including, for instance, the historical conceptions and practices associated with colonialism. This theme challenges the common assumption that time is a background experience that is independent of human agency. The second, *heterotemporalities*, refers to the infinitely varied experiences of time that can coexist and interact simultaneously at multiple locations and scales operating within and against dominant chronopolitical tendencies. This concept challenges the idea that a homogenous dominant globalized experience of time is erasing distinctive local and personal temporalities. The third, *materiality*, explores the multidirectional entanglements of ideas, technical artifacts, bodies, and the natural environment in the interaction of time and globalization. This type of hybridity challenges notions of time as intrinsic to nature, with humans merely elaborating ways to perceive and comply with these unalterable natural forms of order, repetition, and sequencing. The fourth, *global futures*, addresses the impact of the changing interaction between globalization and time on how we imagine, are governed by, or create our futures. As the force of tradition has diminished it is not yet clear whether we let hegemonic conceptions of the future dictate our conduct—as when we comply with risk models—or if the future is vanishing, displaced by the intensity and instantaneity of global flows. By foregrounding the creative ways that we imagine, contest, construct, and live our futures—and by treating the changing future as one part of a larger process of changes in time and globalization—our conception of global futures challenges any notion that such changes are inexorable. Taken together, our themes emphasize that neither globalization nor time are unified or independent forces, but are instead infinitely varied, and fully part of the distinctively human experience and exercise of creativity, imagination, power, resistance, and being in the world. In the remainder of this introduction, we comment on each of our four themes in further detail, and then summarize the articles in this special issue.

Chronopolitics

As Fabian (1983) shows in his seminal work, *Time and the other*, the politics of imperialism and other power relations are bound up with cultural experiences and uses of time. Because colonization is predicated on the temporal frameworks of 'progress, development, and modernity', Fabian argues, '*geopolitics* has its ideological foundations in *chronopolitics*' (p. 144). Thirty years after Fabian's writing, the study of chronopolitics—of the assumptions and power relations inherent in contested notions of time—remains central to understanding the evolution and consequences of globalization. Conceptualizing time as a form of power can usefully illuminate a wide range of relevant issues, from the forms of temporal domination associated with colonialism, to the economic and political relationships between the global North and South, to specific concerns related to corporate power, disease responses, international aid, and social justice movements. The question of who has the ability to impose their preferred temporal frames and ideologies, and the related question of why some forms of time fail to gain traction, is a vital one for considerations of globalization.

Scholars from various disciplines take up the matter of global chronopolitics by examining the difficult negotiations with temporal powers and experiences that occur in a range of contemporary globalized contexts. Theorists including Paul Virilio, Zygmunt Bauman, and Hartmut Rosa have interrogated the ways in which speed increasingly defines global configurations of power by investigating, for example, how high-speed actors are increasingly able to dominate slower actors; in the words of Bauman (2000), 'it is the people who cannot move as quickly [...] who are ruled' (pp. 178–179). Differential access to instantaneity and rapid adaptability can mean the difference between domination and subjugation. Many key processes of globalization—from the manipulation of speed in global financial markets to the role of temporality in the strategic behavior of multinational corporations—entail the manipulation of temporality to serve powerful interests (Porter & Stockdale, in press, this issue).

The dominance of particular social narratives and policies also reflects the contested forms of power associated with global chronopolitics. The network of global cities that was constructed largely for the purpose of accelerating economic globalization also unexpectedly permitted the rapid transmission of severe acute respiratory syndrome (SARS) during the 2003 outbreak—a situation that highlights the importance of thinking beyond the hegemonic vision of economics when it comes to planning and theorizing global connections (Zhou & Coleman, in press, this issue). In a different context, the narrative characteristics of the Live Aid and Live 8 benefit concerts suggest that narratives of global humanitarianism tend to borrow temporal strategies from the genre of melodrama, and that the strategic representation of time within these projects in fact serves partially to legitimate the perpetuation of global inequality (Lousley, in press, this issue). The strategic planning abilities of contemporary global justice movements also exist in tension with the forces of social acceleration; interviews with social activists reveal how the constant pressures of precariousness, urgency, and speed both shape and limit the activists' tactics and priorities (Petrick, in press, this issue).

Heterotemporalities

On the one hand, economic globalization commonly displays a hegemonic and homogenizing force, operating to synchronize or even annihilate diverse temporalities associated with particular cultures, places, histories, and human experiences. On the other hand, it has also led to increasing temporal–spatial disjuncture as well as desynchronization of different groups and segments of society, given their differential capacity to accelerate in a 'high-speed society' (Hassan, 2005; Rosa, 2009). Explaining how this causal relationship can work in both directions, Hope (2009) points out that the structures and activities of global capitalism are riven by contradictions and conflicts between opposing temporal logics, in part because the networks of global capitalism may weaken 'the conjunctures between nation, state, economy, and society, and exacerbate temporal disjunctures within them' (p. 62). Yet heterotemporalities are not solely the product of global capitalism; in fact, the complex relationships among different temporalities have constituted aspects—including manipulation, contestation, and resistance—of contemporary globalization itself.

Indeed, the operation of economic globalization heavily relies on the strategic use—or, exploitation—of multiple temporalities, in such forms as the manipulation of the future in global financial markets, transnational corporations' arrangements of global production activities, and the global e-waste trade between the North and the South (LeBel, in press, this issue; Porter & Stockdale, in press, this issue). In the case of e-waste, different temporalities (such as those based on access to technologies and to economic resources in general) across geographies are the foundation on which the poor countries' or communities' exposure to environmental toxicity, health risk, and an unsustainable future are created, maintained, and reinforced (LeBel, in press, this issue). In the case of infectious diseases such as SARS or Ebola, however, not only the South but also the North are *simultaneously* vulnerable primarily because of heterotemporalities based on nation-states, such as the varied speeds of information flow and differential capacities to respond to the simultaneous health emergency. The accelerated circulation of pathogens through the networks of global cities and international airports thus indicates the urgent need to address temporal disjunctures as well as inequalities in the contexts of international health collaboration and global health crises (Zhou & Coleman, in press, this issue). In this sense, heterotemporality or non-global temporalities also play an important role in interrupting, resisting, and challenging the normative and hegemonic temporal framework of global capitalism, and thus confirming the potential of 'othered' time to diversify the futures of globalization (Li, in press, this issue).

Materiality

Our experience of time involves a relationship between human consciousness of time and material rhythms. Some of these material rhythms, such as the earth's rotation, are independent of humans; others, such as the rotation of a clock's hands, are constructed by humans, constituting temporal artifacts. The interactions of time and globalization have always been linked to technical artifacts, as with the measuring devices that created global time zones in the nineteenth century (Hom, 2010), or today's information technologies that seem to shrink the world and accelerate daily life (Hassan & Purser, 2007). The materiality of the human body interacts with changes in globalization and time, as Li (in press, this issue) shows in exploring the interplay in Don DeLillo's novel *Cosmopolis* between individual bodies, local street life, and the high-speed world of global finance. The expression of ideas or social commitments in material form helps them endure through time and travel across space—as with written documents or money—or embed them locally or nationally—as with urban architectures, and museums. Temporal artifacts can help manage the future, as with planning, scheduling, or risk management technologies. At the same time, the obstinate materiality of people and things can complicate such efforts to plan (O'Brien, in press, this issue). Technical artifacts can also obscure the future. As Urry (2009) has noted, 'as a result of the need for instantaneous responses, particularly because of the speed implied by the telephone, telex, fax, electronic signals, and so on, the future dissolves into an extended present', reducing our capacity to imagine or shape the future (p. 191). These high-speed information and communications technologies (ICTs) that are centrally involved in trans-formations of globalization and time produce a much longer term material legacy in the form of e-waste, which when traded across borders can create a kind of 'slow violence' (Nixon, 2011) from its negative environmental effects. Our experiences of time and globalization thus shape and are shaped by the materiality of production processes and transportation infrastructures, which accel-erate and intensify the cross-border circulation of products and the linkages of our individual journeys through time as workers, consumers, and biological beings. While it is important to recognize the material dimensions of time, we should challenge the notion that it is a natural phenomenon that operates beyond the reach of human creativity, just as assertions that globaliza-tion is a quasi-natural process have been discredited. Humans are continually acting on and through the ideas, technical artifacts, bodies, and natural environments, through which we experience and make use of time and globalization (Porter & Stockdale, in press, this issue).

Global Futures

The future assumes diverse and even contradictory significances in the context of globalization. It is at once *under*valued, overshadowed by a focus on the short term, and *over*valued, its force as an object of speculation exerting a powerful influence on the present. For many critics, globali-zation entails a troubling collapse of futurity as an area of concern. The problem has many related causes, including digital technology that shrinks the temporal horizon by facilitating near-instantaneous connection, and the economic system enabled by that technology. It is not only that capitalist society is geared toward short-term profit, but also that, in the digitized realm of finance, infinitesimal temporal differences can be leveraged to massive advantage (Porter & Stockdale, in press, this issue). The long term recedes in significance in such a digi-tized economy, an effect that reflects and also shapes a surrounding culture that is fixated on the present (Adam, 1998; Bindé, 2000). Within this orientation, driven by the tempos of market rationality, 'future people and environmental sustainability. . . . are not readily encompassed within the boundaries of [our] concerns' (Adam, 1998, p. 15). The problem is exacerbated by the tendency to overestimate the extent to which digital connectedness represents the elimination of time and space. E-waste represents one example of the danger of an unreflexive celebration of technological transcendence (LeBel, in press, this issue).

The long-term health effects of e-waste toxins on workers and ecosystems are still unknown. Such uncertainties are pervasive. Systemic and non-linear changes arising from the 'complex connectivity' of globalization (Tomlinson, 1999) whose symptoms range from environmental events such as climate change to terrorism and global epidemics render the past increasingly useless as a guide to the future. The erosion of scientific and economic certainty, along with the dissolution, via the end of state communism, of any large visible alternative to capitalism, has made the future simply more difficult to conceptualize. This faltering of the imagination constrains people's capacity to invest their hopes in utopian projects such as sustainable development (Lousley, in press, this issue). It also affects progressive movements in smaller, but more practical ways, for example by hampering the ability of actors in such movements to engage in long-term planning (Petrick, in press, this issue).

Clearly, though, in spite of its increasing inscrutability, the future has not receded from view. In fact, even as it is discounted in certain contexts, it has simultaneously become the object of burgeoning speculation (in diverse senses of the word). Key to this engagement is a concept of the future as a zone in which, following from Ulrich Beck's concept of the risk society (1999), 'turbulence [can] not be prevented; it [can] only be managed' (Cooper, 2010, p. 167). Addressing the imperative to manage the future is a raft of technologies ranging from financial instruments like derivatives to risk management strategies such as scenario planning (Cooper, 2010; O'Brien, in press, this issue). These tools ideally work to help individuals and organizations leverage 'black swans' ('high-impact low-probability' events [Taleb, 2010]) as opportunities—a practice that finds its darkest realization in what Naomi Klein (2007) calls 'disaster capitalism'. In a finance economy in which the 'futures' market plays a key role, speculations (e.g. of future volatility) have the capacity to bring about the conditions they forecast, thereby bringing the future to bear on the present in unprecedented ways (Cooper, 2010). The controlling force of (beliefs about) the future on the present finds further manifestation in the widespread adoption in the security realm of the rationale of preemption (Stockdale, 2013). In the light of prevailing thinking on terrorism, according to which it is always 'a matter of not *if* but *when*' the next strike will occur, many states have passed, or are planning, counterterrorism laws that facilitate extensive surveillance, preventive arrest, and other anticipatory measures (Amoore & de Goede, 2008). A key aspect of all these forms of risk management concerns not their success or failure but rather the threat they pose to democracy—a threat that, post-9/11, clearly affects certain racialized populations more than others.

Whether the future is discounted or overvalued, the anxiety it induces reflects the rapidity and complexity of changes occurring within and across the realms of culture, economy, and environment that characterize globalization. These changes combine to produce a future characterized by 'irreducible indeterminacy', which confounds the most rigorous and expansive calculations (Adam, 1998, p. 36).

Summary of Contributions

Victor Li's article, entitled 'The untimely in globalization's time: Don DeLillo's *Cosmopolis*', examines both the temporal framework capitalist globalization imposes on the world and the times outside that framework that, by their 'untimeliness', disturb globalization's temporality.

He argues that just as globalization's spatial framing requires anomalous spaces to be left out, so too does globalization's temporal framing of the world demand the exclusion of those times that do not fit. Viewing the relationship between globalization's time and the persistence of 'untimely' or othered times as unequal yet dynamic, Li emphasizes the importance of the latter in threatening and resisting the former's normativity and naturalization from outside. The existence of the non-global temporalities and the untimely not only calls into question the thesis of the homogeneity of time; it also suggests 'a temporality open to difference, to immiscible times, and to a future that remains undetermined'.

In their article 'The strategic manipulation of transnational temporalities', Tony Porter and Liam Stockdale explore the role of human agency in the interaction of time and globalization by developing the concept of temporal systems, which are assemblages of such temporal artifacts as clocks, time zones, stages of life, and the temporal mechanisms of technological innovations, financial markets, and global governance. Through an analysis of four diverse examples, they illustrate that time, like globalization, is a social construct that is amenable to manipulation by human agency, rather than a natural unalterable structure that limits the behavior of human agents. More importantly, this sort of temporal manipulation plays a key role in certain processes and phenomena that are constitutive of what is broadly known as globalization. Challenging the naturalistic view of time, their discussion brings human actors back to the center of our understanding of the relationship between time, globalization, power, and agency.

Using the transmission in 2003 of SARS as a case study, Yanqiu Rachel Zhou and William D. Coleman's article, 'Accelerated contagion and response', examines the intersections of globalization, time, and diseases—a topic that has become increasingly pertinent in the context of emerging infectious diseases (EIDs) such as H1N1 and Ebola. Questioning traditional spatiality-based approaches in the field, they contend that globalizing processes have changed temporal–spatial dynamics of EIDs like SARS, in such forms as the speed of global transmission, the simultaneity of public health emergency across geographies, and the possibility of accelerating responses on a global level. While the technical infrastructure of global networks has provided a promising condition for accelerating surveillance and information sharing on a global level, other temporality-related challenges—such as differential capacities of the affected countries to respond to the simultaneity of the crisis—are yet to be tackled.

Sabine LeBel's essay, 'Fast machines, slow violence: ICTs, planned obsolescence, and e-waste', analyzes the temporality of the global e-waste recycling trade. Feminist philosopher Zoe Sofia's work on container technologies and environmental literary and cultural theorist Rob Nixon's theory of 'slow violence' offer helpful critical lenses for considering the environmental implications of the ICTs that have facilitated the global extension of fast connectivity. Focusing on the temporality of production that is built around planned obsolescence, along with the unknown, long-term effects of e-waste on the poor communities to which it is shipped, the essay illuminates a chronopolitics of e-waste that significantly complicates the conventional, often celebratory, association of ICTs with speed, acceleration, and simultaneity.

Cheryl Lousley's essay, 'Humanitarian melodramas, globalist nostalgia: Affective temporalities of globalization and uneven development', employs the generic conventions of melodrama to describe the temporal politics of the global humanitarian discourses in Live Aid/Live 8. Highlighting the operation of melodrama's characteristic temporal devices, such as peripeteia, deferral, delay, and missed chances, the essay argues that the Live 8 concert, held 20 years after the original Live Aid event, evinces a 'melancholic attachment to Euro-American global hegemony retroactively and repetitively constructed as a missed chance to do good that always meant well'. Melodrama works, Lousley suggests, to suspend time, patching over discontinuities between the era of international development and neoliberalism, and mobilizing (without resolving) contradictory affects of nostalgia and melancholy, aspiration, and ambivalence.

Susie O'Brien's essay, '"We thought the world was makeable": Scenario planning and postcolonial fiction', employs Indra Sinha's 2007 novel, *Animal's people*, as a critical lens to analyze the discourse of scenario planning. The essay suggests that scenario planning—a strategy of speculation about possible futures—expresses the idea of globalization as an inexorable unfolding of the world as a complex system while eliding the historical processes of colonialism and capitalism. As a fictional representation of the aftermath of the 1984 Union Carbide factory gas leak in Bhopal, India, *Animal's people* brings these erasures into view. The novel contests (thematically and formally) the hegemonic temporality of globalization that informs scenario planning and the model of risk management it inspires.

Kamilla Petrick's article 'Strategic planning in the "empire of speed"' examines the impact of social acceleration on the capacity for long-term strategic planning within contemporary global justice movements. After delineating the widespread changes to the future time perspective wrought by the shift from the modern 'age of progress' ruled by 'clock time', to a global 'network society' characterized by speed, risk, and uncertainty, Petrick draws upon several dozen semi-structured interviews with social activists in order to shed light upon the challenges to contemporary social justice movements posed by the pervasive sense of precarity and futurelessness associated with life in a high-speed, global risk society. Petrick argues that the dominant cultural sense of future precariousness militates against the individual and collective capacity to create plans for the long-term future, and that the shift toward an amorphous, networked mode of political engagement—what she calls 'fast activism'—likewise endangers the capacity for long-term strategic planning among alter-globalization activists.

Conclusion

Harmut Rosa's recent book *Social acceleration* (2013) represents a major accomplishment in the critical study of time in late modern societies. He convincingly demonstrates that the acceleration of a wide range of social processes is quantifiably real, and that social acceleration in fact constitutes the primary mode of experience in contemporary society. 'The experience of modernization', he writes, 'is an experience of acceleration' (p. 21). One of the strengths of Rosa's study is that by understanding modern societies as globally linked networks engaged in accelerative processes, he is able to craft a larger comprehensive model of social acceleration as a dominant global force. Of course, because his book takes such a large-scale approach, it leaves open many opportunities for the development of more nuanced insights into the particular expressions of acceleration in diverse places and circumstances, along with other forms of temporal power. As Sharma (2014) points out in her study of the cultural politics of temporality, 'theoretical critiques of the culture of speed [have] not paid sufficient attention to the institutional, cultural, and economic arrangements that produce specific tempos for different populations' (p. 137). She concludes that the intensive theoretical attention that has often been paid to the concept of acceleration has 'obscured the necessity of tracing how *differential* relationships to time organize and perpetuate inequalities' (p. 137). A fuller critical understanding of the relationships between time and globalization requires accounting for many forms of *difference*. Carrying out this work is one of the goals of this special issue of *Globalizations*.

Both of the subjects under consideration here—time and globalization—cannot be reduced to singular processes, experiences, or disciplines. An adequate understanding of their relationships must address diverse manifestations of both time and globalization across many different places and circumstances. Whether the authors of these articles are investigating the strategies of alter-globalization activist groups, the representation of humanitarian aid to a massive global audience, the temporal implications of the global circulation of computer technologies, or other cultural experiences and activities, these projects seek to illuminate the many different 'worlds' that the connected processes of time and globalization make possible. In the end, perhaps the most significant lesson to draw from this collection of work is that the critical study of time enables us to imagine *different globalizations*. The wide-ranging insights that the authors of this issue put forward suggest that time, perhaps more than any other element of social experience and power, deserves to be understood as the fulcrum of different forms of globalization. The articles in this issue contribute an important degree of complexity to Rosa's fear that the acceleration of society has progressed to such a dangerous and unstoppable degree that 'the time of modern politics has run out' (2013, p. 267). At the same time, these studies also suggest that the global waters of temporal power and possibility run very deep indeed.

Acknowledgements

This work was supported by the Social Sciences and Humanities Research Council of Canada and the Institute on Globalization and the Human Condition at McMaster University. We also thank Barry Gills for his editorial support.

Disclosure Statement

No potential conflict of interest was reported by the authors.

Note

1   Even towering philosophical figures separated by vast chronological and philosophical gulfs seem to agree on this point. For instance, Heidegger once described time as inherently 'unthinkable', while St. Augustine famously claimed to know what time was up until the moment he was made 'to explain it to one that asketh'.

References

Adam, B. (1998). *Timescapes of modernity: The environment and invisible hazards*. London: Routledge.
Allen, T. (2008). *A republic in time: Temporality and social imagination in nineteenth-century America*. Chapel Hill: University of North Carolina Press.
Amoore, L., & de Goede, M. (Eds). (2008). *Risk and the war on terror*. London: Routledge.
Barrows, A. (2011). *The cosmic time of empire*. Berkeley: University of California Press.
Bauman, Z. (2000). Time and space reunited. *Time and Society*, 9(2–3), 171–185.
Beck, U. (1999). *World risk society*. Malden, MA: Blackwell.
Bindé, J. (2000). Toward an ethics of the future. *Public Culture*, 12(1), 51–72.
Cooper, M. (2010). Turbulent worlds: Financial markets and environmental crisis. *Theory, Culture & Society*, 27(2–3), 167–190.
Der Derian, J. (1992). *Antidiplomacy: Spies, terror, speed and war*. Oxford: Blackwell.
Dewdney, C. (2008). *Soul of the world: Unlocking the secrets of time*. Toronto: HarperCollins.
Fabian, J. (1983). *Time and the other: How anthropology makes its object*. New York, NY: Columbia University Press.
Felski, R. (2000). *Doing time: Feminist theory and postmodern culture*. New York, NY: New York University Press.
Friedman, N. (2014, December 31). US oil prices fall 46% this year. *Wall Street Journal*. Retrieved from http://www.wsj.com/articles/oil-prices-hit-again-by-weak-china-data-buildup-in-u-s-stockpiles-1420019256
Giles, C. (2014, December 15). Winners and losers of the oil price plunge. *Financial Times*. Retrieved from http://www.ft.com/intl/cms/s/2/3f5e4914-8490-11e4-ba4f-00144feabdc0.html#axzz3P11RuC4R

Harvey, D. (1992). *The condition of postmodernity*. Oxford: Blackwell.

Hassan, R. (2005). Timescapes of the network society. *Fast Capitalism, 1*(1). Retrieved from http://www.uta.edu/huma/agger/fastcapitalism/1_1/hassan.html

Hassan, R., & Purser, R. (Eds.). (2007). *24/7: Time and temporality in the network society*. Redwood City, CA: Stanford University Press.

Hom, A. (2010). Hegemonic metronome: The ascendancy of Western standard time. *Review of International Studies, 36*, 1145–1170.

Hope, W. (2009). Conflicting temporalities: State, nation, economy and democracy under global capitalism. *Time & Society, 18*(1), 62–85.

Huebener, P., O'Brien, S., Porter, T., Stockdale, L., & Zhou, Y. R. (Eds.). (2012). *Interdisciplinary forum on time and globalization* (Working Paper 12/3). Institute on Globalization and the Human Condition, McMaster University. Retrieved from http://www.socialsciences.mcmaster.ca/institute-on-globalization-and-the-human-condition/documents/IGHC-WPS_12-3_T-G%20Forum.pdf

Khan, I. (2015, January 4). US drone strike in Pakistan said to have killed 6 militants. *New York Times*. Retrieved from http://www.nytimes.com/2015/01/05/world/asia/us-drone-strike-pakistan.html

Klein, N. (2007). *The shock doctrine: The rise of disaster capitalism*. Toronto: Knopf.

LeBel, S. (in press). Fast machines, slow violence: ICTs, planned obsolescence, and e-waste. *Globalizations*. doi:10.1080/14747731.2015.1056492

Li, V. (in press). The untimely in globalization's time: Don DeLillo's Cosmopolis. *Globalizations*. doi:10.1080/14747731.2015.1056493

Lousley, C. (in press). Humanitarian melodramas, globalist nostalgia: Affective temporalities of globalization and uneven development. *Globalizations*. doi:10.1080/14747731.2015.1056494

Nixon, R. (2011). *Slow violence and the environmentalism of the poor*. Cambridge, MA: Harvard University Press.

O'Brien, S. (in press). 'We thought the world was makeable': Scenario planning and postcolonial fiction. *Globalizations*. doi:10.1080/14747731.2015.1056495

Petrick, K. (in press). Strategic planning in the 'empire of speed.' *Globalizations*. doi:10.1080/14747731.2015.1056496

Porter, T., & Stockdale, L. (in press). The strategic manipulation of transnational temporalities. *Globalizations*. doi:10.1080/14747731.2015.1056497

Retracing the steps of the Dallas Ebola patient. (2014, October 8). *New York Times*. Retrieved from http://www.nytimes.com/interactive/2014/10/01/us/retracing-the-steps-of-the-dallas-ebola-patient.html?_r=0

Rosa, H. (2009). Social acceleration: Ethical and political consequences of a desynchronized high-speed society. In H. Rosa & W. E. Scheuerman (Eds.), *High-speed society: Social acceleration, power and modernity* (pp. 77–112). University Park: Pennsylvania State University Press.

Rosa, H. (2013). *Social acceleration: A new theory of modernity*. New York, NY: Columbia University Press.

Rosa, H., & Scheuerman, W. E. (Eds.). (2009). *High-speed society: Social acceleration, power, and modernity*. University Park: Pennsylvania State University Press.

Sassen, S. (2000). Spatialities and temporalities of the global: Elements for a theorization. *Public Culture, 12*(1), 215–232.

Sharma, S. (2014). *In the meantime: Temporality and cultural politics*. Durham, NC: Duke University Press.

Sobel, D. (1995). *Longitude*. New York, NY: Walker.

Stockdale, L. P. D. (2013). Imagined futures and exceptional presents: A conceptual critique of 'pre-emptive security'. *Global Change, Peace & Security, 25*, 141–157.

Taleb, N. N. (2010). *The black swan: The impact of the highly improbable*. New York, NY: Random House.

Tomlinson, J. (1999). *Globalization and culture*. Chicago, IL: University of Chicago Press.

Urry, J. (2009). Speeding up and slowing down. In H. Rose & W. E. Scheuerman, (Eds.), *High-speed society: Social acceleration, power, and modernity* (pp. 179–198). University Park: Pennsylvania State University Press.

US and China strike deal on carbon cuts in push for global climate change pact. (2014, November 12). *The Guardian*. Retrieved from http://www.theguardian.com/environment/2014/nov/12/china-and-us-make-carbon-pledge

White House. (2014, November 11). US-China joint announcement on climate change. Washington, DC: Office of the Press Secretary. Retrieved from http://www.whitehouse.gov/the-press-office/2014/11/11/us-china-joint-announcement-climate-change

Zerubavel, E. (1982). The standardization of time: A sociohistorical perspective. *American Journal of Sociology, 88*(1), 1–23.

Zhou, Y. R., & Coleman, W. D. (in press). Accelerated contagion and response: Understanding the relationships among globalization, time, and disease. *Globalizations*. doi:10.1080/14747731.2015.1056498

The Untimely in Globalization's Time: Don DeLillo's *Cosmopolis*

VICTOR LI

University of Toronto, Toronto, Canada

ABSTRACT   *Globalization's time is made possible through the elision or devaluation of other times and the attempt to control and foreclose the future through the technological acceleration of its own temporality. But global time remains haunted by traces of the non-global and the untimely. My paper will examine both the temporal framework capitalist globalization imposes on the world and the times outside that framework that, by their untimeliness, disturb globalization's time. I will focus my discussion on Don DeLillo's* Cosmopolis, *a novel that not only provides us with a description of capitalist globalization's temporal regime but also tracks the disruptive emergence of the untimely. The untimely emerges as persistent anachronistic matter and the body in pain: both remain resistant to global capitalism's desire to annul time itself. My paper, therefore, attempts to make a case for heterotemporality against capitalist globalization's isochrony, which seeks to put an end to time.*

Descriptions of globalization involve an active framing of the world that brings into visible focus what purports to be a true representation of our contemporary world on condition that other views of the world are excluded or made to disappear. In such a framing of the world, the condition for knowing the world as a whole is paradoxically the exclusion of many aspects of that same world. While studies of globalization have generally focused on the spatial framing of the world, I want in this essay to examine globalization's temporal framing and to argue that just as globalization's spatial framing requires anomalous spaces to be left out, so too globalization's temporal framing of the world demands the exclusion of those times that do not fit, those times that are therefore considered to be untimely. In a talk titled 'In What Time Do We Live?' presented at the 2011 Venice Biennale, Rancière (2012) noted that

> Every description of a 'state of things' gives a major part to time. There is a simple reason for this: a 'state of things' presents itself as an objective given that precludes the possibility of other states of things. And time is the best medium for exclusion. (p. 11)

Rancière's point seems apt for our current 'state of globalization': time is still the best medium for exclusion.

The temporal frame within which capitalist globalization operates emphasizes growth, accumulation, innovation, and the continuous 24/7 functioning of the global market; it is also future-oriented and infatuated with speed. Those times that cannot enter globalization's temporal frame because they do not fit its 24/7 operational mode, future-oriented temporality, and accelerated tempo are (mis)translated as anachronistic—they are literally othered, devalued, deemed obsolete, seen no longer to count. As Lim (2009) points out, 'intractable differences are *temporally managed* by being positioned as already known and surmounted precursors, not something disturbing that persists alongside and within the modern but as relics of superseded chronological antecedents' (p. 16). These 'chronological antecedents' are seen as '*immiscible times*—multiple times that never quite dissolve into the code of modern time consciousness, discrete temporalities incapable of attaining homogeneity with or full incorporation into a uniform chronological present' (Lim, 2009, p. 12). But these so-called anachronistic times that are immiscible and unassimilable to global capitalist time cannot be so easily managed or dismissed as they are precisely the constitutive outside that defines and renders recognizable (and thus an outside that continues to haunt) the normative frame within which modern global time functions.

In this essay, I show how Don DeLillo's novel, *Cosmopolis*, tracks the ways in which capitalist globalization's temporal frame, inscribed in the billionaire currency trader Eric Packer's hypersubjective future-oriented worldview, remains haunted and troubled by those very temporalities that have been dismissed as anachronistic and obsolete, those other times that now return to put a brake on global capitalism's acceleration into the future. DeLillo's novel shows how the times outside globalization's temporal frame function as the untimely, as those out-of-step elements that both define and question the temporal frame from which they have been excluded. I discuss, in some detail, two sites in the novel where globalization's temporal frame is disturbed by the untimely, by times that remain immiscible: the persistence of anachronistic life forms and objects and the body in pain. Finally, I argue that DeLillo's novel is aware that global capitalism's acceleration into the future is also, paradoxically, an attempt to annul time itself—and thus to annul the possibility of a politics of time—since it aspires to what Paul Virilio calls 'the futurism of the instant', a future that is technologically mediated and captured in the present, not an undeterminable future, but a future already anticipated or foreclosed, a future without a future. DeLillo's (2003) novel (which is set in the year 2000) offers, in its portrayal of the self-destructive trajectory of a Wall Street 'master of the universe', an insightful and premonitory account of the nihilistic hubris secreted in late capitalism that resulted in the criminal scandals and losses of 2008, a hubris that does not mark the triumphant 'future without a future' of global capitalism, but, in its self-destructiveness, opens the way, perhaps, to another future that Cazdyn and Szeman (2011) have termed the *after* of globalization .

Framing Global Time

Globalization's temporal framework, it can be argued, was established with the standardization of global time. In 1884, representatives from 25 countries attended the International Meridian

Conference in Washington, DC, where they 'proposed to establish Greenwich as the zero meridian, determined the exact length of the day, divided the earth into 24 time zones one hour apart, and fixed a precise beginning of the universal day' (Kern, 1983, p. 12). Though many countries were slow to adopt the global standard time recommended by the conference (France, notably, refused to accept such an arrangement till 1911), the Washington consensus (or what can be called the *original* Washington consensus) was a significant step in facilitating the global growth and expansion of capital insofar as it allowed for the rationalization and coordination of transportation, information, commerce, stock trading, and financial transactions. Lim (2009) notes that the adoption of standard time zones not only made modern homogeneous time (i.e. clock time's uniform, measurable units that are applicable everywhere because they have been separated from context and emptied of all specific content) appear 'natural and incontrovertible', it also provided 'the indispensable advantages of synchronizing people, information, and markets in a simultaneous global present' (p. 11). Adam (2002) offers a similar observation: 'Standard time, time zones and world time became essential material preconditions for the global network of trade, finance, transport and communication. Today, they underpin the daily operations and transactions of local businesses, global institutions and TNCs' (p. 16).

The social and economic advantages gained by the global standardization of time are offset, however, as both Lim and Adam point out, by the elision of other temporalities that are local, contextual, and embodied, temporalities linked to seasonal variations or biological rhythms. Drawing on the work of Fabian (1983) and Chakrabarty (2000), Lim (2009) contends that global standard time exercises social, political, and economic control over how we work and live by obscuring and suppressing 'the ceaselessly changing plurality of our existence in time' (p. 11). The isochrony achieved by global standard time, Lim argues, requires the denial of temporal coevalness—that is, the devaluation or subordination of other views of time—that both Fabian and Chakrabarty have traced in Western colonial disciplines such as anthropology and historiography. From a feminist and social justice perspective, Adam (2002) warns that the naturalization of clock time and global standard time not only causes other temporalities to fade from view, it also furthers the agenda of global capitalism:

> [A]bsolute decontextualization is the ideal condition for money to flow freely and for capital and operations to be moved unencumbered where the circumstances for wealth generation are optimal. In such decontextualized conditions, real people living in particular places with specific needs are sidelined out of the frame of reference: they have no place in a decontextualized world. (p. 17)

The decontextualized world of global capitalism thus has little use for other times as it institutes a desynchronization (the temporal equivalent of deterritorialization) that disrupts the daily rhythms of local lifeworlds with often damaging consequences to people's health and social life.[1] As we shall see, such a desynchronization (which is also a despoliation) of local lifeworlds is accompanied by the emergence of a restless hypersubject and the resynchronization and reframing of time into a 24/7 world that requires at once an accelerated temporality and an unchanging global uniformity.

The Hypersubject in a 24/7 World

It is in such a world of global capitalism with its decontextualized and desynchronized time that Eric Packer, the currency trader protagonist of Don DeLillo's *Cosmopolis*, lives. The opening pages of the novel introduce us to a sleepless Packer for whom insomnia has become a regular occurrence. Though he is not a night-shift worker, Packer's routines do not follow a normal diurnal rhythm since, as a currency trader, his work never stops. We are shown Packer's nocturnal habit of pacing through his 48-room apartment, stopping only to visit his annex-office 'where there were currencies to track and research reports to examine' (DeLillo, 2003, p. 7). When he is asked if the Japanese yen ever sleeps, he replies: 'Currency markets never close. And the Nikkei runs all day and night now. All the major exchanges. Seven days a week' (p. 29). The decontextualized 24/7 time of global currency trading seems to be the cause of Packer's insomnia.

But there is more to Packer's sleeplessness. We are told that in his state of wakefulness 'Nothing existed around him. There was only the noise in his head, *the mind in time*. When he died, he would not end. The world would end' (p. 6; my emphasis). DeLillo's description of Packer's sleepless state renders a portrait of a Cartesian self that desires to master the world and subject time to a controlling consciousness. Packer *is* because there is only his ravenous mind, his restless consciousness. Time is made secondary to mind; *in* time, we can only find the mind. Time becomes an object that exists only because it is represented by the Cartesian subject. That is why Packer's hyper-Cartesianism allows him to believe that when he dies, it is the object world, along with time, that will end, not him. As I will discuss in detail later, Packer believes that he can achieve immortality through the conversion of his mind into cyber-data that can be preserved on a disk, thereby ensuring 'a consciousness saved from [the] void' (p. 206). What is of interest, for the moment, is that Packer's wide-awake Cartesianism matches precisely Heidegger's description of how the modern mind has made itself into the referential center, the subject before whom beings stand as objects that can be measured and mastered. It is this Cartesian attitude that allows man to grasp the world as a 'world picture', something he can represent. As Heidegger (2002) puts it:

> Understood in an essential way, 'world picture' does not mean 'picture of the world' but, rather, the world grasped as picture. Beings as a whole are now taken in such a way that a being is first and only in being insofar as it is set in place by representing-producing [*vorstellend-herstellenden*] humanity … And what goes along with this is that man sets himself forth as the scene in which, henceforth, beings must set-themselves-before, present themselves—be, that is to say, in the picture. (pp. 67–69)

The temporal equivalent of the 'world picture' is modern global time. Here, time becomes an 'object' that the human subject can represent, manipulate, and compel to become part of the 'picture'. A sense of mastery and domination is evident as different temporalities, like different beings, have to present themselves and be set in place by the representing subject. Those times that do not enter the picture, that are not represented because they remain outside the temporal framework of global modernity are literally 'othered', devalued, no longer seen to count.

In Packer, we see the logical evolution of Heidegger's modern Cartesian subject into the hypersubject of late capitalism.[2] According to Fischbach (2011), the concern, expressed in the 1960s, over threats posed to the subject's autonomy by political institutions and mass culture has, since the 1980s, given way to an extravagant affirmation of the subject. It is as if the managers of late capitalism, in response to the 1960s' demand for the emancipation of the self, have ended up saying, 'You want the autonomous subject? Well, we will give it to you'. Rather than the negation of the subject (a negation social theory has traditionally defined as 'reification'), we encounter, on the contrary, an aggrandizement or inflation of the subject, an 'ultra-subjectivation' (Fischbach, 2011, pp. 34–35). The contemporary hypersubject seeks its fulfilment in an incessant affirmation of its own agency and performativity; it is a free-floating, mobile subject indifferent to any form of attachment, loyal only to its own changing desires.

Rejecting any kind of fixity or stability, the hypersubject is a figure of pure restlessness, forever detaching itself from any current commitment or project so that it can pursue other, newer projects. As Fischbach (2011) succinctly notes, 'Pour l'hypersujet, le repos, c'est la mort' (p. 38).

The hypersubject whose identity requires the denial of repose is featured prominently in Jonathan Crary's recent book *24/7: Late capitalism and the ends of sleep*. Observing that contemporary capitalist society demands 'the uninterrupted operation of markets, information networks and other systems', Crary (2013) describes how a world formed by a nonstop 24/7 temporality inscribes 'human life into duration without breaks, defined by a principle of continuous functioning' (p. 8). A 24/7 world is a world without pause, a world in which the only time that matters is the indifferent time of networks and systems that operate around the clock. In such a world, sleep is a scandalous waste of time, an interruption of productivity and profit.

The 24/7 world of contemporary capitalism helps us to understand not only Packer's sleeplessness but also his hypersubjectivity, his constant need to act and assert himself. Crary (2013) explains cogently how in a 24/7 world 'there are now very few significant interludes of human existence (with the colossal exception of sleep) that have not been penetrated and taken over as work time, consumption time, or marketing time' and that such a world esteems 'the individual who is constantly engaged, interfacing, interacting, communicating, responding, or processing within some telematic milieu' (p. 15).

Like the hypersubject who needs to eliminate forms of otherness that block its self-determination, so too the 24/7 world of capitalism seeks to eradicate alternate temporalities that prevent its smooth functioning. Crary (2013) perceptively notes, for example, that

> 24/7 announces a time without time, a time extracted from any material or identifiable demarcations ... In its peremptory reductiveness, it celebrates a hallucination of presence, of an unalterable permanence composed of incessant, frictionless operations. It belongs to the aftermath of a common life made into the object of technics. (p. 29)

Forcing different lived temporalities into a technologically mediated homogeneous time that is everywhere identical to itself, contemporary capitalism inhabits a paradoxical temporality: it flattens and reduces heterotemporalities to the uniform regimen of a 24/7 world while, simultaneously, embracing an accelerated temporality that can accommodate the rapid, ceaseless flow of communication, information, and commodities in a global market. Capitalist globalization's temporal framing is deliberately paradoxical insofar as its desire to include every object and every form of life can also be seen as a controlled or strategic process of selecting, filtering, and reshaping all that is gathered into its frame, thereby turning inclusion into a form of inclusive exclusion as well.

To a currency trader and speculator like Packer, whose nonstop 24/7 world requires him to monitor constantly a rapid stream of electronic data on currency prices and exchange rates, only the present and, more crucially, the future count. The only time that matters is the technologically mediated 'real' time information about the global market streamed day and night, seven days a week. A selective inclusion that also acts as a form of exclusion is clearly present in this temporal framing. The following description captures well the global temporal frame which dominates Packer's life:

> [T]iers of data running concurrently and swiftly about a hundred feet above the street. Financial news, stock prices, currency markets. The action was unflagging. The hellbent sprint of numbers and symbols, the fractions, decimals, stylized dollar signs, the streaming release of words, of multinational news, all too fleet to be absorbed .... Beneath the data strips, or tickers, there were fixed digits marking the time in the major cities of the world .... Never mind the speed that makes it

hard to follow what passes before the eye. The speed is the point . . . .This is the point, the thrust, the future. (p. 80)

There are a couple of important points to note in the description above. First, the different temporal rhythms of the world have either been decontextualized, abstracted, and simplified into 'fixed digits' that only mark the time of major world cities (i.e. those cities with stock exchanges that are globally interconnected) or converted into so many fleeting fractions, decimals, and symbols that make sense only to stock brokers and currency traders. In short, the world is interpreted, framed, and represented according to the time and tempo set by global capital. It is a world stripped of alternate temporalities and colonized by a 24/7 temporal regime that focuses solely on the uninterrupted functioning of the market.

The second point to note is that the time of global capital is the future and its tempo is acceleration. Vija Kinski, Packer's 'chief of theory', awed by the power of capitalist globalization, describes how it has conquered time by commodifying it—that is, by installing money as time's maker and master—and how the new time of global capital is devoted to speeding up the future which holds the promise of profit:

The idea is time. Living in the future. Look at those numbers running . . . .It's cyber-capital that creates the future . . . .Because time is a corporate asset now. It belongs to the free market system. The present is harder to find. It is being sucked out of the world to make way for the future of uncontrolled markets and huge investment potential. The future becomes insistent. (pp. 78–79)

What excites Kinski in this new theory of time is what worries DeLillo (2001) who, in an essay titled 'In the ruins of the future', gloomily echoes Kinski's words

In the past decade the surge of capital markets has dominated discourse and shapes global consciousness . . . .The dramatic climb of the Dow and the speed of the Internet summoned us all to live permanently in the future, in the utopian glow of cyber-capital, because there is no memory there and this is where markets are uncontrolled and investment has no limit. (p. 33)

What happens then, one may ask, to those other times that do not fit the temporal framework demanded by capitalist globalization or keep up with the accelerated clock-time of nanoseconds, or what Packer further describes as 'zeptoseconds', or 'yoctoseconds'? (p. 79). What happens to the past and present when turbo-charged cyber-capital is only interested in the future? Crary (2013) sees capitalism's 24/7 routines as shaping a 'disenchanted' world that seeks to exorcise or neutralize any sign of the 'spectral' which he describes as 'the intrusion or disruption of the present by something out of time and by the ghosts of what has been deleted by modernity, of victims who will not be forgotten, of unfulfilled emancipation' (pp. 19–20). Similarly, in *Cosmopolis*, Packer dismisses as anachronistic, obsolete, and useless those time-saturated, finite objects and lifeworlds that do not belong to the futural thrust of cyber-capitalism. He does not concede that they are forms of untranslatable or immiscible temporalities, although, as we shall see, they persist as stubborn, recalcitrant differences that continue to haunt and trouble him.

The Persistence of Untimely Matter

Packer's assassin and shadow-self, Richard Sheets (who wants to be known as Benno Levin and who, significantly, does not possess a watch or any other timepiece), describes Packer as 'always ahead, thinking past what is new . . . .Things wear out impatiently in his hands . . . .He wants to be one civilization ahead of this one' (p. 152). As a futurist, Packer likes the idea of buildings that lack density and materiality, buildings 'made empty, designed to hasten the future'.

He admires architecture that signals 'the end of the outside world', that bypasses the 'here' for 'the future, a time beyond geography and touchable money and the people who stack and count it' (p. 36). Objects, technological devices, even words are seen by him as anachronistic or obsolete when they do not measure up to the futurism of his worldview. Phone devices are seen as already 'vestigial' and 'degenerate structures' (p. 19); stethoscopes are 'lost tools of antiquity, quaint as blood-sucking worms' (p. 43); ATMs are 'anti-futuristic, so cumbrous and mechanical that even the acronym seemed dated' (54); the word 'skyscraper' has an 'anachronistic quality' that belongs to the 'olden soul of awe' (9); and computers are 'dying in their present form' and 'even the word computer sounds backward and dumb' (p. 104).

The global future Packer desires is confronted, however, by what he sees as the stubborn anachronism of New York's street life. His soundproofed stretch limousine cannot quite keep out the noise of blowing horns which reminds him of 'a lament so old it sounded aboriginal' (p. 14). Turning his attention away from the computer screens in his car, Packer notices New York's diamond district full of 'Hasidim in frock coats and tall felt hats' dealing with 'a form of money so obsolete Eric did not know how to think about it'. We are told that he senses

> in the grain of the street ... the Lower East Side of the 1920s and the diamond centers of Europe before the second war, Amsterdam and Antwerp .... This was the souk, the shtetl. Here were the hagglers and talebearers, the scrapmongers, the dealers in stray talk. The street was an offense to the truth of the future. (pp. 64–65)

A little later in the novel, Packer turns his attention once again to the street where he sees more local forms of life rooted in a stubborn anachronistic materiality that defies the globe-spanning speed and numeric immateriality of financial information. Packer sees 'the cockney selling children's books from a cardboard box, making his pitch from his knees', 'the old Chinese ... doing acupoint massage, and the repair crew passing fiber-optic cable down a manhole from an enormous yellow spool'. The sight disturbs him and makes him think 'about the amassments, the material crush, days and nights of bumper to bumper, red light, green light, the fixedness of things, the obsolescences .... How things persist, the habits of gravity and time, in this new and fluid reality' (p. 83). Despite the new reality of accelerated global time, old temporalities, other ways of living in time persist. Discrete, immiscible temporalities remain to proclaim their difference, their otherness to Packer's technologically mediated global time. The cockney selling children's books out of a cardboard box inhabits a time and technology different from the stream of financial data that roll across the multiple screens in Packer's office and limousine. The archaic art of Chinese acupoint massage with its emphasis on the tactile belongs to a world and time very different from the objectifying medical technology of the echo-cardiogram that visually represents, at a remove, Packer's beating heart (p. 44). Differences of class are also clearly inscribed in the different temporalities.

Though Packer is oriented to the immaterial and virtual futurity of global capital, we find that he cannot fully elide or ignore the other temporalities that exist in the world. Despite his beliefs, he is still paradoxically drawn to 'the local, the mixed, ... the old brawl, the old seethe' (p. 129). He is impressed by the missing finger of a Sikh taxi-driver, the index of a different temporality: 'Eric regarded the stub, impressive, a serious thing, a body ruin that carried history and pain' (p. 17). Packer is similarly fascinated by the damaged eye of his limousine driver, Ibrahim Hamadou. He guesses that Ibrahim's wound signifies a history and depth of experience alien to him: 'He tried to read the man's ravaged eye, the bloodshot strip beneath the hooded lid. He respected the eye. There was a story there, a brooding folklore of time and fate' (p. 170).

Packer's attraction to other times is also evident in his desire to get a haircut across town at a barbershop his father took him to when he was a child. Just as the term 'haircut' signifies 'taking a loss' in financial slang, Packer's quest for a 'haircut' expresses perhaps a search for 'lost times', those times that do not fit into the single timeframe of capitalist globalization. The barbershop is situated in a street from another time of poverty and crowded tenements. Packer's father had grown up on that street and we are told that '[t]here were times when Eric was compelled to come and let the street breathe on him' (p. 159). He likes the unchanged, old-fashioned decor of the barbershop and the old stories about his father the barber likes to recount: 'This is what he wanted from Anthony. The same words. The oil company calendar on the wall. The mirror that needed silvering' (p. 161). Interestingly, Packer's insomnia—a symptom of the temporal decontextualization and dislocation necessary to global currency trading—is lifted when he enters the other time of Anthony Adubato's barbershop: 'In time the voices [of Anthony and Ibrahim] became a single vowel sound and this would be the medium of his escape, a breathy passage out of the long pall of wakefulness that had marked so many nights' (p. 165). Moreover, Packer, the man who believes only in the future, feels strangely drawn to trust Anthony and Ibrahim, men from the past. The barbershop in all its materiality, suspended in time and filled with memory, becomes for Packer a refuge rather than an anachronistic and useless relic: 'It felt good to trust someone. It felt right to expose the matter [the threat to his life] in this particular place, where *elapsed time hangs in the air*, suffusing solid objects and men's faces. This is where *he felt safe*' (p. 166; my emphases). Thus, as the novel clearly shows, other times inhabited by other social classes not only persist in Packer's world of capitalist globalization but also suggest other possibilities, other ways of life than the one demanded by a 24/7 temporal regime oriented to technological progress and financial profit.

One further point should be made about the persistence of untimely matter. An irony that escapes Packer but not the reader of the novel is that of the unavoidable materiality of the book *Cosmopolis* itself and of the time it takes to read it. Though Packer may be a hypersubject who wishes to attain the condition of immateriality, virtuality, and instantaneity, he is also a character contained in the material pages of a book subjected to the temporality of reading. In fact, in the opening pages of the novel, we are presented with an interesting description of a scene of reading. A sleepless Packer 'tries to read his way into sleep' by reading 'science and poetry' (p. 5). But reading only makes him more wakeful by engaging him in the temporality of reading and the materiality of the page. We are told that he liked 'poems sited minutely in white space, ranks of alphabetic strokes burnt into paper. Poems make him conscious of his breathing. A poem bared the moment to things he was not normally prepared to notice' (p. 5). But the materiality of the poem's page and the surprising revelatory 'moment' it makes possible are set aside by Packer, in the same way that he puts down the book he is reading on Einstein's Special Theory of Relativity, so that he can retreat into an immaterial idealism in which 'nothing existed around him' (p. 6). By doing so, he fails to recognize the materiality of literature, the temporality of reading, and the revelations they make possible, as troubling untimely matter that resists any totalizing or globalizing attempt to put an end to time's many possibilities. As such, picking up a copy of *Cosmopolis* and reading it can perhaps be regarded as an untimely act of resistance as well.

The Untimely Body

The body is the other site that remains immiscible and unassimilable to the temporal regime of global capitalism. To understand the resistance of the body, we must again examine the futurism that drives global capitalism. We have already noted Vija Kinski's assertion that cyber-capital creates the future and that the future is replacing both the past and the present (p. 79). She also argues that technology, especially computer technology, can help us eliminate doubt and thus enable us to better understand and control the future: 'Computer power eliminates doubt: All doubt rises from past experience. But the past is disappearing. We used to know the past but not the future. This is changing ....We need a new theory of time' (p. 86). The new theory of time Kinski calls for is a theory that seeks knowledge and mastery of the future through technology, especially cybernetic telecommunications. This imperative to master the future is of course built into the very being of a currency trader like Eric Packer. We are told that he 'liked knowing what was coming. It confirmed the presence of some heredi-tary script available to those who could decode it' (p. 38). Packer's financial empire depends on his ability to calculate future prices and profits and to place the right bets on future trades. As Adam (2002) reminds us, most money today 'is made on the speculative market that trades not with goods, but with time. This involves bets on future prices of the stock market, currency prices, interest rates, even on the entire stock market indices' (p. 22). According to a 2010 survey by the Swiss-based Bank of International Settlements, the average daily turnover in the global foreign exchange market amounted to 4 trillion US dollars, while daily transactions in over-the-counter interest rate derivatives amounted to 2.1 trillion dollars.[3]

Given the staggering sums of money involved in this global trade in time, we can understand why capitalist society seeks a better understanding and control of the future. The temporal regime of global capitalism seeks to lessen, if not eliminate, the contingent, unpredictable aspects of the future and, in attempting to do so, paradoxically seeks an end to chronological time itself. Not only does it seek to dismiss the times of the Other as primitive superstitions or surpassed anachronisms, it also wishes to foreclose the future through the triumph of instan-taneity. Virilio (2012), for example, sees global capitalist time as complicit with cybernetic informational technology in the 'acceleration of reality', an acceleration that seeks to close the gap between the present and the future (p. 33). Virilio (2010) notes that in the twenty-first century, 'the interactive telecommunications of cybernetics' result in what he calls, 'Instantane-ity': 'Past, present and future contract in the omnipresent instant, just as the expanse of the ter-restrial globe does these days in the excessive speed of the constant acceleration of our travels and our telecommunications' (pp. 70–71). Instantaneity, achieved through the power of cyber-netic telecommunications, is the time of global capitalism, an omnipresent instant in which the future is captured and harnessed for financial profit. Using computer-driven algorithms that can process huge amounts of information, financial traders can come to a decision and execute an order to buy or sell millions of stocks or currency in a nanosecond or less. But the acceleration of reality can also have unforeseen consequences, as when mistakes in the nano-timed inter-action between automated execution programs and algorithmic trading models resulted in the 'flash crash' of 2010.[4]

The desire to capture or colonize an uncertain future by compressing time into the instant speaks not just to financial greed but to a greater need to eliminate time altogether. What Virilio (2010) calls 'the futurism of the instant' is nothing less than the desire for 'a future with no future' (p. 96). Global financial time aims for a kind of atemporality, 'the creation of non-temporal time' (Adam, 1998, p. 66). In an insightful passage, Adam (1998) describes how the money economy is related to the desire to transform that which is temporal and perish-able into something permanent:

> The transformation of nature into money can . . . be understood as the pursuit of alchemy. Embedded in that quest is the desire for the control of earthly conditions of existence, for unboundedness and permanence, for cheating entropy and death, for future security and certainty. (pp. 70–71)

Such a search for order and permanence is present in Packer's actions. He places his faith in 'techniques of charting that [can predict] the movements of money itself' (p. 75). Driving his financial speculation is his belief that he can decipher and chart a deep correspondence between the biosphere's rhythms and the movement of the market. Packer believes that 'There's an order at some deep level . . . .A pattern that wants to be seen . . . .There's a common surface, an affinity between market movements and the natural world' (p. 86). He searches for 'cross-harmonies between nature and data . . . .How market cycles can be inter-changeable with the time cycles of grasshopper breeding, wheat harvesting' (p. 200). This search for 'cross-harmonies between nature and data' reveals Packer's belief that with the tech-nologies available to him he can understand nature's temporal order, allowing him to secure a known future protected from contingency and uncertainty. Moreover, his Faustian wish to control and conquer time is also a desire to escape mortality: 'When he died he would not end' (p. 6).

What one can call Packer's pursuit of immortality, for a futurism without a future, involves the dematerialization of the body in time and its conversion into timeless data. Early in the novel, we are told that Packer believes that human life, in fact the whole biosphere itself, can be converted (in Heidegger's terms 'pictured' or 'represented') into digitized data:

> This was the eloquence of alphabets and numeric systems, now fully realized in electronic form, in the zero-oneness of the world, the digital imperative that defined every breath of the planet's bil-lions. Here was the heave of the biosphere. Our bodies and oceans were here knowable and whole. (p. 24)

Achieving what can be called biopolitical globalitarianism—a totalizing and governing knowl-edge of the whole world—would require not only the dematerialization of objects into digital electronic data but also the delimitation of time, converting time into a universal timeless system of zeros and ones. Vija Kinski explains this necroidealism, this conversion of the mortal body into immortal data thus:

> People will not die. Isn't this the creed of the new culture? People will be absorbed in streams of information . . . .Why die when you can live on disk? A disk, not a tomb. An idea beyond the body. A mind that's everything you ever were and will be, but never weary or confused or impaired. (pp. 104–105)

The faint echo of Keatsian yearning in Kinski's speculation is replaced by a more pragmatic, economic idiom in Packer's reflections on immortality:

> He'd always wanted to become quantum dust, transcending his body mass, the soft tissue over the bones, the muscle and fat. The idea was to live outside the given limits, in a chip, on a disk, as data, in whirl, in radiant spin, a consciousness saved from void . . . .It would be the master thrust of cyber-capital, to extend the human experience toward infinity as a medium for corporate growth and invest-ment, for the accumulation of profits and vigorous reinvestment. (p. 207)

Cyber-capitalism's desire to transcend temporality by controlling the future, its global biopoli-tical dream of immortality is resisted, however, by the very materiality it seeks to transcend—the body.

While having his prostate probed by his doctor, Packer realizes that it is not that easy to dismiss the body and convert it into a timeless array of information:

He felt the pain. It traveled the pathways. It informed the ganglion and spinal cord. He was here in his body, the structure he wanted to dismiss in theory even when he was shaping it under the measured effect of barbells and weights. He wanted to judge it redundant and transferable. (p. 48)

But the body is not made easily redundant or transferable into immaterial, timeless data. The body's pain insists that he is still 'living in the gland, in the scalding fact of his biology' (p. 50). Later, after he shoots his own hand during the confrontation with his assassin, he is made aware that pain anchors him in the here and now, in his body. He realizes that 'The pain was the world. The mind could not find a place outside it' (p. 201). He finally understands that the cyber-capitalist dream of endless economic globalization, of replacing finitude with immortality is impossible in the face of the recalcitrant body *in time* with its own unique biological rhythms and personal history:

But his pain interfered with his immortality. It was crucial to his distinctiveness, too vital to be bypassed and not susceptible, he didn't think, to computer emulation. The things that made him who he was could hardly be identified much less converted to data, the things that lived and milled in his body, everywhere, random, riotous, billions of trillions, in the neurons and peptides, the throbbing temple vein, in the veer of his libidinous intellect . . . .He'd come to know himself, untranslatably, through his pain . . . and so much else that's not convertible to some high sublime, the technology of mind-without-end. (pp. 207–208)

The body's pain situates the body inescapably in the present; the body's immanence is untranslatable, untransferable, not capable of being converted into the atemporality of cyber-data, of a 'mind-without-end'.

The corporeal being that suffers pain in the here and now questions and interrupts the future-less futurism of cyber-capitalism's atemporal vision of a 24/7 global market. The body in time— changeable, vulnerable, mortal—acts to disrupt capitalist globalization's non-temporal temporal regime. In that sense, the body proves to be untimely. The untimely, Nietzsche (1983) once wrote, has to do with 'acting counter to our time and thereby acting on our time and, let us hope, for the benefit of a time to come'(p. 60). The body is untimely because it acts counter to the atemporality of globalization. Packer's own bodily organ, what his doctor describes as an asymmetrical prostate, becomes an example of the untimely. Packer is fascinated by the idea of asymmetry: 'It was intriguing in the world outside the body, a counterforce to balance and calm, the riddling little twist . . . .There was the serpentine word itself, slightly off kilter, with the single additional letter that changes everything' (p. 52). The 'off kilter' asymmetry of Packer's prostate provides, later in the novel, an explanation for why his attempts to chart the yen fail. His assassin Sheets offers this analysis:

You tried to predict movements in the yen by drawing on patterns from nature . . . .The mathematical properties of tree rings, sunflower seeds, the limbs of galactic spirals . . . .You made this form of analysis horribly and sadistically precise. But you forgot something along the way . . . .The importance of the lopsided, the thing's that skewed a little. You were looking for balance, beautiful balance, equal parts, equal sides . . . .But you should have been tracking the yen in its tics and quirks. The little quirk. The misshape . . . .That's where the answer was, in your body, in your prostate. (p. 200)

Packer agrees with this assessment of his mistake: 'He [Sheets] was probably right. There was something in what he said' (p. 200). Packer's mistake lies in his belief that he possesses a temporal metric that will allow him to chart with precision orderly patterns and rhythms in the financial world as in nature, and, through those measurements, to predict and control the future. But what he forgets is the intervention of the untimely, that which is 'lopsided' and 'skewed a little', that which is misshapen and moves in unpredictable and uncharitable 'tics and quirks'.[5]

23

At the end of the novel, we see again how the untimely body acts as a counterforce to the annulment of time in the foreclosed future of cyber-technology. We are told that Packer's watch contains an electron camera 'so microscopically refined it was almost pure information. It was almost metaphysics. It operated inside the watch body, collecting images in the immediate vicinity and displaying them on the crystal' (pp. 204–205). Accidentally activating the camera during his encounter with his assassin, Packer sees on his watch's display screen a body that resembles his though no actual body is present in plain sight. The watch-camera also picks up a beetle climbing up a wire, maintaining 'its old dumb leaf-eating arcadian pace' (p. 205), a form of life indifferent to cyber-capital's speed and faithful to its own slow, alternate temporality.[6] Packer can see the beetle with his own eyes, but the body can be seen only on the watch's screen. Suddenly, he realizes that the dead body on the screen is his and that the electron camera of his watch has imaged his death before it has actually occurred. The watch-camera's technology has somehow accelerated reality and foreclosed the future by imaging it instantaneously in the present. This telemediated future is an annulment of the passage of time and, therefore, *not* a future to come that is yet to be known, a future that remains other. Žižek (2012), for example, has pointed out that in French there are two words for the 'future'. *Futur* stands as 'the full actualization of tendencies which are already present, while *avenir* points more towards a radical break … *avenir* is what is to come (*à venir*), not just what will be' (p. 264). The future imaged by the watch-camera is not *avenir*, not one that remains open to other possibilities; it is more like a *futur* already framed and determined by a technological will to knowledge. The watch-camera's future manifests what Virilio (2012) calls 'megaloscopy':

> [The] continual increase in speed has led to the development of a megaloscopy which has caused a real infirmity because it reduces the field of vision. The faster we go, the more we look ahead in anticipation and lose our lateral vision. Screens are like windshields in a car; with increased speed, we lose the sense of lateralization, which is an infirmity in our being in the world . . . . Augmented reality is a fool's game, a televisual glaucoma. Screens have become blind. (pp. 36–37)

The watch-camera's imaging of the future, like the teleological futurism of capitalist globalization, thus remains blind to the reality of the material or biological present in its rush to anticipate and control the otherness of the future. In DeLillo's novel, it is the untimely body that once again proves disruptive as it puts the brakes on cyber-capitalism's acceleration of time. The pain in Packer's hand roots him in the present even as his watch displays the image of his future death.

The final paragraph of *Cosmopolis* reads:

> His murderer, Richard Sheets, sits facing him. He has lost interest in the man. His hand contains the pain of his life, all of it, emotional and other, and he closes his eyes one more time. This is not the end. He is dead inside the crystal of his watch but still alive in original space, waiting for the shot to sound. (p. 209)

By describing the future as a still-born image that has to wait for a present that remains suspended, the novel disrupts the teleological belief of capitalist globalization in a future already known and mastered. What is interesting to note is that the persistence of bodily pain in the present prevents a foreseen and foreclosed future from taking immediate hold. The wait or interval that the present of bodily pain introduces is the untimely counterforce that resists the already determined future envisaged by technology and cyber-capital.

The Beetle's Arcadian Pace

Like those stubbornly anachronistic things that Packer is quick to dismiss, those things that inhabit what one can call 'slow time', the untimeliness of the body's pain is that which allows time to free itself from the futurism of the instant, the accelerated yet atemporal frame-work imposed on the globe by cyber-capital. It is the untimely—all those forms of temporal otherness excluded by capitalist global time—that makes possible a politics of time and that allows for what Derrida (2003) has described as '*à-venir*', a 'to come', a future in which we are irreducibly exposed to that which is other and unknown, a future 'that opens itself, that opens us to time, to what comes upon us, to what arrives or happens, to the event' (p. 120). Vija Kinski is quite right when she says that we need a new theory of time, even if the theory she recommends is not the one we need. To challenge the atemporal futurism of capitalist glo-balization, we need a theory and politics of time that will welcome a temporality that is not one, a temporality open to difference, to immiscible times, and to a future that remains undetermined. Rancière (2012) has usefully reminded us that the way out of any logic of domination 'should be a way out of its time, a way out of the plot of the homogeneity of time and of the incapacity of those who live in it. It has to call in to question the thesis of the homogeneity of time. There is no global process subjecting all the rhythms of the individual and collective time to its rule. There are several times in one time' (p. 26). It seems, therefore, that there are still political lessons we can learn from anachronistic objects and forms of life that in their multifarious heterotemporality offend 'the truth of the future', such as 'the old Chinese doing acupoint massage', the slow mate-riality of reading a book (like *Cosmopolis*, for instance), the inescapable pain of the body in time, or the 'old dumb leaf-eating arcadian pace' of a beetle.

Acknowledgements

I wish to thank the editors of this issue of *Globalizations*, the journal's anonymous reviewers, and all the participants of the two workshops on 'Time and Globalization' organized by the Insti-tute on Globalization and the Human Condition at McMaster University for their helpful com-ments on earlier drafts of this paper.

Disclosure Statement

No potential conflict of interest was reported by the author.

Notes

1 See, for example, Birth (2007) and Nadeem (2009).
2 The hypersubject in *Cosmopolis* is gendered male. DeLillo's novel is androcentric in focus since its protagonist, Packer, operates in the predominantly male-gendered world of speculative finance. Women, to Packer, are mere objects of carnal desire or function merely as interlocutors. Nonetheless, there is a moment during the meeting between Packer and Jane Melman (his 'chief of finance') that allows the reader an opportunity to question the male-gendered temporality that governs the financial world. Summoned to meet Packer on her day off, Melman complains that Packer can't possibly know 'what it's like … [to be] a single struggling mother' (p. 40). Her remark clearly indicates the existence of other temporalities like those of re/productive, domestic labor and non-profit care-giving, temporalities still often gendered as female in our society. For a compelling analysis of gender as a significant component of a time-politics that has been neglected in accounts of globalization, see Adam (2002).
3 See the foreign exchange statistics page of the Bank of International Settlements' website: http://www.bis.org/publ/rpfx10.htm.
4 See Contenta (2012) and Virilio (2012, p. 34). For an illuminating account of the 'flash crash' of 6 May 2010 and of artificial intelligence trading machines that can process incredible amounts of data and information and place orders to sell or buy hundreds of thousands of shares in less than the blink of an eye, see Patterson (2012).
5 The search for a deep pattern or for some kind of orderly explanation is often present in DeLillo's other novels where it takes on a paranoid urge to uncover conspiracies that resist definitive proof, or results in comic deflation, as in

White Noise, in which Jack Gladney, desiring to hear something of cosmic import in his sleeping daughter's muttered words, discovers that she is actually intoning an automotive brand name, 'Toyota Celica' (DeLillo, 1985, p. 155). A similar comic deflation of the cosmic occurs in *Cosmopolis* when Packer is reminded that the deep pattern he is looking for is to be found in his lowly misshapen prostate.

6   It should be noted that the beetle's 'arcadian pace' does not suggest some golden-age longing for a nature untouched and unsullied by humanity. The beetle, after all, is described as crawling up a wire in an inescapably technologized world. But even if globalization, through its powerful chronotechnologies, has more or less altered, accelerated, and unified the different times of the world, the beetle's slowness reminds us of other life forms that persist, however precariously, as anachronistic alternatives to global capitalism's need for speed and instantaneity.

References

Adam, B. (1998). *Timescapes of modernity: The environment and invisible hazards*. London: Routledge.

Adam, B. (2002). The gendered time politics of globalization: Of shadowlands and elusive justice. *Feminist Review, 70*, 3–29.

Birth, K. (2007). Time and the biological consequences of globalization. *Current Anthropology, 48*, 215–226.

Cazdyn, E., & Szeman, I. (2011). *After globalization*. Chichester: Wiley-Blackwell.

Chakrabarty, D. (2000). *Provincializing Europe: Postcolonial thought and historical difference*. Princeton, NJ: Princeton University Press.

Contenta, S. (2012, April 29). The Speed of Money. *Toronto Star*, p. IN1 and IN4–5.

Crary, J. (2013). *24/7: Late capitalism and the ends of sleep*. London: Verso.

DeLillo, D. (1985). *White noise*. New York: Viking Penguin.

DeLillo, D. (2001, December). In the ruins of the future: Reflections on terror and loss in the shadow of September. *Harper's Magazine*, p. 33–40.

DeLillo, D. (2003). *Cosmopolis*. New York: Scribner.

Derrida, J. (2003). Autoimmunity: Real and symbolic suicides. In G. Borradori (Ed.), *Philosophy in a time of terror: Dialogues with Jürgen Habermas and Jacques Derrida* (pp. 85–136). Chicago, IL: University of Chicago Press.

Fabian, J. (1983). *Time and the other: How anthropology makes its objects*. New York, NY: Columbia University Press.

Fischbach, F. (2011). *La Privation De Monde: Temps, Espace Et Capital*. Paris: Vrin.

Heidegger, M. (2002). The age of the world picture. In J. Young & K. Haynes (Eds. and Trans.), *Off the beaten track* (pp. 57–85). Cambridge: Cambridge University Press.

Kern, S. (1983). *The culture of time and space 1880–1918*. Cambridge, MA: Harvard University Press.

Lim, B. C. (2009). *Translating time: Cinema, the fantastic, and temporal critique*. Durham, NC: Duke University Press.

Nadeem, S. (2009). The uses and abuses of time: Globalization and time arbitrage in India's outsourcing industries. *Global Networks, 9*, 20–40.

Nietzsche, F. (1983). *Untimely Meditations*. (R. J. Hollingdale, Trans.). Cambridge: Cambridge University Press.

Patterson, S. (2012). *Dark pools: The rise of A. I. trading machines and the looming threat to Wall Street*. London: Random House.

Rancière, J. (2012). In what time do we live? In M. Kuzma, P. Lafuente, & P. Osborne (Eds.), *The state of things* (pp. 10–37). London: Koenig Books.

Virilio, P. (2010). *The futurism of the instant: Stop-eject*. (J. Rose, Trans.). Cambridge: Polity.

Virilio, P. (2012). *The Administration of Fear*. (A. Hodge, Trans.). Los Angeles, CA: Semiotext(e).

Žižek, S. (2012). *Less than nothing: Hegel and the shadow of dialectical materialism*. London: Verso.

The Strategic Manipulation of Transnational Temporalities

TONY PORTER* & LIAM STOCKDALE**

*Department of Political Science, McMaster University, Hamilton, Canada
**Institute on Globalization and the Human Condition, McMaster University, Hamilton, Canada

ABSTRACT   While it is now widely recognized that globalization is socially constructed, time is often still seen as a natural unalterable force. Drawing on the literature on the social construction of time, we explore the role of human agency in the interaction of time and globalization by developing the concept of temporal systems. These systems are assemblages that bring together temporal artefacts such as clocks and schedules, the temporalities of the natural world and the body, and social practices involving agency, power, and organization. We then explore, through four illustrative examples, how such systems interact with and constitute globalization. These examples are: the initial emergence and contemporary operation of world standard time; the manipulation of the future and speed in global financial markets; the rise of informal international organizations in global governance; and the role of temporality in the strategic behaviour of multinational corporations.

Introduction

An important feature of research on globalization in recent years has been a shift away from earlier characterizations that saw globalization as an unstoppable quasi-natural or structural force, operating independently of human volition. A now large and diverse literature has highlighted the active role in globalization played by states (Helleiner, 1994; Weiss, 2003), business actors (Carroll, 2010), citizens (Pleyers, 2010), and individuals associated with international institutions (Avant, Finnemore, & Sell, 2010). Today, it is therefore uncontroversial to say that globalization is politically or socially constructed through the strategic behaviour of certain key actors, even though there is still much work to be done to understand the potential and limitations of these actors in shaping globalization. Building upon this direction in globalization scholarship, this article explores the relationship between temporality and globalization, with the particular aim of highlighting how the social construction of globalization is closely bound up with the exercise of human agency with respect to time. 'Agency' here refers simply to the capacity of an actor to imagine a course of action and act to bring it about; though we are specifically interested in the strategic manipulation of temporalities by human agents, and how such processes help constitute globalization.

A challenge in analysing the ability of human actors to construct time is that time seems intuitively to originate in the natural world, unfolding largely independently of human agency. Although there is a wealth of theoretical work on time that challenges this intuitive understanding (for instance, Bender & Wellbery, 1991; Elias, 1992), this has not been integrated sufficiently with theoretical work on globalization, with the partial exception of claims about the compression of time in a globalized world (Harvey, 1989). Globalization theorists have very effectively criticized the idea that there are quasi-natural drivers of globalization that are impervious to human agency, such as technological determinism or the operation of mysterious invisible market forces, but the social construction of these drivers is more easily demonstrated than is the social construction of our temporal relationship to such natural phenomena as the rotation of our planet.

Drawing on the literature on the social construction of time, we address this challenge by emphasizing, in the specific context of globalization, the extent to which our experience of time is mediated through temporal artefacts and systems which humans construct. This includes clocks, schedules, timelines, time zones, routines, stages of life, typologies of pre-historic eras, and infinitely many others. Moreover, these temporal artefacts and systems often interact with the technical artefacts and systems associated with globalization; and while all technologies are constructed by human agents, they can also constrain human agency: 'technology is power made durable' (Latour, 1991). Actors can therefore alter the human experience of time in ways that are similar and related to the way they construct or restrain globalization. In other words, the temporal agency of human actors is an important factor in the constitution of globalization, and thus merits greater attention in the literature.

This article moves in this direction, first theoretically, and then through four illustrative examples. In order, these examples are: the initial emergence and contemporary operation of world standard time and the associated global time zone regime; the manipulation of the future in global financial markets; the rise of informal international organizations in global governance; and the role of temporality in the strategic behaviour of multinational corporations. These examples have been chosen for their variety, as they respectively involve time systems inherited from the past, future-oriented uses of time, political governance, and economic production.

Conceptualizing Agency, Time, and Globalization

Although human agency is often discussed without reference to time, there are good reasons to see them as inseparable. For instance, at the most basic level, the key features of agency are forethought and choice, which are explicitly temporal notions. Moreover, actions take place in time, and agents draw on their inherited capacities and the prior and existing expectations of others to choose and bring about a future course of action—which can itself include the preservation of existing practices through time. As Emirbayer and Mische argue, 'the agentic dimension of social action can only be captured in its full complexity if it is analytically situated within the flow of time' (1998, p. 963; see also Gell, 1996, p. 154).

Empirically oriented research has supported this view by identifying numerous creative ways in which humans have been able to alter time through the exercise of agency. For instance, extensive interview research by Flaherty (2003) on this question found that individuals most often reported efforts to control the duration of events, followed by frequency, sequencing, timing, and the allocation of time to them—although, importantly, the idea that they were in fact capable of acting on time in such ways was never questioned. Similarly, Hitlin and Elder (2007) have identified different time horizons that human agency is oriented towards, from the 'pragmatic' which involves innovation when routines break down, to the longer 'life course' horizon. More generally, what can be termed 'temporal agency' is reflected in a myriad of everyday activities: individuals may construct a schedule, coordinate a routine with someone else, find a distraction to make time pass, change their child's bedtime, restrict the time they spend online, or slow down to smell the roses. All of these actions involve acting strategically on time, thus highlighting humanity's ability not merely to construct time, but to manipulate it for predetermined purposes (Elias, 1992, p. 13). This is the sort of temporal agency with which we are concerned in this article, particularly as it relates to the construction of globalization.

Conceptually speaking, it should be clear that this understanding of temporal agency challenges the conception of time as an unalterable natural force. Of course, this is by no means a novel perspective; rather, it situates our analysis firmly within the extensive theoretical literature on time that emphasizes how 'time is not given but ... fabricated in an ongoing process' (Bender & Wellbery, 1991, p. 4). Indeed, the exercise of temporal agency is an important mechanism through which the social construction of time takes place, since it involves the strategic creation of temporalities by social actors for a particular purpose. Yet, our perspective deviates from a purely constructivist understanding of time, in that these strategic actions frequently involve interactions between human actors and 'natural' temporalities. In other words, the exercise of temporal agency often consists of mediating the temporalities of the natural world through systems or artefacts of human creation in ways that benefit the agents in question.[1] This creation of 'temporal systems' that draw upon both human and natural temporalities is a crucial dimension of the social construction of time more generally, as discussed further below. However, the point here is to situate our analysis conceptually by emphasizing that our notion of temporal agency implies a theory of time that recognizes the latter's natural *and* social dimensions, and which views these as mutually constitutive in the context of humanity's broader experience of time. In short, analysing temporal agency—whether in general or in the specific context of globalization—requires acknowledging the natural (or 'objective') aspect of time while also recognizing that, as Thomas Luckmann puts it, 'the objective categories of time ... cannot be imagined to have come into existence without some prior social interaction' (1991, p. 158).

The suitability of such a conceptual approach for our analysis can be further emphasized by considering how the temporalities of human society include both an infinite number of rhythms and other temporal features of nature and specific temporal artefacts constructed by humans—ranging from heartbeats, to atomic frequencies, to lunar orbits, and the rotating hands of a clock. Many of these emerge and operate independently of human agency; yet, human agency in many forms often also involves the creative linking of rules and understandings to these material temporalities (Elias, 1992, pp. 2–4). Indeed, this aspect of temporal agency is crucial to coordinating human activity and changes in nature, such as through a calendar that helps to determine when to plant crops (Luckmann, 1991, p. 159). But it can also be a way of controlling human behaviour for more social or political purposes and establishing relations of power and domination, such as through a punch clock in a factory (Gell, 1996, pp. 312–313; Thompson, 1967). These are examples of how the exercise of human agency with respect to natural temporalities serves to construct time as experienced by humans. However, it is also important to emphasize that this sort of agency requires the creation and use of particular technical artefacts, such as clocks and schedules (Birth, 2012). These artefacts can become 'black-boxed', and the degree to which they were created by humans may be forgotten, leading natural temporalities to appear to operate automatically as they are filtered through these artefacts to create our experience of time. This obscures the extent to which temporalities are socially constructed, which can in turn serve to reinforce relations of power and domination. The exercise of human agency is thus crucial to the intertwining of natural and social temporalities that underpins the overall human experience of time.

In short, human agency helps to create, and interacts with, temporal systems, which condition how time is apprehended and experienced in human affairs and enable powerful actors to harness or manipulate particular temporalities for strategic purposes. Temporal systems can be defined as assemblages of temporal artefacts such as clocks or printed schedules, together with the natural rhythms, objects, practices, and ideas associated with these artefacts. There are three main ways that human agency interacts with temporal systems. First, actors may create such systems, and these systems may then independently organize human activities. A schedule that becomes routine is an example. Second, actors may work creatively within these systems, drawing on them to organize their own conduct and that of others. The decision to intervene strategically at a particular time in an existing schedule is an example. Third, actors may use a temporal system to dominate or manipulate actors who are external to it. The use of a schedule to coordinate a military strike is an example. Temporal systems can also be nested within other temporal systems, and more than one of these types of temporal agency may be present in any particular activity.

Building upon this conceptual architecture, the remaining sections of the paper will attempt to illustrate that these types of interactions between human agency and temporal systems are crucial to understanding the broader relationship between time and globalization. In this respect, the discussion thus far has shown how the human experience of time is constituted by ongoing interactions between human agents and the natural world, mediated through a complex array of social institutions, systems, and artefacts; however, in the twenty-first-century world of instantaneous global communication and worldwide networks (Slaughter, 2004), these interactions inevitably extend in varying ways across local and global spaces. The practices, processes, and phenomena collectively known as globalization are then at least in part constituted through the exercise of human agency in relation to time, while even ostensibly mundane exercises of temporal agency can have important global dimensions. Indeed, the strategies of powerful actors often incorporate both the spatial and temporal properties of the globe and the technical systems that extend across it, thereby constructing time and globalization. The remainder of the paper explores the interaction of human agency with temporal systems of global significance across the four highly diverse contexts outlined in the Introduction.

The Emergence of Universal Standard Time and the Global Time Zone Regime

An instructive illustration of how agency is exercised in relation to time and globalization can be found in how world standard time and the attendant global time zone regime emerged in the late nineteenth century, and in the way it continues to operate today. As will become clear, this example especially illustrates the first type of interaction between agency and temporal systems that we identified above: actors' creation of temporal systems with global reach that then independently work to organize human conduct.

While the contemporary universal mechanism of temporal reckoning is often presented as an inevitably natural consequence of scientific advancement and worldwide human necessity—in other words, as something that would have necessarily occurred regardless of any particular exercise of human agency—its emergence was in fact primarily the result of a protracted campaign by a very small group of powerful individual agents led by prominent Canadian industrialist Sandford Fleming. At the time of its emergence, support for temporal standardization was largely confined to Western professionals working in industries that stood to benefit from it—such as cartography, telegraphy, and railroad operation—and economic elites with a financial interest in the facilitation of global capital flows. In fact, it was 'met with indifference or antagonism' by most others (Barrows, 2011, p. 34; Zerubavel, 1982, pp. 12–14). Advocates therefore realized that the global community had to be 'unconsciously educated to the desirability of uniform standard time' if their project was to be brought to fruition (Barrows, 2011, p. 34). Fleming led the charge in this respect, devoting his life to advocating global temporal standardization. He amassed 'a powerful arsenal of arguments' that combined extensive research with rhetorical flourish, through which he attempted to convert other, more sceptical political and economic elites to his cause (Barrows, 2011, p. 36). It is important to note that while Fleming and his followers framed their campaign in the language of global public service and universal human interest, they also had significant strategic reasons for supporting it, stemming particularly from their own personal financial interests in further enabling the global flow of investment capital (Barrows, 2011, p. 45).[2] As Adam Barrows puts it, universal time is best understood not 'as a technologically determined fact emerging inevitably out of the orderly march of scientific laws', but rather as the result of 'political intervention of a handful of advocates to facilitate the operation of global commerce' (Barrows, 2011, p. 27).

While we are not claiming that universal time could not have been created without Fleming and his followers, we are drawing attention to how it involved agency and was not an inevitably natural occurrence. At the same time, this global time system did interact with properties of the natural world, including the curved terrain of the earth's surfaces and the earth's rotation. Moreover, as the system developed and became institutionalized through the early twentieth century, it was embedded in countless artefacts, imbuing it with more independence from individual actors, including its architects, than at the outset. However, it should also be noted that ongoing agency is needed to preserve the coherence and effectiveness of the system. Such activities range from properly maintaining the global time reckoning system—as in the actions of the International Earth Rotation and Reference Systems Service, which works to determine when leap seconds should be inserted to reconcile clock time systems and the variable rotation of the earth (Luzum, 2013)—to those countless everyday activities that rely upon temporal coordination across the globe—such as cross-border financial transactions or transcontinental conference calls. These global interactions that help constitute globalization thus do not take place in a time that is independently unfolding, but instead involve, and indeed require, the construction of global 'temporal systems'.

Moreover, the correlation between Fleming's temporal agency and his own financial interests demonstrates that these global temporal systems can serve to enhance the power of those actors whose agency underlies their constitution. Consider in this respect how global temporal systems empower globally mobile actors—who tend overwhelmingly to be the affluent beneficiaries of globalization—relative to locally situated actors—who are primarily poorer and located at the margins of the world economy. This involves the second and third ways that agency interacts with temporal systems: working strategically within such systems and using such systems to dominate or manipulate others. A clear example of this phenomenon is how firms located in the time zones associated with more powerful states can demand that those in other time zones adjust their lived temporalities to match up, as in the case of Indian contact centre workers servicing firms with customer bases in North America, Europe, and Australia. These workers are required to radically alter their local lives in order to 'adapt to global demands' that often include serving a 'clientele located in remote time zones' (Aneesh, 2012, p. 516). The resulting day/night inversion and the associated disconnect from the temporalities of local life can have serious consequences for the physical and mental well-being of the workers (Aneesh, 2012, pp. 527–528).

For our purposes, it is important to note that these sorts of economic relationships are enabled by multiple socially constructed global temporal systems—from universal standard time itself to the particular mechanisms that coordinate the flow of information across telephone and internet networks in real time. In particular, contact centres involve numerous scheduling and other temporal challenges, including matching anticipated volume of calls with staff availability, planning around differences in holidays across jurisdictions, efficiently matching calls to staff expertise, and monitoring and managing performance measures such as average call-handling time. These often clash with local time systems, embedded in social temporalities such as family routines, or natural temporalities such as biorhythms and the passage of dawn and dusk across neighbourhoods, which can be accompanied by the exercise of temporal agency by local managers and workers.

This discussion of global standard time and the time zone regime thus illustrates how human agency mediated through technical artefacts is key to the construction of the global temporal systems that underpin globalization itself. Understanding this relationship is important, because it highlights both the social construction of time more generally, and the extent to which the exercise of strategic temporal agency by powerful actors is constitutive of globalization.

Strategic Manipulation of the Future in Global Finance

The globalization of finance has been seen as emblematic of globalization as a whole. Since the 1960s, cross-border financial flows have grown dramatically in volume, volatility, and complexity, drawing the world together in new ways. Importantly, there is an inadequately recognized temporal dimension to this, as strategic manipulation of the speed of financial transactions is a central characteristic of the system. To better illustrate these points, we consider two aspects of this sort of strategic temporal manipulation in global finance. The first concerns the manipulation of expectations about the future—particularly in the context of the global derivatives market. This is an example of the first and third ways that agency interacts with temporal systems discussed above, in that financial actors are constructing temporal systems which then act relatively independently to organize human conduct, but they also construct temporal systems to manipulate others who are external to them. The second relates to the ongoing competition over speed involved with rise of 'high-frequency trading' (HFT). This is an example of the second type of interaction between agency and temporal systems that we have identified, since financial actors in this context are working strategically within temporal systems. In both cases, however, it is clear that human agency interacts with technical artefacts to construct the temporalities of global finance, which are in turn constitutive of globalization more broadly.

A central function of contemporary finance is to manage the future through the buying and selling of risk. A simple example is home insurance, which alters the likelihood that a homeowner will be left homeless in the future if a catastrophic scenario comes to pass. A more complex example is the 'over-the-counter' (OTC) derivatives market, which in 2012 was estimated at $565 trillion in notional amounts outstanding (International Swaps and Derivatives Association, 2013). Derivatives are contracts, the values of which are determined by the values of some other product. In effect, they are used to trade pieces of risk, such as when someone swaps the risk of an interest rate changing with the risk of an exchange rate changing. The complexity and intangibility of these financial mechanisms for managing the future provide extraordinary opportunities for knowledgeable actors to manipulate the less knowledgeable, thus exercising a form of strategic temporal agency for their own benefit.

The OTC derivatives market is dominated by a small number of powerful global economic actors. In 2010, for instance, the 14 banks that were the largest dealers held 82% of the global notional amount outstanding (Mengle, 2010). These dealers therefore benefit from the complexity and opacity of the market (Litan, 2010), and following the global financial crisis that began in 2007, they have used their relative power to resist efforts by governments to channel OTC derivatives trading onto more transparent and standardized exchanges and clearing arrangements. A high-profile demonstration of the strategic temporal manipulation that can occur with complex financial products was the Abacus AC1 collateralized-debt obligation (CDO), which influential speculator John Paulson worked to create in 2007 in order to bet against the sub-prime mortgage market. Abacus CDOs were then sold by investment bank Goldman Sachs, which itself had already been betting against that market. The product was sold to less well-connected investors who assumed that the market was still healthy. These transactions earned Goldman $15 million in transaction fees (Fontevecchia, 2013). In 2010, Goldman agreed to pay a $550 million penalty to settle the charges that the authorities had brought against it for its role in these sales (Grocer, 2013).

These examples are useful for our purposes because financial products such as CDOs are underpinned by contracts that specify obligations to make payments at particular moments in time, and thus involve the construction (and manipulation) of the sorts of temporal systems discussed earlier. In this case, the key temporal artefacts are the financial contracts, documents, and electronic systems that facilitate their trading (Riles, 2008). Like the global time zone regime, the temporal systems at the core of global finance are constructed by the agency of powerful human actors interacting with temporal artefacts, and facilitate the exploitation of weaker economic actors by the strategic behaviour of the more powerful. This is demonstrated by the dynamics of the sub-prime mortgage crisis, where the CDOs linked financially stretched homeowners in the USA to a complex chain of other actors, each scheduled to intervene at particular times and under particular conditions—to the benefit of some at the expense of others. Importantly, this financial temporal system and its associated processes also had a global dimension, since many investors from outside the USA were heavily involved in financing this machine. This included European banks, which were seen by some US traders as convenient places to dump toxic products, thus transmitting the crisis to Europe. The crisis was also fuelled by the Chinese government, which was heavily financing US debt at the time.

This type of temporal and global strategic agency could be illustrated in many other areas of global finance as well. An example is HFT. HFT involves automated trading at speeds of milliseconds and volumes up to a billion shares a day (Creswell, 2010)—far beyond the capacity of humans to monitor or carry out. High-frequency traders operate within ultra-fast machine temporalities to take advantage of investors limited by slower human temporalities, thus further highlighting the importance of technical artefacts to the exercise of temporal agency in global finance. These technologically facilitated interactions also take place across borders, highlighting their global dimension. For instance, Hibernia Atlantic initiated a $300 million project to run a new undersea fibre-optic cable between New York and London in order to reduce travel time to 30 milliseconds—a gain of only a couple of milliseconds over the existing connection, but which can lead to massive increases in trading returns (Schneider, 2012).

The centrality of strategic temporal agency to the operation of global finance thus highlights the extent to which time is socially constructed through the agentic creation and manipulation of temporal systems; and because global finance is emblematic of globalization more generally, it also suggests that such exercises of temporal agency are constitutive of globalization itself.

Temporality, Informality, and Global Governance

A third example of how both time and globalization are constituted through the exercise of temporal agency by powerful actors can be found in the recent rise to prominence of more informal international organizations comprised largely of the most powerful states. Exemplified initially by the G7/8, and now by the G20, the creation and operation of such institutions can be understood as involving all three of the ways that agency interacts with temporal systems that we identified above. As temporal systems, the G7/8 and the G20 facilitate the intervention of their member-states within the larger and much slower temporal system associated with traditional international law and organization, while also enabling the manipulation and domination of actors who are external to the G7/8 and G20 temporal systems. The larger and more traditional temporal system of global governance, much like time zones, is inherited from its construction in the past, operating presently somewhat independently to organize and constrain those working within it. Although the temporalities of the G7/8 and G20 are framed as being in the broader global interest—with the accelerated temporalities of a globalized and digitized world cast as increasingly at odds with the languid temporalities of traditional governance mechanisms—action towards this end is primarily premised upon the most powerful states asserting their exclusive prerogative to set the global governance agenda. Indeed, by including only the most powerful states ostensibly in the name of speed and efficiency, these institutions reaffirm the prominent positions of their members at the top of the global political and economic hierarchy, since it is their exclusionary character that is deemed crucial to their success (Heinbecker, 2011, p. 4).

To elaborate upon these points, it should first be acknowledged that the rise of informal global governance mechanisms such as the G7/8 and the G20 resulted from many interrelated geopolitical and global economic factors; however, this trend can also in part be understood in terms of temporality. Specifically, the latter decades of the twentieth century were characterized by a significant expansion of the international states system, primarily through decolonization. This created a large number of economically and militarily weak states that were nevertheless entitled to representation in the primary global governmental bodies—such as the United Nations and International Monetary Fund (IMF)—and inclusion in a proliferation of global formal treaty-making processes (Denemark & Hoffmann, 2008). This served to exacerbate the bureaucratic sluggishness of these and other traditional global governance mechanism, such that even so seemingly uncontroversial a proposition as the International Covenant on Civil and Political Rights took over two decades from the opening of negotiations to its entering into force in 1976. The already-slow temporalities of global governance therefore seemed to decelerate further. Conversely, the transportation and information technology revolutions of the same era greatly accelerated the temporalities of everyday life across the globe—particularly in the realm of economics and finance—thus creating a serious temporal disconnect between the capacities of existing global governance institutions and the phenomena most urgently in need of governing. A key result was a significant shift in the foundations of international law-making and global governance away from formal mechanisms based on tradition and universalism and towards more informal and exclusive institutions and channels comprising only the most powerful states and focusing on developing future-oriented policies rather than preserving past practices, as had been the case with treaties and customary international law.

The influence of the G7/8 and G20 has thus grown to the extent that these institutions often set the directions that the more formal and universal organizations are then enlisted to implement. This is enabled by the influence that the G7/8 and G20 can exercise in the universal organizations when they act together, as well as by the agenda-setting work that is done before policies reach those organizations. The formal international institutions subsequently promote compliance with these policies over the longer run. This was evident, for instance, in the response to the global financial crisis of 1997/1998, which involved new standards and codes initiated and managed by the G7/8 and a set of small groupings organized around the Bank for International Settlements in Basel that eventually worked through the IMF and World Bank to promote these new standards and codes in developing countries. Often, the formulation and implementation of such policies involve tools such as benchmarking and peer review, which are far better able to adjust to change over time than are more formal bureaucratic mechanisms (Porter, 2012). In short, it is generally the case that powerful actors in the realm of global governance work through speedier and more informal mechanisms than do smaller or weaker actors.

It is also important to note that these changes are not simply taking place within an accelerating world emerging independently of them; rather, these emerging international governance mechanisms contain and further construct particular temporal systems and legal artefacts. For instance, in the Vienna Convention on the Law of Treaties—which is a prototypical example of more traditional global governance mechanisms—Article 62 relating to 'fundamental change of circumstances' significantly constrains the ability of states party to the treaty to alter it over time. This reflects the orientation of formal treaties towards stabilizing relationships temporally. In contrast, an explanation of peer review by the OECD—which is another notable informal international organization that pioneered and heavily influenced the use of peer review in international affairs—notes that, 'unlike a legal enforcement body, examiners in a peer review have the flexibility to take into account a country's policy objectives, and to look at its performance in a historical and political context', including working with 'trends' with regard to compliance (Pagani, 2002). Informal transnational governance mechanisms thus construct particular temporal systems consisting of specific timelines and sequencing, which organize international actors temporally, empowering some and controlling or excluding others.

This discussion of informalization in global governance thus illustrates how powerful actors are able to exercise temporal agency in pursuit of particular strategic aims—in this case, the maintenance of the most powerful states' capacity to shape the global governance agenda and thus adequately manage key problems. Indeed, by constructing informal, flexible, exclusive, and future-oriented governance institutions, the most powerful states in the international system have exercised agency with respect to time, and engaged in practices that have helped to constitute globalization.

Strategic Temporal Manipulation in Transnational Production Processes

The strategic character of the globalization of production is well recognized (Harvey, 1989), as when a firm decides to source offshore to reduce costs, or to accelerate production processes by investing in robotic technology. However, the degree to which such strategic action involves the manipulation of temporalities is often overlooked. Indeed, when a firm works to move its products across the world more quickly in order to compete with more local or slower competitors, it is manipulating the temporalities of the global economy for its own benefit. Moreover, this exercise of temporal agency helps to construct globalization by expanding the transnational flow of economic activity. This suggests that both time and globalization are not simply background conditions to the transnational production activities of multinational firms, but are instead being constructed and modified by these powerful actors. To illustrate these points, consider the following two examples of the interaction of agency, temporality, and globalization in production processes.

Our first example is Walmart's innovative use of extensive electronic data to coordinate and control its global product supply chain (Hansen & Porter, 2012). Now the world's largest corporation (CNN Money, 2011) Walmart pioneered the collection of data from the point of sale (POS) in 1971. Its electronic data interchange (EDI) allows it to closely control its suppliers (Johnson, 2002). In particular, it permits the control of the temporal aspects of Walmart's products, linking the production of new products more immediately to real-time sales trends. This temporal dimension is even clearer in the way that POS data are combined with forecasting models to project market trends and direct suppliers to adjust before those trends appear. POS data also allow precise measurement of the time taken by suppliers to deliver products (Foote & Krishnamurthi, 2001). These electronic systems are temporal artefacts that structure time, much like calendars and clocks, and thus create a particular temporal system within which Walmart's product supply operations function. These processes involve the first and third ways that agency interacts with temporal systems: the Walmart system was deliberately created and then exhibited a degree of independence in organizing those included in it; but it has also been used to dominate or manipulate actors external to it, such as suppliers and competitors. Indeed, the global reach of these temporal technologies has been a crucial factor in Walmart's market dominance, as the EDI system integrates 100,000 global suppliers into its control systems, including in low cost production locations as far away as China (Wailgum, 2009; Wang, 2006).

The global dimension of the system has increased in recent years, going beyond Walmart, which has now begun to work with other large multinational firms to coordinate their efforts to control production chains. For instance, a Global Commerce Initiative (GCI) was launched in 1999 to develop global supply chain standards, and its most prominent working group, on EDI, was co-chaired by Kraft Foods and Walmart (Nairn, 2003). In 2009, the GCI merged with the International Committee of Food Chains (CIES)—the primary food and consumer goods industry association—and the Global CEO Forum to create the Consumer Goods Forum (CGF). The CGF has worked with GS1 global supply chain standards regime to promote a standardized global model of close integration similar to the one that Walmart had developed. Again, the standards and mechanism involved in these developments create temporal systems with a global reach by, for example, establishing timelines, delivery dates, production lead times, along with locational information. By actively manipulating the temporal dimensions of global production for its own strategic benefit, Walmart has thus modified the temporalities of the global economy in such a way that also contributes to the broader constitution of globalization.

A second example of these sorts of dynamics can be found in the global smartphone market, which has involved global and temporal struggles for market share between Blackberry, Apple, Samsung and other companies. The life cycles and timing of the phones these companies produce are related to one another and to the material properties of the phones themselves, thereby constituting a temporal system. The system as a whole is not constructed deliberately, but a great deal of effort is devoted to the choice of when to insert a new product into this evolving temporal system, and the longevity of that product relative to that temporal system. This corresponds to the second way that agency interacts with temporal systems: acting strategically within a temporal system. The temporal aspects of the competition are especially evident in the insertion of each new model into a rapidly evolving global market where novelty and timing are crucial. For instance, the Samsung's Galaxy S4 launch 'didn't quite capture the "wow" factor as the Galaxy S3 first did' (senior market analyst Clement Teo, cited in Choudhury, 2013), illustrating the importance of maximizing the opportunities that a succession of particular moments in time offer. Similarly, after unveiling its new Z10 in New York, Blackberry delayed two months before making it available, 'a delay that allowed some of the excitement from the launch to dissipate' (Slater, 2013). Such failures to properly manage the temporalities of the market can have negative impacts on customers and investors. Moreover, the smartphone industry itself is positioned in a very particular time period located between an earlier time where consumers were spending on laptops and 'dumb' phones, and the imminent saturation of the market for high-end smartphones: 'once a status symbol, the smartphone is quickly becoming a commodity product', with customers unwilling to pay for new features that seem to do more than they need (El Akkad & Marlow, 2013). The temporal sequencing of products is thus crucial for attracting customers, but also for defending the patent rights in the technology, as evidenced in the 2012 US court decision that Samsung owed over $1 billion in damages for infringing on six Apple patents (Gobble, 2012). Apple had previously offered to license its patents to Samsung for a substantial cost of $30 per smartphone (Gupta & Prinzinger, 2013).

This temporal competition also plays out globally. For example, the market began with high-end smartphones dominated at late as 2011 by three Western companies, Apple, Nokia and BlackBerry, but by 2013, Nokia and BlackBerry had been outranked by five Asian companies: Samsung, LG, Lenovo, Huawei and ZTE (Pfanner, 2013). Initially, the Western companies had benefitted from reducing production costs by manufacturing in Asia and selling in the developed world. But, by 2013, the Asian companies had benefited from their ability to produce cheaper phones with fewer features for developing markets, as well as their connections to suppliers or networks in Asia or the developing world, where market growth was strongest (Pfanner, 2013; Yang, 2013).

What do these examples from the realm of transnational production tell us about the relationship between agency, time, and globalization? Firstly, both cases involve highly strategic decisions with explicitly temporal and global dimensions on the part of the firms' executives and employees. These actors are able to reduce the temporal constraints of global distances by constructing linkages across them, as in Walmart's use of supplier technologies. The firms also operate within a temporal narrative, where market events are linked in distinctive irreversible sequences. This is particularly evident in the case of smartphones. While this partly confronts the firms as a temporal structure that they cannot change, it is simultaneously constructed by the firms' strategic agency via decisions regarding when new products are introduced. There is a materiality to this as well in the properties of the devices themselves, which can be altered to add new features, but not in ways fully in control of the firms. Ultimately, the ability of powerful corporations to construct and manipulate the temporalities of transnational production indicates a significant capacity for temporal agency, while the global reach of these agentic exercises suggests that the latter are a key component of the economic processes that constitute globalization.

Conclusion

This article began with a concern about an enduring tendency in the social sciences to treat time as something of a background condition, a naturally constituted structure that limits the behaviour of human agents. Building upon the existing conceptual literature on the construction of time, we asserted that understandings of time should follow a trajectory similar to recent understandings of globalization, with this naturalistic view being replaced by one that sees time as socially constructed and thus amenable to manipulation by human agency. The parallel to globalization was deliberate, however, since we proceeded to argue through four illustrative examples that this sort of strategic temporal manipulation plays a key role in certain processes and phenomena that are constitutive of what is broadly known as globalization. In other words, neither globalization nor time is simply a natural or structural force acting independently of humans; rather, both are to a significant extent socially constructed through the exercise of human agency—though their 'natural' aspects are still relevant to their effect on human society. The relationship between human agency, globalization, and time thus involves a complex set of interactions, whereby temporal systems are produced by human actors, linking agency to the material aspects of time in the natural world and in objects that humans construct. Understanding these relationships can productively advance our broader understandings of time, globalization, and the interaction between the two.

To help further such an understanding, we identified three ways that agency interacts with temporal systems: in creating them, working within them, and using them against actors external to them. Our four case studies illustrated these interactions. The case of global temporal standardization especially illustrated the way in which an exercise of agency by Sandford Fleming in the past created an institution, linked to the planet's rotation, that continues to organize our experience of time and globalization—the first way that agency interacts with temporal systems. We then showed how financial actors manipulate the perception and experience of temporality by concealing future risks and quickly departing with their profits before the costs of those risks became apparent—the second and third ways that agency interacts with temporal systems. The case of informalization in global governance illustrated the capacity of powerful states to harness their own accelerated governance capacities to work around or through more universal but slower institutions to govern the globe. This involved the temporal systems of the G7/8 and G20 working within and against the slower temporal systems of traditional international law and organization—processes that involve all three ways that agency interacts with temporal systems. We then turned to how the supply chain technologies developed by Walmart and now being adopted by other large global firms have linked suppliers around the world to disciplining and forecasting mechanisms that empower these firms relative to competitors and suppliers. Much like the G7/8 and G20, this involved the creation of a temporal system that organized Walmart and empowered it relative to its suppliers and competitors, a mix of all three ways that agency interacts with temporal systems. Similarly, the competition among smartphone companies is unfolding across time and global economic spaces, as it both creates and operates within a globalized temporal system where temporal positioning is crucial to success. This reflects the second way that agency interacts with temporal systems.

There are an abundance of equally diverse examples that could be explored in subsequent research. We have especially focused on the strategic temporal agency of powerful actors, but less powerful actors can also act strategically on time, such as when an alternative global future is imagined and worked towards, or when the speed that favours powerful actors is actively resisted. These strategic actions of less powerful actors deserve more attention in future research. More generally, however, it is clear that very specific examination of the inter-actions of agency, time, and globalization—in even more detail than we have provided in our cases—will be important to understanding key events and practices in the twenty-first-century world. Indeed, when the purpose is to understand institutional changes over longer stretches of time and space, sensitivity to the interactions of agency, time, and globalization will be an important complement to other ways of using social theory or literary imagination. In all cases, we should challenge prevailing tendencies to treat time as simply a background condition. Instead, we must recognize how, as with globalization, its treatment as such in fact obscures the creative and strategic actions that humans have taken—and are capable of taking—which work to construct such seemingly natural, unalterable phenomena and our experiences thereof.

Acknowledgements

The helpful comments of two anonymous referees from this journal and from participants in the Time and Globalization workshops held at McMaster University in October 2012 and September 2013 are gratefully acknowledged.

Disclosure Statement

No potential conflict of interest was reported by the authors.

Funding

This work was supported by the Social Sciences and Humanities Research Council of Canada [grant numbers 410-2011-2376 and 611-2012-0098].

Notes

1 This is the point made by Norbert Elias in the preface to his celebrated essay on time, as he discusses how the clocks and calendars through which humans apprehend and mediate natural temporalities—and thus the very concept of 'time' itself, which is constructed through this process—developed out of the strategic organizational requirements of human civilization (Elias, 1992, pp. 4, 13; see also Luckmann, 1991, p. 161).

2 This is epitomized by Fleming's involvement in high-risk investments in Brazilian railroad and mining ventures in the late 1880s, as these potentially lucrative schemes 'employed the very transportation and communication technologies that necessitated [temporal] standardization' (Barrows, 2011, p. 46).

References

Aneesh, A. (2012). Negotiating globalization: Men and women of India's call centers. *Journal of Social Issues, 68*(3), 514–533.

Avant, D. V., Finnemore, M., & Sell, S. K. (2010). *Who governs the globe?* Cambridge: Cambridge University Press.

Barrows, A. (2011). *The cosmic time of empire.* Berkeley: University of California Press.

Bender, J., & Wellbery, D. E. (1991). Introduction. In J. Bender & D. E. Wellbery (Eds.), *Chronotypes: The construction of time* (pp. 1–15). Stanford, CA: Stanford University Press.

Birth, K. K. (2012). *Objects of time: How things shape temporality.* New York, NY: Palgrave Macmillan.

Carroll, W. K. (2010). *The making of a transnational capitalist class: Corporate power in the 21st century.* London: Zed Books.

Choudhury, A. R. (2013, July 6). Samsung hammered as profit falls below expectations; analysts point to concerns about smartphone market nearing saturation, TV price war. *Business Times Singapore.* Retrieved from LexisNexis.

CNN Money. (2011). *Global 500: Our annual ranking of the world's largest corporations.* Retrieved from http://money. cnn.com/magazines/fortune/global500/2011/full_list/

Creswell, J. (2010, May 16). Speedy new traders make waves far from Wall Street. *New York Times.* Retrieved from LexisNexis.

Denemark, R. A., & Hoffmann, M. J. (2008). Just scraps of paper? The dynamics of multilateral treaty-making. *Cooperation and Conflict, 43*(2), 185–219.

El Akkad, O., & Marlow, I. (2013, June 1). Commodity boom: The smartphone's global price war. *Globe and Mail* (Canada), p. B4.

Elias, N. (1992). *Time: An essay.* Oxford: Blackwell.

Emirbayer, M., & Mische, A. (1998). What is agency? *American Journal of Sociology, 103*(4), 962–1023.

Flaherty, M. G. (2003). Time work: Customizing temporal experience. *Social Psychology Quarterly, 66*(1), 17–33.

Fontevecchia, A. (2013, August 1). Ex-Goldmanite 'Fabulous Fab' Tourre takes the heat as jury finds him liable for securities fraud. *Forbes.* Retrieved from http://www.forbes.com/sites/afontevecchia/2013/08/01/ex-goldmanite-fabulous-fab-tourre-takes-the-heat-as-jury-finds-him-liable-of-civil-fraud/

Foote, P. S., & Krishnamurthi, M. (2001). Forecasting using data warehousing model: Wal-Mart's experience. *Journal of Business Forecasting, 20*(3), 13–17.

Gell, A. (1996). *The anthropology of time.* Washington DC: Berg.

Gobble, M. A. (2012, November–December 4–5). Apple scores a win in the smartphone wars. *Research-Technology Management.*

Grocer, S. (2013, July 15). 'Fabulous fab', Goldman and abacus—a timeline. *Wall Street Journal.* Retrieved from http://blogs.wsj.com/moneybeat/2013/07/15/fabulous-fab-goldman-and-abacus-a-timeline/

Gupta, A., & Prinzinger, J. (2013). Apple Inc.: Where is it going from here? *Journal of Business Case Studies, 9*(3), 215–220.

Hansen, H. K., & Porter, T. (2012). What do numbers do in transnational governance? *International Political Sociology, 6*(4), 409–426.

Harvey, D. (1989). *The condition of postmodernity: An enquiry into the origins of cultural change.* Cambridge: Blackwell.

Heinbecker, P. (2011). *The future of the G20 and its place in global governance* (CIGI G20 Papers, No. 5). Waterloo: Centre for International Governance and Innovation.

Helleiner, E. (1994). *States and the reemergence of global finance: From Bretton Woods to the 1990s.* Ithaca, NY: Cornell University Press.

Hitlin, S., & Elder, G. H., Jr. (2007). Time, self, and the curiously abstract concept of agency. *Sociological Theory, 25*(2), 170–191.

International Swaps and Derivatives Association. (2013, June 20). ISDA publishes year-end 2012 market analysis: Portfolio compression and central clearing continue to impact size of OTC derivatives market (news release). Retrieved from http://www2.isda.org/news/isda-publishes-year-end-2012-market-analysisportfolio-compression-and-central-clearing-continue-to-impact-size-of-otc-derivatives-market

Johnson, B. (2002). The Wal-Mart effect: Information technology isn't the whole story behind productivity. *The McKinsey Quarterly,* (Winter), 40–43.

Latour, B. (1991). Technology is power made durable. In J. Law (Ed.), *Sociology of monsters: Essays on power, technology and domination* (pp. 103–132). London: Routledge.

Litan, R. E. (2010, April 7). *The derivatives dealers' club and derivatives markets reform: A guide for policy makers, citizens and other interested parties.* Brookings. Retrieved from http://www.brookings.edu/research/papers/2010/04/07-derivatives-litan

Luckmann, T. (1991). The constitution of human life in time. In J. Bender & D. E. Wellbery (Eds.), *Chronotypes: The construction of time* (pp. 151–166). Stanford, CA: Stanford University Press.

Luzum, B. (2013). The role of the IERS in the leap second. *ITU News Magazine.* Retrieved from http://www.iers.org/IERS/EN/Organization/About/Biblio/biblio.html

Mengle, D. (2010). Concentration of OTC derivatives among major dealers. *ISDA Research Notes.* Issue 4. Retrieved from http://www.isda.org/researchnotes/pdf/ConcentrationRN_4-10.pdf

Nairn, G. (2003, May 3). Forum to boost supply chain standards: Global Commerce Initiative. *Financial Times*. Retrieved from LexisNexis.

Pagani, F. (2002). *Peer review: A tool for co-operation and change* (Directorate for Legal Affairs, OECD, SG/LEG(2002)1). Retrieved from www.oecd.org

Pfanner, E. (2013, July 27). Competition heats up in smartphones. *International Herald Tribune*, p. 11.

Pleyers, G. (2010). *Alter-globalization: Becoming actors in a global age*. Cambridge: Polity Press.

Porter, T. (2012). Making serious measures: Numerical indices, peer review and transnational actor networks. *Journal of International Relations and Development, 15*, 532–557.

Riles, A. (2008). The anti-network: Private global governance, legal knowledge, and the legitimacy of the state. *American Journal of Comparative Law, 56*(3), Special Symposium Issue, Summer, 605–630.

Schneider, D. (2012). The microsecond market. *IEEE Spectrum*. Retrieved from http://spectrum.ieee.org/computing/networks/the-microsecond-market/4

Slater, J. (2013, August 13). The BlackBerry comeback that wasn't; the company's decision to launch a review of strategy—including a possible sale—is a tacit admission that BB10 phones aren't catching on. *Globe and Mail* (Canada), p. B1.

Slaughter, A.-M. (2004). Disaggregated sovereignty: Toward the public accountability of global government networks. *Government and Opposition, 39*(2), 159–190.

Thompson, E. P. (1967). Time, work-discipline, and industrial capitalism. *Past and Present, 38*, 56–97.

Wailgum, T. (2009, July 12). Will Wal-Mart suppliers see red at green edict? *Computer World*. Retrieved from http://www.computerworlduk.com/in-depth/it-business/2386/will-wal-mart-suppliers-see-red-at-green-edict/

Wang, J. (2006). Economies of IT systems at Wal-Mart—an historical perspective. *Academy of Information and Management Sciences Journal, 9*(1), 45–66.

Weiss, L. (Ed.). (2003). *States in the global economy: Bringing domestic institutions back in*. Cambridge: Cambridge University Press.

Yang, L. (2013, January 7). Providing a template to challenge Apple. *New York Times*. Retrieved from LexisNexis.

Zerubavel, E. (1982). The standardization of time: A sociohistorical perspective. *American Journal of Sociology, 88*(1), 1–23.

Accelerated Contagion and Response: Understanding the Relationships among Globalization, Time, and Disease

YANQIU RACHEL ZHOU* & WILLIAM D. COLEMAN**

*McMaster University, Hamilton, ON, Canada
**University of Waterloo, Waterloo, ON, Canada

ABSTRACT   *The rapid global transmission of Severe Acute Respiratory Syndrome (SARS) in 2003 raises questions about the intersections of globalization, time, and diseases. Viewing it as a disease of speed, this article examines SARS as a case of emerging infectious diseases in the context of contemporary globalization. We contend that the SARS crisis exposed the limitations of traditional spatiality-based approaches to infectious diseases, disease control, and health governance. When the advances in information and communication technologies (ICTs) in recent decades have accelerated the diffusion of pathogens, actors at all levels of global public health are pressed to keep up with the new temporalities. While cognitive and organizational innovations arising from technological changes show some hope for addressing these issues on a global level, other temporality-related challenges—such as differential capacities of the affected countries to respond to the simultaneity of the crisis— are yet to be tackled.*

Introduction

The transmission in 2003 of Severe Acute Respiratory Syndrome (SARS) around the world 'at the speed of a jet airplane' (Health Canada, 2003, p. 23) raises questions about the complex intersections of globalization, time, and diseases. Contemporary globalization processes have deterritorialized the world through global financial markets and rapid expansion in modes of travel in all parts of the sphere (Aaltola, 2012). Through the emergence of global networks of transportation and communication that link countries and cities in new, more integrated ways, increasing transnational contacts, travel, and integration have given rise to new health threats. Not surprisingly, international and global health organizations have framed the new challenges in terms of security. Primarily, they use spatiality-based measures (e.g. border control); this framing, however, overlooks the important changes in the nature and experience of time that have accompanied economic, political, cultural, and social globalizing processes. These processes have led to the 'speeding up' of time, to new forms of time, and to changes in the relationship between time and space/place, as well as between different temporalities. These changes, in turn, produce such phenomena as 'time-space compression', 'timeless time', 'spaces of flow', 'simultaneity', and 'multi-temporality' (Castells, 2009; Harvey, 1990; Rosa, 2009; Scholte, 2005).

In recent years, the emerging infectious diseases (EIDs) such as SARS, avian flu, H1N1, Ebola, and MERS testify to the difficulties globalizing processes present for public health surveillance and interventions. The increased global movements of people and microbes have generated temporal uncertainties when it comes to the speed of transmission and the pressure to respond quickly to disease outbreaks. The fast trans-border transmission of infectious agents arises from steep increases in the volume, frequency, and scope of international travels of humans and of animals and plants which spread pathogens. These difficulties generate questions about traditional state-centric, often spatiality-based, approaches to disease control and health governance.

Technological advances since the 1970s have accelerated contemporary globalizing processes that, in turn, have changed the speed of the circulation of pathogens. In response, actors at all levels of global public health are pressed to speed up their responses. Differences in the experiences of, and capacities for, 'speeding up' of time have created profound new challenges to both domestic responses and global collaboration to control the spread of infectious diseases. Despite proliferation of globalizing linkages among national economies, the continued legitimacy and importance of state borders also pose challenges to addressing trans-border phenomena related to health and disease.

Situating the SARS crisis in 2003 as a case study of EIDs in the context of contemporary globalization, our analysis primarily draws on theories of 'acceleration' and the 'global cities network' found in the globalization (including global health) literature. This theoretical framework allows us to understand time as both a standardized overarching system (e.g. 'universal' clock time) and as a multi-dimensional construct associated with technology, place, politics, and history. It also assists in studying the interconnected relationships among globalization, time, and disease. Guided by these theories, we present our case study in two parts. First, we review the 2003 SARS crisis from a temporal perspective—in particular, its accelerated spread through the global cities network—and second, the rapid, yet temporally contested, responses by some major affected countries to the simultaneity of the crisis. In the section that follows, we examine how the response to SARS at a global level suggests a promising new approach to managing temporal challenges posed by EIDs. We contend that the accelerated transmission of SARS has exposed the limitations of traditional spatiality-based approaches to infectious diseases and disease control. In contrast, cognitive and organizational innovations arising from technological changes show some hope for addressing these challenges.

Conceptualizing the Relationships among Globalization, Time, and Disease

In their book *Timespace: Geographies of Temporality*, May and Thrift (2001) view the late twentieth century as one of the historical periods, when society witnessed 'a significant acceleration in the pace of life concomitant with a dissolution or collapse of traditional spatial co-ordinates (changes usually expressed via some kind of discourse on *speed*—or space divided by time)' (p. 7). Viewing modern societies as acceleration societies, Rosa (2013) also depicts three main, mutually reinforcing types of acceleration that constitute a 'circle of acceleration'. That is,

> *technological acceleration* tends to increase the pace of *social change*, which in turn unavoidably increases the experienced *pace of life*, which then induces an ongoing demand for technical acceleration in the hopes of saving time, and so on back around the circle. (p. xx, emphasis added)

In addition, disease transmission is accelerating due to the pace of ecological and environmental change that brings about new animal–human interfaces, and increasing human mobility (Bashford, 2006; Weiss & McLean, 2005).

In discussing the relationship between globalization and health, Lee (2003) argues that three types of boundary—spatial, temporal, and cognitive—have eroded and been redefined, because globalization processes have changed the nature of human interaction by intensifying the interactions across these boundaries that 'have hitherto separated individuals and population groups from each other' (p. 21). The intensification and diversification of human contacts have generated two forms of spatial changes: (i) a redefinition of existing territorially based geographies and (ii) an increasing degree of social interaction that is detached from territorial spaces, such as e-commerce (Lee, 2003). Viewing EIDs, for example, as a security issue has motivated nation-states to reinforce national borders, on one hand. On the other hand, the deterritorialized potential of EIDs also calls for collaboration that goes beyond national and regional levels of border control (Aaltola, 2012; Ingram, 2005; World Health Organization [WHO], 2006). Enabled by technological advances, geographical deterritorialization in the context of accelerated human interaction leads to the spread of changes in lifestyles (including related health conditions) and the quick movement of infectious agents across geographies (Lee, 2003). Spatial and temporal changes also result in alterations to the creation and exchange of information, ideas, beliefs, norms, and other thought processes. For example, sharing of knowledge globally through information and communication technologies (ICTs) can lead to more rapid adjustments in knowledge and practices in health interventions and governance (Lee, 2003). During the SARS crisis, the WHO's travel advisory targeted individual travelers rather than nation-states, and thereby facilitated faster dissemination of information (WHO, 2006).

Coining the concept of 'time–space compression', Harvey (1990) links acceleration with the history of capitalism, which 'has been characterized by speed-up in the pace of life' (p. 240). He points to changes in time arising from large corporations moving away from vertical structures to outsourcing and sub-contracting, which, in turn, quickened the production and assembling of goods. When the spatial barriers are overcome by technologies, in effect, the distances between places—measured by, for example, travel time or cost—are reduced or even annihilated, and time horizons are 'shortened to the point where the present is all there is' (Harvey, 1990). Consequently, at a global level, 'space appears to shrink to a "global village" of telecommunications and a "spaceship earth" of economic and ecological interdependences' (Harvey, 1990). On a social level, however, people have to learn how to cope with 'an overwhelming sense of *compression* of our spatial and temporal worlds' (Harvey, 1990, author's emphasis). The rapidity of the global spread of SARS through international air travel speaks to the relevance of the concept of time–space compression.

Historically, time was defined as the sequencing of practices, in such terms as 'biological time', 'clock time' (the industrial age), and 'social time' (Castells, 2009, pp. 34–35). In contrast, in the present era, as time 'accelerates', sequencing is lost. Novel ICTs compress time to the point that the sequences of social practices (past, present, future) blur. The instantaneity of information transmission means that all events appear to be simultaneous in digital communication. In these respects, time becomes 'timeless' (Castells, 2009, p. 35). More and more parts of the world experience the same phenomena as 'no time' and 'at the same time' (Scholte, 2005, p. 62), whether these be a banking crisis, extreme weather, or an EID. Under these circumstances, individuals' actions also illustrate a growth in 'the scope and depth of consciousness of the world as a single place' (Scholte, 2005, p. 267), including 'a place' that might fight the same EID anywhere in the world at the same time.

Taking Harvey's observations further, Castells (2009) develops the concept of 'spaces of flows' to capture the new spatial reality: 'the technological and organizational possibility of practicing simultaneity without continuity' (p. 34). Spaces of flows are made of the articulation between three elements: 'the places where activities (and people enacting them) are located; the material communication networks linking these activities; and the content and geometry of the flows of information that perform the activities in terms of function and meaning' (Castells, 2009) Built as they are on 'timeless time', such social spaces also mean 'the possibility of asynchronous (not synchronous) interactions in chosen time' (Castells, 2009). The spaces of flows, working through the social form of the *network*, are increasingly used to respond quickly to the accelerated spread of infectious diseases.

The network geographies of spaces of flows and of the experience of timeless time map onto, in turn, the 'global cities network'. Building on Sassen's research on 'global cities' that was limited to a few key nodes like New York, London, and Tokyo (2001), Taylor (2004) argues that a growing number of cities, including former 'third world' cities like Hong Kong, Shanghai, Singapore, and Taipei, have become the central nodes of the globalizing processes, as he explains:

> The experience of cyberspace is not essentially hierarchical; it operates as innumerable networks, albeit across an uneven globalization. In this sense, then, all cities are global: they operate in a contemporary space of flows that enables them to have a global reach when circumstances require such connections. (p. 43)

This specification of new social structures built around global cities adds to our analysis, because these same horizontal city-to-city networks become the primary conduits for the rapid global spread of infectious diseases. In their study of emerging infections of SARS in global cities, Ali and Keil (2008) argue that, the global cities network could also potentially 'serve as a network for disease transmission' (p. 5), given the intensified flow of people in these ever-dynamic hubs.

While space can be 'annihilated' by time, the role of place as a geographical site or physical space in constituting temporalities has remained important. According to Sassen (2000), in a global city, we can see the coexistence of an old, or collapsing, temporality (the time of the nation state as a historical institution) and a new temporality (the time of economic globalization). The intersection of these different expressions of time generates new dynamics and opportunities that drive economic, political, and social globalizations, and 'can be thought of as partly de-nationalized temporalities' (p. 20). For example, global networks of finance, transnational corporations, and international organizations routinely impose their temporal priorities in local contexts, in which there exist not only different temporalities but also different capacities to respond to globally desirable temporal frameworks. Given that different groups and segments of society have different capacities to synchronize with global processes, these changes result in an increasing multi-temporality (Rosa, 2009):

> This desynchronization entails an increasing 'simultaneity of the non-simultaneous': high-tech and stone-age methods of warfare, transport, or communication persist side by side, not only between different countries, but even within the same society, and fast and slow paces of life can be observed on one and the same street. (pp. 103–104)

In short, uneven globalizing processes have complicated the temporal relationships—in such forms as temporal inequality and disjuncture—among people and societies. In the next section, we explore the impacts of such relationships on the experiences of SARS that demanded fast, simultaneous action across geographies.

The Temporalities of Contagion: The Case of SARS

Accelerated Transmission: The Global Spread of SARS

Emerging in southern China in November 2002, SARS, a viral respiratory disease caused by a novel coronavirus, encompassed the globe, to varying degrees, within weeks. November 16 marked the first retroactively identified case, in Foshan city in China. In less than two months, it broke out in southern China, with similar outbreaks about one month later in other parts of China and Asia (e.g. Hong Kong, Viet Nam, and Singapore) and in Vancouver and Toronto in Canada (Health Canada, 2003; WHO, 2006). The speed with which SARS spread was explicitly linked with 'the age of globalization' in the WHO's 307-page report titled 'SARS: How a global epidemic was stopped'. Specifically, mass, rapid, international travel enabled the transformation of SARS from a local outbreak into a global pandemic; in the absence of accelerated transworld travel, 'it would probably have remained a localized problem, with few consequences for global health' (WHO, 2006, p. VIII).

As one of the 'technologies of speed', jet passenger aircrafts were instrumental in the rapid spread of SARS across countries and continents. Fast air travel means that it takes only hours for a SARS-infected individual, either symptomatic or asymptomatic, to move from one place to another. Such a move becomes even more dangerous when the time used for travel is much less than the 2–10-day incubation and infection period of the SARS Co-Virus (Ali, 2008, p. 244). During the three-hour travel time of Flight CA112 from Hong Kong to Beijing, widespread SARS transmission occurred. In turn, the passing on of the infection is sufficiently rapid that the carrier of the disease to Beijing easily infected both travelers remaining in Beijing or flying on to other cities, such as Taipei, Singapore, and Bangkok (WHO, 2006). Furthermore, the aircraft itself constitutes a distinct environment: one in which passengers are vulnerable to airborne pathogens due to its confined space, little physical mobility, and shared, recirculated air (Ali & Keil, 2006; Budd, Bell, & Brown, 2009; Mangili & Gendreau, 2005). In short, the high degree of mobility of infected, asymptomatic individuals through the networks of international airlines increased the risk of widespread transmission, despite control measures at airports (Mangili & Gendreau, 2005; WHO, 2006). Although the specific patterns of in-flight transmission are yet to be determined, SARS exemplifies the real potential for aircrafts to function as disease 'amplifiers' for 'borderless' transmission (Mangili & Gendreau, 2005).

In addition, the global hub-and-spoke networks of air transportation overlap directly with the networks of 'global cities' (Sassen, 2001; Taylor, 2004, 2013). Providing the infrastructure for global capitalism, the frequent, very fast movement of business and support experts increases the probability of further infection. For example, 78-year-old Ms KSC returned to Toronto, a global city, from Hong Kong, also a global city, on 23 February, and passed the virus on to four members of her extended family before she died; these infections, in turn, sparked the Toronto outbreak (Health Canada, 2003, WHO, 2006). Mr LSK, who acquired SARS in Hong Kong, transmitted it to at least 22 passengers and 2 crewmembers (including residents from Hong Kong, Taiwan, Singapore, and a passenger who flew on to Bangkok) on flight CA112 on 15 March 2003; and at least 59 people were infected after his arrival in Beijing (WHO, 2006). As a result, *simultaneous*, multi-directional transmission took place in these cities.

Unlike the 'spatially contagious diffusion' (spread from major regional epicenters to smaller places) of HIV at an international level, the global spread of SARS occurred between global cities moving along their global economic connections (Ali & Keil, 2006). Given Hong Kong's status as a top 'global city' (Alpha plus) that is more integrated with the global economy than any other city except London and New York (Globalization and World Cities Research Network [GaWC], 2012), it is not surprising that the city became 'an important interchange site' for the global spread of SARS (Ali & Keil, 2006, p. 500). It is not a coincidence, either, that accelerated SARS transmission did not take place until the index case of the Metropole Hotel outbreak arrived in the global city of Hong Kong from Guangdong Province on 21 February 2003. Although the virus had stayed in Guangdong since its first case in mid-November 2002, the diffusion of the disease was accelerated immensely once it arrived in the global cities network. After arriving in Hong Kong, it only took two days to reach Toronto (on 24 February 2003), and three more weeks to massively arrive in Beijing (on 15 March 2003) (WHO, 2006). Although the global media focused on Asia or China as the cause of the pandemic, they overlooked the temporal significance of Hong Kong as a lead node in the global cities network. This network also includes other SARS-affected cities that are classified as first-tier (Alpha category) global cities, such as Beijing (Alpha plus), Singapore (Alpha plus), Toronto (Alpha), Bangkok (Alpha minus) and Taipei (Alpha minus). This ranking means that their contributions to supporting the global economy are of the highest degree (GaWC, 2012). Had the infection not been identified and contained by April 2003, the global cities network could have facilitated even wider disease outbreaks, given its considerable potential for accelerating the pandemic.

The fluidity of human flows in the global cities network accelerated the rapid spread of SARS. Indeed, most of the 'index cases', or 'super-spreaders', who passed the virus on to many others, and thus sparked local outbreaks, were frequent travelers. The index case that started the global spread of SARS was a professor of medicine who went to Hong Kong for a relative's wedding from Guangzhou (China), where he was treating SARS-infected patients. The Hanoi index case was a New York businessman who had traveled to China and Hong Kong before arriving in Viet Nam. The source case on flight SQ 25 (from New York to Singapore) was a doctor who treated SARS cases in Singapore, and then attended a medical conference in New York. The source cases on flight TG614 (from Bangkok to Beijing) were two Chinese officials who became infected on flight CA112, and passed the virus on to a Finnish official of the International Labor Organization, who had traveled in Europe and Bangkok before going to Beijing (WHO, 2006).

The rapid expansion and intensification of global air traffic flows along global cities networks have been instrumental in reconstructing the relationship between space and time. Global cities have grown 'closer' through increased speed of travel, as well as the intensity of the connectivity among them. The 'increasing flows of new kinds' (Ingram, 2005, p. 527) in the space of global networks add to vulnerability and risk. 'Whereas some places are more likely to become conducive to a pandemic disease, there are some travelers who are more exposed as well as more likely to pass the disease on to others' (Aaltola, 2012, p. 63).

Coping with the Simultaneity of the Crisis: Local Responses to the Pandemic

When the SARS Co-Virus arrived in localities around the world, the major temporal charac-teristics of this disease became more about simultaneity, including what Rosa (2009) calls 'simultaneity of the non-simultaneous'. All of the affected countries were forced to respond to the common crisis simultaneously, despite their greatly varied economic, technical, political, and social capacities to do so. The process of time–space compression noted previously sig-nificantly reduced or, even, annihilated the time available for the development of the 'best' reactions at a local/national level. Even though a synchronized emergency response across countries might be desirable, it is difficult in practice because of the 'multi-temporality' associ-ated with the economy, politics, history, and people in different places. We illustrate these issues by focusing on China and Canada, two of the hardest-hit countries that are geographi-cally distant and became temporally 'closer', or interconnected, because of this global pandemic.

After the first SARS case in November 2002, the virus spread unreported in Guangdong Pro-vince for a couple of months before moving to Hong Kong and other parts of the world. On 28 March 2003, one day after Beijing was added by the WHO to its list of affected areas, the Chinese Ministry of Health agreed to provide the WHO with regular, up-to-date reports from all provinces beginning 1 April. With all other affected areas having already done so, this step symbolized that the country had 'become, very clearly, part of the global network in dealing with the disease' (WHO, 2006, p. 24). Although Western media tended to attribute the Chinese government's delay and the inefficient flow of information to its non-democratic system (Huang & Leung, 2005), there were other reasons, too. In addition to China's inexperi-ence in responding to this previously unknown disease, the local health authorities faced bar-riers, at both systematic (a decentralized system of disease surveillance) and personal (undermining of prospects for job promotion) levels, to the timely reporting of the outbreak to higher authorities. Furthermore, the government's decision on the timing of publicizing the outbreak was influenced by its implications for domestic economic and social stability, and for its already problematic international image (Ahmad, Krumkamp, & Reintjes, 2009; Tai & Sun, 2007).

The huge international pressure to contain the virus induced a high degree of politicization of the battle against SARS in China in order for the government to quickly mobilize the entire society. On 14 April, President Hu Jintao declared a 'people's war' against SARS (WHO, 2006). On 20 April, both the health minister and the mayor of Beijing were removed from their posts (Zhao, 2003). Adopting a strategy analogous to that of the traditional 'patriotic health movement' that relies heavily on mass mobilization, China was able to somewhat com-pensate for the inadequacy of its resources (e.g. time, technology, and personnel) for SARS sur-veillance and prevention (Liu, 2003; WHO, 2006). Becoming the government's 'top priority', SARS responses came directly under the leadership of the vice-premier Wu Yi, who was *also* made the new health minister. The result was faster coordination of resources, communication and collaboration across sectors (including mass media), places, and hierarchies of the govern-mental systems (Liu, 2003; WHO, 2006; Zhao, 2003). In late April, it took only seven days for China to build a 1000-bed hospital for SARS patients in a northern suburb of Beijing, at a cost of 160 million *yuan* (US$19.33 million) (Zhao, 2003). With the wide dissemination of information and surveillance by the public, the time between onset of symptoms and hospitalization in Beijing was reduced to two from the five to six days that was the norm before the outbreak (Pang et al., 2003).

Similar to China, Canada's initial responses to SARS were delayed. As early as 27 November 2002, the Canada-based Global Public Health Intelligence Network (GPHIN), an Internet-based early warning system for worldwide public health threats, received a Chinese-language report of a flu outbreak in mainland China. While the Chinese report was sent to the WHO with a translated English title, the full report was not translated until 21 January 2003, in part because the GPHIN system then in use could not accommodate the information in languages other than English and French (Blench, 2008; Health Canada, 2003). As a result, an early opportunity to learn about SARS was missed by Health Canada and WHO (Health Canada, 2003). The arrival of SARS in Canada in late February quickly transformed airports into the first and foremost frontiers of disease control. On 18 March, quarantine officers were deployed, and 'Health Alert Notices' were distributed to air travel passengers arriving in and returning to Canada from Asia at Toronto's Pearson and Vancouver International airports. On 23 April, the WHO extended its travel advisory to Toronto, which was removed soon after Canada's strong objection (WHO, 2006). As a condition of this removal, the level of monitoring of passengers at major airports was increased, and multiple expensive thermal scanners were installed at Toronto's Pearson and Vancouver airports in May (Health Canada, 2003; Keil & Ali, 2006). Given the nature of the disease, however, the effectiveness of these airport screening measures was unclear. As of 27 August 2003, out of an estimated 6.5 million passengers screened at Canadian airports, roughly 9100 were referred for further assessment by screening nurses or quarantine officers: but none had SARS. Out of the approximately 2.4 million passengers screened by the pilot thermal scanner project, only 832 required further assessment, and (again) none was found to have SARS (Health Canada, 2003).

On one hand, the massive use of border control regimens, as well as other infection-control instruments (contact tracing and quarantine[1]), for SARS control reflects the decision-makers' intention to err on the side of caution and safety in the context of uncertainties (e.g. the difficulty of identifying people with SARS and predicting their movements) (Affonso, Andrews, & Jeffs, 2004). On the other hand, however, it also signals 'a return to an unhappy past', when 'dangerousness'—unpredictable danger that somehow inheres in certain individuals (e.g. people from 'Third-World' countries)—was the central logic of public health governance, and attention was devoted to 'locating and neutralizing all sources of danger' threatening public health (Hooker, 2001, 2006, pp. 179–180). The transnational movement of SARS was too fast for the classical approach to risk management that required more time to widen 'our field of vision' and improve the accuracy of 'our prediction' (Cooper, 2006, p. 119). Ironically, at a time when the world has become increasingly deterritorialized due to global capitalism, the importance of border control in disease control was resumed in the context of EIDs.

Being listed by the WHO as one of the 'affected areas', and the only such location[2] outside Asia, meant that Toronto also had a hard time adapting to its multiple and contested 'temporal' identities. In contrast to a long-standing projected identity as a 'safe, North American city', Toronto was constructed during the SARS crisis by the international media as an 'exotic plague town', a 'backward place' that was 'not quite up to modern standards of hygiene and scientific rationality' (Strange, 2006, pp. 221–223). To protest the WHO's travel advisory, which had tremendous negative impacts on Toronto's image and economy, the governments, along with Canadian media, tried to externalize the disease through, for example, defining the virus as an exotic invasion (SARS as a Chinese or Asian disease), thereby distinguishing Toronto from other affected places (Keil & Ali, 2006; Leung, 2004; Strange, 2006). The city's Chief Medical Officer of Health diplomatically commented on Toronto's link with other 'pre-modern' SARS-affected Asian areas as 'a gross misrepresentation of the facts'; the province's commissioner of public health simply said: 'We're not some rinky-dink Third-World country' (Strange, 2006, pp. 224–225).

The racialization of the disease, along with intensified public fear, reactivated historic anti-Asian (in particular, anti-Chinese) and anti-immigrant attitudes in Canada (Keil & Ali, 2006; Strange, 2006). In addition to the surveillance measures targeting travelers from Asia, social distancing from the Chinese and Asian communities in Toronto was widely observed (Leung, 2004). To some extent, the racism during the SARS crisis can also be understood in terms of people's inability to cope with what Harvey (1990) calls 'an overwhelming sense of compression', caused by this fast, borderless, and contagious disease. At a material level, the gap between the accelerated global spread of SARS and the lack of effective vaccine and treatment for the disease certainly generated public anxiety and panic. At a cognitive level, reduced travel times between Canada and the 'Third-World' countries and the permeability of the traditional state borders in the context of EIDs also challenged people's sense of security, given the impaired ability to separate or protect themselves from the 'dangerous' others. Although Toronto's ethnic and cultural diversity and transnational ties with other global cities in Asia were negatively presented in the dominant media discourses on SARS, its post-SARS promotional campaigns, ironically, resumed this pre-SARS identity by using the logo, 'Toronto: the World Within a City' (Keil & Ali, 2006; Strange, 2006).

Simultaneously confronting the public health emergency, China, as the 'source' of the pandemic and a relatively resource-limited country, had to resort to a traditional 'patriotic movement' to mobilize its resources; and Canada, as a wealthy country 'unpreparedly' hit by this disease 'from Asia', struggled with the effectiveness of using border control for disease control. We should also note that the mobilization strategy in China was simply impossible in Canada, given the latter's decentralized federal system and institutional arrangement of the healthcare system (Health Canada, 2003; Van Wagner, 2008). These two countries' experiences of coping with the simultaneity of the crisis illustrate the challenges ensuing from the coexistence of, and disjunction between, multiple temporalities (Rosa, 2009; Sassen, 2000). These include the accelerated SARS transmission facilitated by the global cities network, when compared with the slower responsiveness of older systems of disease control. Even longer is the time needed for immigrant or diaspora communities to be integrated and accepted into a host country. In the next section, we review the global response to the challenges arising from this newly emergent infectious disease.

Containing SARS at a Global Level: Networked Responses in the 'Spaces of Flow'

Our discussion above highlights the rapidity and global extensity of EID infections through air travel built around global cities network and population density. The same conditions of time–space compression made possible rapid scientific identification of the disease and the development of effective approaches to confining the virus. Once the outbreak began to cross borders in February 2003, it was fully contained within five months. The institutional tools and networks needed for containing the SARS Co-Virus grew out of 'speeding up time' in the containment of EIDs and other infectious diseases, thanks to several steps taken beginning in the early 1990s. The Program for Monitoring Emerging Diseases, launched in 1994, was a first attempt at devising a global Internet-based reporting system on outbreaks of contagious diseases and exposures to toxins. Within 12 years of its founding, it had 30,000 subscribers in 150 countries (Zacher & Keefe, 2008). In 1997, the Canadian government set up the aforementioned GPHIN in cooperation with the WHO. Over time, after overcoming linguistic limitations, it built the capacity to scan news sources 24 hours a day, 7 days a week in Arabic, English, French, Russian, simplified and traditional Chinese, Farsi, and Spanish (Zacher & Keefe, 2008). Meanwhile, six groups of actors took steps to set in place the arrangements needed for rapid construction of response networks for pandemic infectious diseases: the WHO in hiring its own experts; the expansion of trained persons at the six regional offices of the WHO; the involvement and linking together of national research laboratories like the Centers for Disease Control (CDC) in Atlanta and in China; NGOs like MSF (Doctors without Borders), International Federation of Red Cross and Red Crescent Societies, and Merlin; Ministries of Health in WHO member states; and other UN bodies like UNICEF (Zacher & Keefe, 2008, pp. 60–64).

Gradually, these six types of organization developed an informal network for better communication and responses to problems including disease outbreaks. In April 2000, the network was formalized under the direction of the WHO as the Global Outbreak and Response Network (GOARN). The Network cooperates on four tasks: conducting epidemic intelligence, verifying outbreak rumors, alerting appropriate groups in outbreak situations, and organizing rapid response reactions (Zacher & Keefe, 2008). GOARN has been involved in 70 global outbreaks in 42 countries since its founding: 'By assembling missions that rapidly provide critical expertise and resources to countries affected by disease outbreaks, GOARN serves a critical role in containing contagious disease and providing back up capacity' (Ansell, Sondorp, & Stevens, 2012, p. 332).

GOARN and SARS: Information Flows 'Outpacing' the Virus

When compared to the past, acceleration in time 'was used to an advantage during the global SARS response, since the sharing of information via the instant time of computer networks vastly outpaced the biologically defined time of viral reproduction and travel' (Ali, 2008, p. 247). Ali (2008) adds that the:

> hallmark of this response was the rapid formation of a virtual network of international scientists who joined forces to identify the causal agent of the disease, develop a universal case definition for the disease, and characterize the genetic code of the virus—all within one month. (p. 247)

The first network formed brought together researchers from 13 laboratories in 10 countries to tackle the question of the etiology of the virus. One of these laboratories, the British Columbia Cancer Agency in Canada, announced that it had isolated the previously unknown coronavirus and released the data on 12 April 2003. Two days later, the CDC in Atlanta built on the Canadian agency's work, providing further information to the WHO, which, in turn, released the data internationally on 16 April. A second network of 50 clinicians in 14 countries developed a definition of the disease and some control guidelines. The WHO set up a third virtual network of 32 epidemiologists from 11 countries, which brought together public health institutions, ministries of health, and WHO country offices to define appropriate public health measures for containing the spread of SARS (Zacher & Kiefe, 2008). These networks drew upon the new ICTs to give life to global spaces of flows that linked both nation-states and other transnational actors in the gathering and sharing of information.

Ansell et al. (2012) identify additional advantages arising from the acceleration of time and the rapid filling of global spaces by networks of experts. First, it permitted the mobilization of partner institutions as a 'technical community', which facilitated rapid coordination due to the 'direct and sustained contact' among these institutions (p. 324). Second, with such an arrangement, information and influence can flow both down from the WHO but also up from the technical partners to multilateral institutions like the WHO. The independence of the GOARN network added to the effectiveness and efficiency of these transactions. Third, the network form allows the direct integration of quasi-public and even private institutions into virtual pathways for sharing knowledge rapidly and independently. The acceleration of scientific exploration and analysis 'via the instant time of computer networks vastly outpaced the biologically defined time of viral reproduction and travel' (Ali, 2008, p. 247). Finally, the accelerated formation of scientific and clinical networks gave an organization like the WHO the capability to manage multilateral, regional and bilateral responses. The WHO's Executive Director of Communicable Diseases explained: 'I think that it would be fair to say that this is the first global outbreak where there was a 24 hour availability of information and information was continuously coming in through networks of doctors, of clinicians, of virologists, of epidemiologists' (cited in Ali, 2008, p. 242).

Accordingly, working 24 hours a day in 'timeless time', GOARN was able to locate and mobilize available and relevant expertise and resources; communicate directly with national ministries of health on needs and terms of reference; mobilize multilateral resources and then deploy them as field teams where needed; and provide a two-way flow of coordination between WHO headquarters and the various field teams involved at anytime and anywhere (Ansell et al., 2012).

GOARN was built upon the timeless time that existed between researchers around the world. The WHO was able to challenge the nation-state monopoly on the control of time and thus space. It harnessed the new technologies and their rapid adoption by non-state actors for global public health purposes. As Fidler (2005) observes: 'The revolution in information technologies changed the context for state calculations about whether to report or try to cover up an outbreak' (p. 346). Ali (2008) adds: 'As a consequence by "outpacing" the virus, the scientific establishment was able to break the chain of transmission of the SARS-CoV quite handily—an outcome that was no doubt assisted by the presence of other fortuitous factors' (p. 247). In this respect GOARN's taking advantage of space–time compression represented a profound break with the state controlled surveillance found in the traditional approach to infectious disease control in the preceding century. In this regard, GOARN provided additional evidence of the need to reform the International Health Regulations (IHR) built in an earlier world of clock time in limited spaces defined by nation-state and imperial boundaries.

Reforming IHR: Toward an Accelerated Response to Future EID Outbreaks

Simultaneous to the various steps taken in the 1990s that led to the founding of GOARN in 2000, the WHO had embarked upon the reform of the IHR. These regulations trace their history to the nine sanitary conferences held by various world powers beginning in 1851 and finishing early in the twentieth century. Their objective was to minimize the negative impact of several key infectious diseases on international trade, most notably cholera and yellow fever and later influenza. The discussion of how these regulations could be brought up to date was profoundly influenced by the SARS crisis and the emergence of GOARN.

Backed up consistently by the World Health Assembly, the WHO, carved out a new approach built on health 'security', on the speeding up of time made possible by ICTs, and on the rapid entry of NGOs into global health governance. Over the same period, the GOARN model needed to be adapted so as to be able to respond to other threats to global health where the acceleration of time and globalization of spaces were having lethal impacts. The global health discussions now expand to such issues as weapons of mass destruction, biological weapons, chemical disasters like Bhopal in India, and failures of atomic reactors.

Accordingly, when the WHO proclaimed the new IHR regulations in 2005, they took 'time and space compression' more fully into account. The particular global health challenges exemplified by the SARS Co-Virus were bought under a new broader concept: *public health emergencies of international concern* defined as follows: 'an extraordinary event which is determined, as provided in these Regulations: (i) to constitute a public health risk to other States through the international spread of disease; and (ii) to potentially require a coordinated international response' (cited in Fidler, 2005, p. 362). Subsequent legal interpretation of the concept suggests that it would include human-made disasters like Bhopal, the use of weapons of mass destruction, and planned use of biological agents as well as EIDs (Fidler, 2005, pp. 365–367).

The speeding up of time for the spread of EIDs like SARS and the lessons learned about accelerating responses to such outbreaks from the performance of GOARN led to further innovations in the new regulations. They legitimized the practice of States working in global networks in tandem with non-state actors and public health authorities at all levels. The WHO gained the authority to declare these 'public health emergencies of international concern' and to issue non-binding recommendations concerning appropriate health measures (Fidler, 2005). IHR 2005's surveillance strategy ... has been specifically designed to make IHR 2005 directly applicable to EID events, which are usually unexpected and often threaten to spread internationally (Baker & Fidler, 2006, pp. 1059–1060).

Conclusion

ICTs that came together in the 1970s, along with advances in the speed and volume of airplanes, created what Castells (2009) calls 'timeless time'; thus, many human activities now take place in 'no time'. Building on Harvey's concept of time–space compression, our article argues that contemporary temporality stretches space: the linkages between people are more and more 'transplanetary' to use Scholte's term: they reach increasingly from any one place in the world to any other place. These changes exemplify globalization in action and they are most evident along the pathways of global cities networks.

We argue that globalizing processes have changed temporal–spatial dynamics of EIDs like SARS, in such forms as the speed of global transmission, the simultaneity of public health emergency across geographies, and the possibility of accelerating responses on a global level. Taking into account the intersection of globalization, time and disease, it is clear that contemporary globalization has not only shaped the temporal nature of EIDs like SARS but also been shaped by the processes of global health responses (e.g. cross-country collaboration and the reform of related international organizations). While the technical infrastructure of global networks has provided a promising condition for accelerating surveillance and information sharing on a global level, other temporality-related challenges—such as differential capacities of the affected countries to respond to the simultaneity of the crisis—are yet to be tackled.

In 2012, the WHO organized an IHR Committee to monitor a new coronavirus, Middle East respiratory syndrome, which first appeared in the Middle East. By 2015, it had expanded to Europe, North Africa, Southeast Asia, China, South Korea, and North America (*Coronavirus infections*, 2015). Even more concerning, in 2014, the lethal Ebola virus, which has occurred off and on in rural areas of West Africa for a number of years, reached large cities for the first time, including Lagos, Nigeria with its 21 million population. Lagos was first classified as a global city (gamma category) in 2008 and had climbed to the 'Beta minus' category by

2012. Ebola's reaching a global city was sufficiently concerning that the WHO declared the outbreak to be a *public health emergency of international concern* under the IHR in August 2014 (Kennedy, 2014).

In conclusion, the increasing potential for the rapid and global spread of EIDs arising from new temporalities has been our principal concern. The possibility of viruses going *anywhere* in *no time* along global cities pathways heightens tremendously the probability of infectious disease pandemics. The factors that came together in the global outbreak of SARS outlined in this article have become even more probable in the ensuing 13 years. More in-depth analysis of the interactions between different temporalities and expanding spaces arising from globalization has become a challenge, if not a necessity, for global health research and globalization studies.

Acknowledgements

We thank our colleagues of the Time and Globalization Working Project at McMaster University and anonymous reviewers for their comments on a draft of this paper.

Disclosure Statement

No potential conflict of interest was reported by the authors.

Notes

1   According to Health Canada (2003), about 25,000 residents of the Great Toronto Area were placed in quarantine during the SARS crisis.
2   Vancouver was removed from the list of 'affected areas' three days after the WHO released its first list on 16 March 2003 (WHO, 2006).

References

Aaltola, M. (2012). Contagious insecurity: War, SARS and global air mobility. *Contemporary Politics, 18*, 53–70.
Affonso, D. D., Andrews, G. J., & Jeffs, L. (2004). The urban geography of SARS: Paradoxes and dilemmas in Toronto's health care. *Journal of Advanced Nursing, 45*(6), 568–578.
Ahmad, A., Krumkamp, R., & Reintjes, R. (2009). Controlling SARS: A review on China's response compared with other SARS-affected countries. *Tropical Medicine & International Health, 14*, S36–S45.
Ali, S. H. (2008). SARS as an emergent complex: Toward a networked approach to urban infectious disease. In S. H. Ali & R. Keil (Eds.), *Networked disease: Emerging infections in the global city* (pp. 235–249). Malden MA: Wiley-Blackwell.
Ali, S. H., & Keil, R. (2006). Global cities and the spread of infectious disease: The case of severe acute respiratory syndrome (SARS) in Toronto, Canada. *Urban Studies, 43*, 491–509.
Ali, S. H., & Keil, R. (2008). Introduction: Networked disease. In S. H. Ali & R. Keil (Eds.), *Networked disease: Emerging infections in the global city* (pp. 1–7). Malden MA: Wiley-Blackwell.
Ansell, C., Sondorp, E., & Stevens, R. H. (2012). The promise and challenge of global network governance: The Global Outbreak Alert and Response Network. *Global Governance, 18*, 317–337.
Baker, M. G., & Fidler, D. (2006). Global public health surveillance under new international health regulations. *Emerging Infectious Diseases, 12*(7), 1058–1065.
Bashford, A. (2006). "Age of universal contagion": Disease, history and globalization. In A. Bashford (Ed.), *Medicine at the border: Disease, globalization and security, 1850 to the present* (pp. 1–18). New York: Palgrave Macmillan.
Blench, M. (2008). *Global Public Health Intelligence Network (GPHIN)*. Retrieved from http://www.amtaweb.org/papers/4.02_Blench2008.pdf

Budd, L., Bell, M., & Brown, T. (2009). Of plagues, planes and politics: Controlling the global spread of infectious diseases by air. *Political Geography*, 28(7), 426–435.

Castells, M. l. (2009). *Communication power*. Oxford: Oxford University Press.

Cooper, M. (2006). Pre-empting emergence: The biological turn in the war on terror. *Theory, Culture & Society*, 23, 113–135.

Coronavirus infections. (2015, June 12). Retrieved from www.who.int/csr/disease/coronavirus_infections/en/index.html

Fidler, D. P. (2005). From international sanitary conventions to global health security: The new international health regulations. *Chinese Journal of International Law*, 4, 325–392.

Globalization and World Cities Research Network. (2012). *The world according to GaWC 2012*. Retrieved from http://www.lboro.ac.uk/gawc/world2012t.html

Harvey, D. (1990). *The condition of postmodernity: An enquiry into the origins of cultural change*. Oxford: Blackwell.

Health Canada. (2003). *Learning from SARS: Renewal of public health in Canada* (a report of the National Advisory Committee on SARS and Public Health). Ottawa: Author.

Hooker, C. (2001). Sanitary failure and risk: Pasteurisation, immunisation and the logics of prevention. In A. Bashford & C. Hooker (Eds.), *Contagion: Historical and cultural studies* (pp. 129–152). London: Routledge.

Hooker, C. (2006). Drawing the lines: Danger and risk in the age of SARS. In A. Bashford (Ed.), *Medicine at the border: Disease, globalization and security, 1850 to the present* (pp. 179–195). New York: Palgrave Macmillan.

Huang, Y., & Leung, C. C. M. (2005). Western-led press coverage of mainland China and Vietnam during the SARS crisis: Reassessing the concept of "media representation of the Other". *Asian Journal of Communication*, 15, 302–318.

Ingram, A. (2005). The new geopolitics of disease: Between global health and global security. *Geopolitics*, 10, 522–545.

Keil, R., & Ali, S. H. (2006). Multiculturalism, racism and infectious disease in the global city: The experience of the 2003 SARS outbreak in Toronto. *Topia*, 16, 23–49.

Kennedy, M. (2014, August 8). WHO declares Ebola outbreak an international public health emergency. *The Guardian*. Retrieved from http://www.theguardian.com/society/2014/aug/08/who-ebola-outbreak-international-public-health-emergency

Lee, K. (2003). *Globalization and health: An introduction*. New York: Palgrave Macmillan.

Leung, C. (2004). *Yellow peril revisited: Impact of SARS on the Chinese and Southeast Asian Canadian communities*. Retrieved from http://www.ccnc.ca/sars/SARSReport.pdf

Liu, C. (2003). The battle against SARS: A Chinese story. *Australian Health Review*, 26(3), 3–13.

Mangili, A., & Gendreau, M. A. (2005). Transmission of infectious diseases during commercial air travel. *The Lancet*, 365(9463), 989–996.

May, J., & Thrift, N. (2001). Introduction. In J. May & N. Thrift (Eds.), *Timespace: Geographies of temporality* (pp. 1–46). London: Routledge.

Pang, X., Zhu, Z., Xu, F. Guo, J., Gong, X., Liu, D., ... Feikin, D. R. (2003). Evaluation of control measures implemented in the severe acute respiratory syndrome outbreak in Beijing 2003. *JAMA*, 290, 3215–3221.

Rosa, H. (2009). Social acceleration: Ethical and political consequences of a desynchronized high-speed society. In H. Rosa & W. E. Scheuerman (Eds.), *High-speed society: Social acceleration, power and modernity* (pp. 77–112). University Park: Pennsylvania State University Press.

Rosa, H. (2013). *Social acceleration: A new theory of modernity*. New York: Columbia University Press.

Sassen, S. (2000). The global city: The de-nationalizing of time and space. In J. Ockman (Ed.), *The pragmatist imagination: Thinking about "things in the making"* (pp. 254–265). Princeton, NJ: Princeton Architectural Press.

Sassen, S. (2001). *The global city: New York, London, Tokyo*. Princeton, NJ: Princeton University Press.

Scholte, J. (2005). *Globalization: A critical introduction* (2nd ed.). Basingstoke: Palgrave Macmillan.

Strange, C. (2006). Postcard from plaguetown: SARS and the exoticisation of Toronto. In A. Bashford (Ed.), *Medicine at the border: Disease, globalization and security, 1850 to the present* (pp. 219–239). New York: Palgrave Macmillan.

Tai, Z., & Sun, T. (2007). Media dependencies in a changing media environment: The case of the 2003 SARS epidemic in China. *New Media & Society*, 9, 987–1009.

Taylor, P. J. (2004). *World city network: A global urban analysis*. London: Routledge.

Taylor, P. J. (2013). *Extraordinary cities: Millennia of moral syndromes, world-systems and city/state relations*. Cheltenham: Edward Elgar Publishing.

Van Wagner, E. (2008). Toward a dialectical understanding of networked disease in the global city: Vulnerability, connectivity, topologies. In S. H. Ali & R. Keil (Eds.), *Networked disease: Emerging infections in the global city* (pp. 13–26). Malden, MA: Wiley-Blackwell.

Weiss, R. A., & McLean, A. R. (2005). What have we learnt from SARS? In A. R. McLean, R. M. May, J. Pattison, & R. A. Weiss (Eds.), *SARS: A case study in emerging infections* (pp. 112–116). New York, NY: Oxford University Press.

World Health Organization. (2006). *SRAS: How a global epidemic was stopped*. Manila, The Philippines: WHO Regional Office for the Western Pacific Region.

Zacher, M. W., & Keefe, T. J. (2008). *The politics of global health governance*: *United by contagion*. London: Palgrave Macmillan.

Zhao, Q.-Z. (Minister of the State Council Information Office). (2003, July 1). A hard won victory by China and its people. *People's Daily*. Retrieved from http://english.peopledaily.com.cn/200307/01/eng20030701_119229.shtm

Fast Machines, Slow Violence: ICTs, Planned Obsolescence, and E-waste

SABINE LEBEL

University of Toronto, Toronto, Ontario, Canada

ABSTRACT   *This paper brings the temporalities of the global e-waste recycling trade into the temporal reckonings of speed, acceleration, and simultaneity typically associated with information and communications technologies (ICTs). Following feminist philosopher Sofia, it begins with a reconsideration of theories of technology as they relate to time and the environment. The second part of the paper suggests that recycling practices do not address the tempos of production, especially planned obsolescence. Bringing together Nixon's concept of slow violence with Sofia's theory of container technologies, this paper interrogates the speed, acceleration, and simultaneity often attributed to ICTs and globalization to argue that planned obsolescence functions as a type of slow violence, and that it structures the environmental politics of the information age.*

It takes a container ship 8 days to cross the Atlantic Ocean, and 12 days to cross the Pacific (Sekula, 1995). The speedy communications engendered by cyberspace, email, and rapid data transfer cannot overcome the actual space and time, not to mention the infrastructure, needed to distribute goods across the globe. Information and communications technologies (ICTs) are fundamentally technologies of globalization; not only are they manufactured through global production chains, but they are also contributors to changes associated with globalization, especially the increasing interconnectedness of people, capital, and data. These technologies of the information age are said to compress time and space: we can instantly communicate with someone in another time zone and capital can move across economies multiple times in the space of a few seconds. As a result, ICTs are typically described by timelessness, acceleration, and simultaneity. The slower, global flows of the production, distribution, and disposal of ICTs as they circle the globe in container ships are then concurrent to, and indeed part of, data and information flows.

The global waste trade is a product of globalization, its development most significantly aided by advancements in transportation technologies and changes to environmental regulations in wealthier countries (Alexander & Reno, 2012). E-waste is the fastest growing waste stream in the 'developed' world (Basel Action Network, 2011). The total volume of e-waste traded in 2012 was estimated to be over one billion kilograms (Lepawsky, 2014). Computers, laptops, cell phones, and other ICTs are largely responsible for the expanding e-waste stream and contain many toxic materials, elements of which cause serious health and ecological problems. While the global trade in e-waste was historically defined by flows from rich to poor countries, more recently trade *between* developing countries has emerged (Lepawsky, 2014). E-waste, and especially the unsafe e-waste reclamation that happens more often in poorer communities, exemplifies what Nixon (2011) terms slow violence: or the often hidden ecological damage that poor communities are increasingly burdened with over the long term. Unlike the ever-increasing speed of ICTs in use, e-waste comprising ICTs cannot be understood as fast. Rather, e-waste must be described in terms of the longer time frames needed for ecological remediation. Bringing the implications of slow violence into discussions of the global penetration of ICTs telescopes their timescale outwards. This more inclusive global temporal accounting of ICTs includes the following speeds: the simultaneity and real time associated with ICTs; the actual time needed to transport materials (both goods and waste) around the world; and the slow violence caused by the toxic pollution of e-waste.[1] However, acceleration must also be included because ICTs are said to accelerate our pace of life and they are also accelerating in terms of pace of production, and speed and efficiency in use. Policies of planned obsolescence dictate that computers and other ICTs be 'death dated' so that existing models are not backwards compatible. New, 'improved', and faster models are marketed every few months and, as a result, functioning ICTs are routinely upgraded and discarded. Planned obsolescence accelerates the accumulation of trashed electronics.

This paper brings the speeds of e-waste, in particular the global trade in e-waste, into the temporal reckonings typically associated with ICTs and globalization. I use computers as a sort of placeholder, intending them to indicate the larger social, economic, and political changes associated with the information age globally, and to represent the many changes related to ICTs generally. Underlying the global and temporal aspects of ICTs are traditional theories of technology that frame our discussions in particular and limited ways. This paper begins with a reconsideration of those theories of technology as they relate to time and the environment following feminist philosopher Sofia (2010). Recycling, the focus of the second part of the paper, is central to global strategies of waste management (Alexander & Reno, 2012). Bringing together slow violence and container technologies into a theoretical framework, this paper interrogates the speed, acceleration, and simultaneity often attributed to ICTs and globalization. I argue that planned obsolescence functions as a type of slow violence, and is also a structuring paradigm of the information age that obscures the environmental problems it causes behind the veneer of technological progress.

Container Technologies

In the realm of ICTs, both the speed of information transmission, and the amount of information in circulation are constantly increasing. A characteristic of information society is that users of technology are often overwhelmed by the volume and speed of information and consequently unable to make sense of it. As Nixon (2011) says, the

> digital world ... threatens to 'info-whelm' us into a state of perpetual distraction. If an awareness of the Great Acceleration is (to put it mildly) unevenly distributed, the experience of accelerated connectivity (and the paradoxical disconnects that can accompany it) is increasingly widespread. In an age of degraded attention spans it becomes doubly difficult yet increasingly urgent that we focus on the toll exacted, over time, by the slow violence of ecological degradation. (pp. 12–13)

Access to the digital realms means living in a state of perpetual information overload, which is not conducive to the longer term planning needed to deal with ecological problems. Time and our experiences of time are fundamentally connected to the technologies of globalization and to the quality of our participation in the information age.

In our consideration of slow violence, or the long-term ecological degradation of the Great Acceleration, as Nixon calls it, there are many factors, effects, and casualties to consider that are often excluded from discussions of the information age. ICTs require vast amounts of natural resources, and so we might include those mines, their workers, and the ecosystems that produce the precious metals in ICTs such as coltan, nickel, gold, and literally hundreds of others. Manufacturers, past and present, from Silicon Valley, USA, to Shenzhen, China, produce legacies of worker illness and ecosystem pollution with the toxic chemicals necessary to produce semiconductors and other components (see Grossman, 2006; Pellow & Park, 2002; Smith, Sonnenfeld, & Pellow, 2006). These too must be included. So too must we include the emissions-producing transportation networks necessary to connect products to consumers, natural resources to factories, and trash to waste disposal sites. Information infrastructures, from wireless hubs to data farms, facilitate our participation or marginalization in the Great Acceleration. Finally, e-waste reclamation, the focus of this paper, needs to be included. ICTs are central to the global restructuring of our manufacturing and disposal centers and peripheries, communications infrastructures, and increasingly define access or lack thereof to the information economy. They configure fast places and slow places, which correspond to global social, economic, and environmental power relations.

In her essay, 'Container technologies', Sofia (2010) suggests that by rethinking how foundational philosophers such as Heidegger and Mumford understand technology we can begin to shift how technology is conceptualized, especially in relation to the environment. She expands Heidegger's theory of technology that suggests technology has a revealing action, which commands nature into a stockpile (or standing-reserve) in the service of human intent and needs. Sofia's (2010) intervention brings in production processes. For example, in Heidegger's discussion of the chalice, the tools and other materials in the shop of the smithy making the chalice are absent (Sofia, 2010). Sofia (2010) argues that the processes of extraction, transportation, and supply—and I would add disposal—are crucial to understanding that object, the chalice. Sofia further locates Heidegger, with Mumford and McLuhan, in a theoretical tradition in which technology is part of a lineage of tools that stretch the limits of the human body. The body connects to the hammer, the spear, and even the car, things that reach out, emphasizing speed, motion, and extension. In contrast, containers keep and preserve their contents over time and act as a technology of re-sourcing and storage (Sofia, 2010). Container technologies such as jugs, urns, sieves, or chalices designed to hold, spill out, or act as filters are omitted from these earlier discussions.

Technologies, then, also have temporal qualities: tools are usually associated with speed and efficiency, whereas containers are meant to preserve, last through time, or to have a timed release of their contents. Both types of technology are fundamentally connected to particular temporal characteristics: tools tend to be connected with speed and containers with duration (of time). Part of the action of container technologies is that they tend to elude our awareness, to be unnoticed and in the background (Sofia, 2010). Often, the only time we become aware of them is when they fail in some way: the glass breaks, spilling red wine all over the white rug; the underground chemical storage tank leaks, polluting a community's groundwater. When a given technology functions both as a container and as a tool, often the 'tool' aspect is reinforced while the 'container' aspect is obscured.

As containers, personal computers are essentially storage devices for data and yet they tend only to be conceived of as 'flying vehicles' for 'surfing the internet' (Sofia, 2010, p. 188). In order for the computer to be used properly and safely by the user, he or she must also be kept safe from exposure to the materials, some toxic, contained by the computer chassis. As the chassis conceals the interior, it also withdraws from our awareness as we use its virtual functions to write emails, use software applications, connect to the internet, or access the 'cloud'. (This lovely, soft, natural image in actuality signifies a massive infrastructure of huge, energy-hogging server farms.) These virtual functions can be understood as part of the tool function as they extend the human body and our ability to write and communicate across space. The expanded definition of the computer, as both tool and container technology, also redefines the computer as a container that stores and re-sources information. As with the broken glass that spills wine, computers are often only understood as data storage units when their hard drives fail and data are lost. With cloud computing, data storage is increasingly off-site and corporately mediated. Rather than computers being understood as containers for data *and* communications devices, they are better understood as networked containers with both tool and container *aspects*. Sofia's theory of technology enables a more comprehensive understanding of tool and container technologies, especially their interdependence with culture, time, and the environment, and, as I will discuss in the following, with nature.

Inarguably, the materialities and virtualities of globalization are, in part at least, made possible by the extension and motion technologies of ships and trucks that crisscross the globe. However, those ships and trucks are also, and even predominantly, technologies of containment.[2] We tend to take for granted those container technologies that enable changes such as the safe storage and containment of petrochemicals over time and, similarly, the storage, organization, and containment of vast quantities of data. Just as ICTs are understood as tool technologies of communication and speed, the container ship is foregrounded as a tool technology, with its motor and ability to cross the oceans, not as a container technology, with its ability to stack massive numbers of containers and to keep those shipments safe from elements, spoilage, and piracy.

Technology does not determine larger social, political, and economic structures; rather, our ideas about technologies subtly reinforce larger structures of inclusion and exclusion. As Sofia (2010) says:

> The specter of resourcelessness looms ever larger on the horizon as we reach the limits of the planet that had once been imagined as an infinite container of resources, now revealed as a finite resource itself. (p. 181)

In the dominant, but limited, conversation about the information age, a defining feature is the exchange and circulation of information. There is an emphasis on extension, circulation, and speed, especially of information, in which the temporal quality of speed is not just emphasized but valued. Sofia's insight reveals our tendency to theorize ICTs and globalization in terms of speed and acceleration (tools), which in turn tends to conceal some of the larger social, political, and environmental politics at work, including the temporal aspects of containment and its significance for social exclusion and inclusion.

The Speed of E-waste

As a problem for municipalities, waste has historically been solved through containment or disposal: the former characterized by barrels or chemical ponds and the latter by dumps at the edge of town (Baker, 1994). Since the 1980s, the globalized trade in waste has seen poorer communities and countries becoming toxic waste dumps for the rich (Alexander & Reno, 2012; Lepawsky & McNabb, 2010). The high costs of complying with environmental regulations, alongside developments in transportation infrastructure, have meant that in many cases it can be cheaper for wealthier countries to export their waste to poorer countries than to dispose of it domestically (Alexander & Reno, 2012). Coming out of these trends of the 1980s, e-waste is one of the streams of toxic waste included in the Basel Ban, which came into effect in 1992 in an attempt to limit and regulate this flow (Basel Action Network, 2011). Recent research on e-waste, however, suggests that this practice is shifting. Although part of the e-waste trade continues to be intra-regional, from rich to poor countries, a significant component is inter-regional, and between developing countries (Lepawsky, 2014; Lepawsky & McNabb, 2010). As part of global trade patterns, waste has an undeniable spatial aspect that is more complex and multidirectional than suggested in many early, dominant narratives (Lepawsky, 2014; Lepawsky & Billah, 2011; Lepawsky & McNabb, 2010). As I will argue in the following, it is also imbued with a temporal aspect that complicates it even further.

A computer, as garbage, is essentially a container full of complex and toxic elements. In general, computers are made up of plastic, metal, and glass (Grossman, 2006). Opening up a computer reveals a geography of national and international industry regulations, and related jargon. Not only are there hundreds of components, but there are also literally hundreds of materials inside of any given computer. As garbage, computers are also more obvious as container technologies. Their tool aspects are rendered null, useless, or irrelevant. Their data storage function is foregrounded, whether one is attempting to salvage data from a crashed drive, transfer data to a newer machine, or to erase the hard drive to avoid data theft. As a container, the function of the chassis is to protect the parts inside from dust and other elements and to keep the user safe from toxic components. Its temporal quality of containment, keeping those contents safe over time, is contradictory. Once garbage, the data storage capabilities can be a liability, especially in terms of fraud or theft. As recyclable, the valuable components within need to be easily accessed, with limited leakage of toxic elements or contamination of workers and ecosystems.

Gille (2007) notes that although waste often occupies liminal physical places, it also has an important conceptual function: 'waste, to wit, is not merely a matter out of place, as those following Douglas argue, but, more profoundly, a concept out of order' (p. 23). What counts as waste is subject to moral, social, and economic organizations (Gille, 2007). As Lepawsky and Mather (2011) say in their study of e-waste in Canada and Bangladesh:

> We flew to Dhaka, spent four months tracking what we thought was e-waste, but we couldn't find any ... Almost everything had value. Every object. Every component. Every material. They were all being bought and sold, assembled, disassembled and reassembled ... They also dwindled into their constituent materials—plastics, glass, metals ... Then they were sold. Money changed hands. Materials moved. We expected we would end up in dumpsites, in piles of waste. Instead, we wound up in production sites. (pp. 242–243)

One region's waste is another's raw material. Waste is a leaky category, both materially and conceptually. In its global and spatial reorganizations, rather than being worthless trash, e-waste is revalued as a potential source of raw materials and economic opportunity. The global e-waste trade is perhaps better described as the global electronics recycling trade.

Alexander and Reno (2012) note that recycling 'assumes a powerful moral and political salience today because it appears to intercede in [the] transformation and corruption of nature ... ' (p. 1). Recycling has been widely adopted by many countries as the most effective solution to e-waste. Groups such as the Basel Action Network are pushing for extended producer responsibility so that corporations such as Intel, HP, and others will become responsible for taking back obsolete electronics. Studies have shown that this encourages companies to update product design to facilitate recycling and refurbishing of personal computers (Tojo, 2006). This practice encourages them to build a better container. For example, the use of screws instead of plastic snap parts makes computer disassembly faster and easier. Presently, the European Union has the most stringent rules and since 2006 new electronic equipment in the EU cannot contain lead, mercury, cadmium, hexavalent chromium, polybrominated biphenyls, or polybrominated diphenyl ethers (Deathe, MacDonald, & Amos, 2008). As a strategy to deal with waste, recycling seems to have the dual benefits of saving money and saving the environment. However, Alexander and Reno (2012) warn that the realities of the global recycling trade 'defy simple moral narratives' (p. 3).

The temporalities related to waste and recycling are multiple. As corporate policies of planned obsolescence accelerate the production and consumption of computers, more toxic waste is created. Recycling is an object lesson in container technologies, re-sourcing, and containment. Recycling a computer takes materials from their particular configuration as a product, breaks them into their component types (plastics, metals, and glass), and makes them usable, or re-sources them into usable materials. Sabelis and van Loon (1997) argue that economies of recycling are informed by notions of time as both linear and cyclical. In a linear conception, waste happens at the end of a product's life cycle, after production and consumption (Lepawsky & Billah, 2011). More nuanced temporal understandings of waste suggest that it is part of a cycle or circulation of materials (Gille, 2007; Lepawsky & Billah, 2011). Recycling reinserts materials into the flow of the market (Sabelis & van Loon, 1997). As part of this action, it also seems to decelerate the pollution and plunder of natural resources whether by reducing the need for environmentally dangerous resource extraction or stopping the waste from entering landfill. Research with dismantlers in Bangladesh by Lepawsky and Billah (2011) suggests that the typical two- to four-year lifespan of electronics in North America is routinely doubled or tripled through global recycling practices. These three temporalities—linear, cyclical, and deceleration—work to bring the ecological and economic into the same multilayered temporal framework.

Although improving the recyclability of computers and their components diverts some machines from landfill, recycling also typically fails to address the production of waste, in terms of sheer volume. Sabelis and van Loon (1997) observe: 'Recycling deals with matters that are always-already there. *How* they came into being is no longer any concern' (p. 298). The logic of recycling does not include a consideration of the tempos of production, especially planned obsolescence. While recycling seems to decelerate the depletion of natural resources by returning raw materials into the production cycle, the process of production creates more waste, which can be intensified where there is less strain on resources or as more materials are available (Sabelis & van Loon, 1997). As more raw materials enter the market, cost of production decreases, and consumer prices also decrease, which, along with planned obsolescence, increases consumer demand. As recycling becomes economically feasible, it drives the price of raw materials down, thus increasing productivity, and, again, the production of waste. Producing more waste will strain waste management systems, regardless of the reuse or recuperation of materials. It also increases the amount of toxic materials in circulation, whether as by-products of production or recycling or as unsafe components of a product.

A Newtonian conception of time informs many understandings of science and economics (Adam, 1998; Sabelis & van Loon, 1997). This heritage brings with it an understanding of reversibility, or the idea that what can be made can also be unmade. According to Adam (1998):

> ... technological products are premised on the Newtonian principles of decontextualization, isolation, fragmentation, reversible motion, abstract time and space, predictability, and objectivity, on maxims that stand opposed to organic principles such as embedded contextuality, networked interconnectedness, irreversible change and contingency. (p. 41)

Waste has a tendency to 'bite back', or to produce unintended and unforeseen results (Gille, 2007). Waste electronic and electrical equipment includes vast quantities of lead, cadmium, mercury, hexavalent chromium, and brominated flame-retardants, all toxic substances which cause serious health problems in humans, including damage to the kidneys, nervous system, bone structure and brain, allergic reactions, blood disorders, hormonal interference, and DNA problems (Deathe et al., 2008). The Newtonian heritage means that the environmental and health hazards of many synthetic materials were discovered after they had become entrenched in routine industrial practices (Adam, 1998). With some synthetic chemicals, such as endocrine disruptors found in plastics, effects can be transgenerational and can depend on the timing of exposure (Freinkel, 2011). The effects of these substances challenge models of toxicology premised on minimum and maximum allowable exposures, which commonly inform environmental legislation and practice. They also exceed models, like the Newtonian conception, that are premised on reversibility. In other words, missing from these linear and cyclical models that typically inform recycling practices, in which ecology and economy are brought into the same temporal frame, are the temporalities of toxicity that can be time-specific, multigenerational, or contingent.

Even when ICTs are properly disposed of, recycled, and returned to market in the form of products, their environmental and health risks are not necessarily contained. As Lepawsky and Billah (2011) note, what emerges with regard to e-waste is complex, global, and uneven so that the production of waste creates value, through jobs, resources, and technology, but also toxic emissions and health problems. One of Lepawsky and Billah's (2011) Bangladeshi informants offers this analysis: 'We are the poorest of the poor. We need first food for our survival. The environment is not for us, it is for wealthy people' (p. 134). Electronics destined for recycling and refurbishment in poorer global communities structure emerging local economies, are a testament to community resilience, and provide steady employment. In the short to medium terms, the influx of electronics resulting from planned obsolescence can strengthen local economies. Over the longer term, these benefits become more dubious as workers and ecosystems exposed to toxic materials may develop health problems. As seen in Silicon Valley where chip production has largely been exported to other global locations while their groundwater remains polluted and some workers face work-related diseases, there is no guarantee that the recycling and refurbishment business will last as long as the pollution will.[3] Global inequities mean that poorer communities continue to take on the burden of toxicity, even as the long-term health of their bodies and ecosystems is at risk, or subjected to slow violence.

Resourcing and containment are the basic environmental problems of technology. Understanding technology as both container and tool does not change these problems, but it does highlight the temporal aspects of both environmental problems and technologies. It encourages a reframing of the interconnectedness of technology and nature so that their interdependence is highlighted. Environmentally speaking, the incomplete temporal frame is the main problem in current discussions of globalization and ICTs. If we consider the resources that go into the machines, their shrinking useful lifespans, and their subsequent too-quick trashing, a pattern of unsustainability emerges. The discourse of waste management dislocates and obscures the origins of that waste, namely production, use, and consumer culture. The time of ICTs must then include not just speed, simultaneity, and acceleration, but also those longer periods of time needed for ecosystems to regenerate and pollution to be neutralized.

Acceleration

We must also reconfigure our understandings of acceleration to encompass discarded computers and other garbage. Sterne (2007) tells us that because of planned obsolescence, computers are 'designed to be trash' (p. 19). If computers are designed to be trash, then as the proceeding section demonstrates, they are shockingly poorly designed. Given the slow violence associated with e-waste, well-designed trash would be created out of fewer, simpler, nontoxic parts. Apple, those leaders in design and innovation, are thus revealed to be the worst innovators in the industry, as they manufacture and design the most difficult to disassemble, toxic-laden machines, keeping components and materials an industry secret. Apple computers also have the shortest life spans of any computer on the market (see Friends of the Earth et al., 2011).[4]

Instead, death-dating policies introduce acceleration into the timescapes of ICTs. Shortening lifespans make for more poorly designed trash entering the waste stream, but the temporal feature of acceleration is not limited to accumulations of garbage. We must understand the slow violence of e-waste as beginning at the point of innovation. Much slow violence is about the failure of containment. Silicon Valley's long-term environmental problems are because of leaking underground holding tanks, which failed to contain toxic chemicals. The slow violence of e-waste is related to badly designed containers. It is not simply about containers failing, it is also about them being full of the wrong stuff, being too hard to take apart, and the sheer numbers of them overwhelming waste management infrastructures. There is a profound paradox at the root of the acceleration related to ICTs, especially with e-waste, because the more and the faster that ICTs are manufactured and trashed, the more and the faster production of e-waste accelerates. However, the slow violence of e-waste—the toxic contamination of workers and ecosystems that might take years to remediate or neutralize, if it can be effected at all—does not speed up. By its nature, the slow violence of toxic pollution lasts. In some cases, unexpected combinations of chemicals exacerbate their ill effects, and defy the temporal practices and qualities associated with traditional waste management strategies. Slow violence endures and the acceleration of planned obsolescence lengthens and increases that violence, extending it over time, slowing it down. Simply put, planned obsolescence is slow violence. It structures the eco-political paradigm of the information age and is central to understanding the chronopolitics of ICTs and globalization.

Even as it has been left out of some conversations about globalization and ICTs, the slow violence of e-waste is business as usual in the globalized information economy. In *After Globalization*, Cazdyn and Szeman (2011) argue that it is not that the system is broken, it is, in fact, running just as it has been designed to do. The logic of the market dictates expanding consumer markets, shipping trash to the poorest communities, and making trash, that former externality, into a commodity through recycling schemes. Understood on a global scale, the ecological effects of every person on the planet having equal access to ICTs demonstrates not only the unsustainability of the information economy, but makes manifest the gross temporal, economic, and ecological inequities that underpin the ideology and workings of the global information society.

I began this essay with a very Newtonian image of container ships crossing the ocean as a reminder of the slower speeds necessary for the production, maintenance, and disposal of ICTs. The timescapes of ICTs must include speed, simultaneity, and longer ecological remediation periods, but also acceleration. Adam (1998) says:

> a time scape perspective conceives of the conflictual interpenetration of industrial and natural temporalities as an interactive and mutually constituting whole and stresses the fact that each in/action counts and is non-retractable. (p. 56)

She stresses that this approach calls for more caution. Cazdyn and Szeman's (2011) temporal intervention on the discourse of globalization suggests that in order to make sense of globalization, and its attendant problems such as e-waste, we must begin to imagine what comes after it.

The notion of a timescape is particularly useful because it suggests that our current understandings of a globalized information society are grossly inadequate to describe, or even theorize, the penetration and growth of ICTs, let alone the hysterical cheerleading of their efficiencies and communicative capacities by our governments, universities, businesses, and hobbyists, most of whom also enthusiastically endorse e-waste recycling programs. The timescape approach reminds us that although we participate in the accelerations of information society, we are also animals who exist in the temporal flows of ecological time. The slow violence of planned obsolescence must also be integrated into this schema so that we push limits of our cultural imagination to imagine what might come next.

Planned obsolescence drives multiple sets of temporalities associated with ICTs: their speed, acceleration, and simultaneity in use; the time it takes for them to move across the globe as raw materials, components, products, and trash; and the slow violence they enact through long-term pollution, including the time-specific, multigenerational, or contingent effects associated with certain toxic chemicals. A more global approach to ICTs might demonstrate that although recycling programs are beneficial to many communities, a long-term approach must go beyond the notion that recycling is always 'good for the environment'. ICTs need to be brought out of the conceptual realm of speed and acceleration to include actual sites of production, consumption, and disposal, and their accompanying temporalities.

Disclosure Statement

No potential conflict of interest was reported by the author.

Notes

1   There are arguably many other ways of understanding time at work here, but I focus only on the speeds typically associated with ICTs in discussions of time, technology, and globalization. See Nixon's (2011) *Slow violence* and Adam's (1998) *Timescapes of modernity* for discussions of the other timescapes of technology and nature.
2   For a fascinating account of the containment problems of ocean vessels, see *Moby Duck*, which describes the journey of a plastic duck bath toy that travels the oceans after containers are lost at sea.
3   See Smith, Sonnenfeld, and Pellow's *Challenging the chip* (2006).
4   Apple defines 'vintage' computers as those between five and seven years old and 'Genius Bars' will not service them.

References

Adam, B. (1998). *Timescapes of modernity: The environment and invisible hazards.* London: Routledge.

Alexander, C., & Reno, J. (2012). *Economies of recycling: The global transformation of materials, values and social relations.* London: Zed Book.

Baker, J. (1994). Modeling industrial thresholds: Waste at the confluence of social and ecological turbulence. *Cultronix,* 1.1.

Basel Action Network. (2011). Retrieved from http.ban.org

Cazdyn, E., & Szeman, I. (2011). *After globalization.* West Sussex: Wiley-Blackwell.

Deathe, A. L. B., MacDonald, E., & Amos, W. (2008). E-waste management programs and the promotion of design for the environment: Assessing Canada's contributions. *Reciel, 17*(3), 321–336.

Freinkel, S. (2011). *Plastic: A toxic love story.* Boston, MA: Houghton Mifflin Harcourt.

Friends of Nature, Institute of Public and Environmental Affairs, Green Beagle, Envirofriends, & Green Stone Environmental Action Network. (2011). *The other side of Apple II: Pollution spreads through Apple's supply chain.* Retrieved from http://www.metronews.fr/info/apple-la-pollution-est-dans-le-fruit/mkia!6P2HwsiBChDls/Report-IT-V-Apple-II.pdf.

Gille, Z. (2007). *From the cult of waste to the trash heap of history: The politics of waste in socialist and postsocialist Hungary.* Bloomington: University of Indiana Press.

Grossman, E. (2006). *High tech trash: Digital devices, hidden toxics, and human health.* Washington, DC: Island Press/Shearwater Books.

Lepawsky, J. (2014). The changing geography of global trade in electronic discards: Time to rethink the e-waste problem. *The Geographical Journal, 180*(1), 1–13.

Lepawsky, J., & Billah, M. (2011). Making chains that (un)make things: Waste-value relations and the Bangladesh rubbish electronics industry. *Geografiska Annaler: Series B, Human Geography, 93*(2), 121–139.

Lepawsky, J., & Mather, C. (2011). From beginnings and endings to boundaries and edges: Rethinking circulation and exchange through electronic waste. *Area, 43*(2), 242–249.

Lepawsky, J., & McNabb, C. (2010). Mapping international flows of electronic waste. *The Canadian Geographer/Le Géographcanadien, 54*(2), 177–195.

Nixon, R. (2011). *Slow violence and the environmentalism of the poor.* Cambridge, MA: Harvard University Press.

Pellow, D. N., & Sun-Hee Park, L. (2002). *The silicon valley of dreams: Environmental injustice, immigrant workers, and the high-tech global economy.* New York: New York University Press.

Sabelis, I., & van Loon, J. (1997). Recycling time: The temporal complexity of waste management. *Time & Society, 6*(2/3), 287–306.

Sekula, A. (1995). *Fish story: Allan sekula.* Amsterdam: Witte de With, Center for Contemporary Art; Düsseldorf: Richter.

Smith, T., Sonnenfeld, D. A., & Pellow, D. N. (2006). *Challenging the chip: Labor rights and environmental justice in the global electronics industry.* Philadelphia, PA: Temple University Press.

Sofia, Z. (2010). Container technologies. *Hypatia, 15*(2), 181–219.

Sterne, J. (2007). Out with the trash: On the future of new media. In C. R. Acland (Ed.), *Residual media* (pp. 16–31). Minneapolis: University of Minnesota Press.

Tojo, N. (2006). Design change in electrical and electronic equipment: Impacts of the extended producer responsibility legislation in Sweden and Japan. In T. Smith, D. A. Sonnenfeld, & D. N. Pellow (Eds.), *Challenging the chip: Labor rights and environmental justice in the global electronics industry* (pp. 273–284). Philadelphia, PA: Temple University Press.

Humanitarian Melodramas, Globalist Nostalgia: Affective Temporalities of Globalization and Uneven Development

CHERYL LOUSLEY

Lakehead University Orillia, Orillia, ON, Canada

ABSTRACT   *The formal conventions of global humanitarianism when performed as melodrama, structured around temporal devices such as peripeteia, deferral, delay, and missed chances, reveal some of its affect-making roles in globalization. The melodramatic flourishing of Live Aid commemorative events and commodities in the twenty-first century suggests there is a melancholic attachment to Euro-American global hegemony, retroactively and repetitively constructed as a missed chance to do good that always meant well. The melodramatic enactment at Live 8 of the 'end' of global poverty promised by Live Aid patches over the discontinuities between the era of development internationalism and neoliberal globalization, creating a moralized image of Euro-American globalization as a 'long-standing' form of humanitarian power that can be lamented in place of confronting the absence of any alternative explanatory framework for escalating processes of uneven development. By suspending time, melodrama creates a fantasmatic site for aspiration, ambivalence, melancholy, and nostalgia without resolving their contradictions.*

> I want to suggest that globalization ... is experienced as a rather melodramatic process in the post-colonial world.
>
> —Sarkar (2008, p. 11)

The relationship between globalization and humanitarianism has garnered significant critical attention (Barnett & Weiss, 2008; De Waal, 1997; Duffield, 2001; Gopal, 2006; Hardt & Negri, 2000; Kapoor, 2013; Kennedy, 2004), with critics focusing on the ways in which global humanitarian discourse tends to 'rationalize the very global inequality it seeks to redress' (Kapoor, 2013, p. 1). Hardt and Negri (2000), for example, provocatively claim, 'humanitarian NGOs are in effect (even if this runs counter to the intentions of the participants) some of the most powerful pacific weapons of the new world order—the charitable campaigns and the mendicant orders of Empire' (p. 36). Although some use the term 'global humanitarianism' to refer to the shift, following the fall of the Berlin Wall in 1989, toward human rights and Western support for humanitarian-driven military intervention (Härting, 2010, p. 157), I follow those who also emphasize its shifting political economy.[1] Development scholar De Waal (1997) traces the growth in power of what he terms the 'humanitarian international'—donor agencies, aid workers, academics, and journalists—alongside the rise in neoliberalism, arguing that global humanitarianism converges with neoliberalism in 'reorient[ing] governmental accountability towards external financiers' in place of political responsiveness to citizen interests and demands (p. 3). Global humanitarianism as a *celebrity spectacle* figures prominently in many of these critiques for its capacity to ideologically and materially buttress neoliberal policies and practices (Brockington, 2014; De Waal, 2008; Goodman, 2010; Kapoor, 2013; Littler, 2008). Celebritized humanitarianism functions to implicitly promote philanthropy and other forms of voluntary, individualized action (Kapoor, 2013; King, 2006; Littler, 2008); depoliticize the social distribution of wealth, security, and opportunity (Brockington, 2014; Kapoor, 2013); and open and consolidate new markets for the celebrity industry and for international humanitarian and development services (Brockington, 2014; De Waal, 1997; De Waal, 2008; Goodman, 2010; Kapoor, 2013).

The critiques of global humanitarianism as handmaiden to neoliberal globalization tend to emphasize the consolidation of Euro-American economic and geopolitical dominance. In this essay, I read celebrity humanitarian spectacles as 'melodramas of globalization' (Sarkar, 2008, p. 31) that negotiate ambivalence and contradiction for audiences in the purported 'First World' when its status is no longer so homogenously asserted or assured (Dirlik, 2007, pp. 50–51). Do humanitarian spectacles perhaps offer comforting displays of Western 'goodness' during a period of *waning* power? What happens to universalist projects of humanitarianism and development in a historical moment when growing economic inequalities create stark divisions within Western nations? What role do melodramatic *commemorations* of humanitarian intervention—such as the remembering of Live Aid in the 2005 'Live 8' event—play in structuring global identities and affects? Do they provide a sense of moral continuity with the post-war reconstruction and development era in a way that obscures the social and economic polarizations of neoliberalism? Or, does the repeated return to scenes of dying expose the failures of development? By attending to global humanitarianism *as performed as melodrama*, I suggest that its *formal conventions*—structured around temporal devices such as peripeteia, deferral, delay, and missed chances—reveal some of its meaning- and affect-making roles in globalization.

The illusory universalism of globalization has long been critiqued in relation to the *spatial* disparities of globalization, most usefully in Smith's (2008) concept of 'uneven development' to describe the pattern of capital accumulation that simultaneously produces 'development at one pole and underdevelopment at the other' (p. 6). But theorists increasingly note the role of *temporal* discourses in managing these disparities (Cazdyn & Szeman, 2011; Chakrabarty, 2009). Humanitarian melodramas are significant precisely because they stage uneven development as a *temporal* challenge—but not simply to suggest all will be fine 'in the end'. Melodrama is an affective mode that 'moves' its audience, as Moretti (1983) identifies, by way of the temporal structure of the 'too late' (p. 160), when the delayed recognition or communication comes too late, or almost too late, to bring about the happy resolution desired. The affective and ideological work of melodrama, Sarkar (2008) argues, thus lies not only in the construction of desired outcomes but also in their *deferral*—delays in which the very powerlessness to bring about the desired future becomes pleasurable. Development and humanitarian critics often note and decry the presumptuousness of Western audiences 'feeling good' about watching white aid workers 'doing good' for racialized others (De Waal, 2008; Douzinas, 2007; Kapoor, 2013). However, there is also a melodramatic lingering on extended moments of dying—spectacles of *time suspended*—and which thereby accentuate an experience of failure or missed chance. I focus on these temporal dynamics of humanitarian melodramas in order to read them as signs of ambivalence toward globalization and nostalgia for a superseded globalism. To appreciate the significance of these temporal structures in humanitarian melodramas, I first outline the shifting role of time in conceptualizing development and globalization and explain the irrealist dimension of melodramatic meaning-making.

Development, Time, and Globalization

Postcolonial historian Dipesh Chakrabarty (2009) argues that the chronological progression implied in the discourses of modernization and development, such that poor countries could 'develop' (as if living organisms) into economically successful ones, consigned the non-West 'to an imaginary waiting room of history' (p. 8), perpetually playing catch-up to a future that emerges 'first in the West, and then elsewhere' (p. 6). One effect of this historicism, Chakrabarty (2009) argues, is that it makes modernity appear global, and 'something that became global *over time*, by originating in one place and then spreading outside it' (p. 7, italics in original). This temporal narrative depoliticized its Eurocentric premises, or the way that 'first in Europe' was 'somebody's way of saying "not yet" to somebody else' (p. 8): a structuring difference and inequality legitimized by way of a universalized future *promised but deferred*. Dirlik (2007) characterizes globalization in similar terms as 'a promise that is perpetually deferred to the future' (p. 22), but, as he notes, Chakrabarty's (2009) temporal analysis, focused on nineteenth to mid-twentieth century modernization discourses, cannot simply be extended to globalization discourse, since the reconfiguration of relations of time and space are distinguishing features of globalization (Castells, 2010; Harvey, 1990; Jameson, 1991; Smith, 2008). The kind of 'globality' that Chakrabarty (2009) describes 'was conceived under the regime of modernization (capitalist and socialist) as "internationalism" rather than as "globalism"' (Dirlik, 2007, 48; see also Berger & Weber, 2007). Globalization discourse, Dirlik (2007) emphasizes, 'claims to break with ... a Eurocentric teleology of change' (p. 21), especially as the rise of powerful capitalist economies in Asia and Latin America disrupts a Eurocentric account of capitalism and modernization organized into a 'waiting room of history', with the non-West fated to a belated arrival.

The chronopolitical narrative of development as progress from Third-World past to First-World future (Escobar, 1995; Mbembe, 2001) is both perpetuated and complicated with globalization. Moreover, it is important to remember that this is not the only way development has been imagined: alternative, autonomous futures driven by national liberation, Third-World solidarity, and economic de-linking define the 'Bandung era' of the 1950s–1970s, supported by the critical analysis dependency theory offered of the structural interconnection of underdevelopment and capitalist development (Dirlik, 2007; Saldaña-Portillo, 2003; Scott, 1999; Wenzel, 2006). But a chronopolitical narrative of universal progression is evident in Gopal's (2006) reading of the global humanitarianism of the mid-2000s. Discussing the British-organized Commission on Africa, Gopal (2006) notes how 'one of the more pernicious and pervasive tropes about Africa's condition is that it has somehow been "left behind", "excluded" or kept "separate" from the rest of the globe' (p. 89). This temporal trope participates in what anthropologist Johannes Fabian (1983) names the 'denial of coevalness' (p. 31), the form of distancing into a 'different time' that legitimized colonialism's racism:

> Anthropology contributed above all to the intellectual justification of the colonial enterprise . . . a scheme in terms of which not only past cultures, but all living societies were irrevocably placed on a temporal slope, a stream of Time—some upstream, others downstream. (p. 15)

Ferguson (2006) argues that, rather than being 'left behind', African lands are on the forefront of new global extraction economies: 'it is worth asking whether Africa's combination of privately secured mineral-extraction enclaves and weakly governed humanitarian hinterlands might constitute not a lamentably immature form of globalization, but a quite "advanced" and sophisticated mutation of it' (p. 41). In this 'second scramble' for Africa (Nixon, 2011, p. 21), it might not be Africa but Euro-American capital and global hegemony that is being 'left behind'.

More is at stake, of course, than who is 'ahead' in the race. In place of the temporally organized 'waiting room of history', with some nations ahead of others, globalization is a network of spatially dispersed elites whose prosperity is dissociated from the millions excluded and marginalized. The universalist conception of a single historical progression, with time gradually passing in a single, world-historical spatial field, has been superseded by a non-universalist assemblage of economic elites, regionalized economies and so-called surplus populations (Davis, 2007, p. 175; Dirlik, 2007; Sassen, 2008). Bauman (1998) argues that the 'world can no longer be imagined as a totality' in the epoch of globalization (p. 58). 'The one-world ethos of globalization', Cazdyn and Szeman (2011) similarly suggest, has been pivotal to its hegemonic appearance as an 'inevitable' process, yet demonstrably *at odds* with the material effects of globalizing processes (p. 37). Cazdyn and Szeman (2011) thus point to the role of a *temporal* rhetoric in managing this contradiction. The impossibility of imagining an 'after' to globalization, they argue, shows how the foreclosure of alternatives to a singularly imagined 'globalization' emerges from a spatial universalism combined with a temporal suspension: 'a system constituted as both atemporal (once begun, it could never end) and inevitable (here, there, and everywhere)' (Cazdyn & Szeman, 2011, p. 37). Globalization, as Fukuyama's 'end of history' thesis posited, could appear to suspend time by equating itself with 'that universal History in which all of humanity is thought to be moving toward a common end' (Cazdyn & Szeman, 2011, p. 37). That 'common end', however, looks less and less about sharing anything 'in common'.

Indeed, Dirlik (2007) warns that the relinquishment of the Eurocentric temporal narrative of development has also involved the abandonment of its 'universalist aspirations' (p. 49); most evident, perhaps, is the waning of support for the principle of universal development, as neoliberal globalization ushers in a new normative horizon in which inequality is considered beneficial and acceptable (Payne & Phillips, 2010, p. 161). De Waal (1997) similarly notes that an underlying social Darwinism in neoliberalism "reduces the moral and political shock of famine" (p. 3). "The end result of this process," De Waal (1997) writes, "may be that famine is somehow considered inevitably or politically acceptable, in the way that Euro-American electorates have come to tolerate a certain degree of unemployment or homelessness" (p. 3).

Now tenuous is the very *promise* of a prosperous future for all, much less its actual material achievement. Dirlik (2007) points out that Third-World and postcolonial critiques of humanitarianism and development as Eurocentric perspectives disguised as universalisms are not as relevant in the context of globalization. Indeed, to critique universalisms *as such* risks undermining alternative *aspirational* universalisms and the forms of solidarity they might enable (see also Cheah, 2003; Robbins, 1999; Tsing, 2005). For example, the solidarity of the nation assumed in competing visions of national development in the post-1945 version of international development has been increasingly abandoned: 'under contemporary conditions, national economic development no longer means the development of the whole nation but rather development only of those sectors of the economy and population that … are components of a global network society' (Dirlik, 2007, p. 137; see also Berger & Weber, 2007).

The combination of social and economic polarization with tenuous universalizing discourses oriented temporally toward the future has marked the entire post-1945 period. Despite the economic and geopolitical reconfigurations of the past 20–30 years, it remains a core contradiction of globalization, even as many of those universalizing discourses begin to lose their salience. Melodrama's temporal dynamics of delay and deferral, as Sarkar (2008) notes, are thus peculiarly appropriate for navigating between the conflicting possibilities, aspirations, identities, and subject positions of postcoloniality, modernization, and globalization, enabling spectators, who experience the contradictions *affectively* in the realms of fantasy, desire, and cultural consumption, to defer the end or closure of their dreams.

Melodramas of Globalization

Working from Chakrabarty's (2009) temporal analysis, film theorist Bhaskar Sarkar (2008) reads contemporary Indian melodramatic cinema as a genre that foregrounds and reconciles the contradictions of developmentalist logic as organized and experienced under globalization. Deferrals, delays, and missed chances, Sarkar (2008) points out, provide the structuring logic of melodrama, a performative mode often disparaged in Western criticism precisely because of its reliance on chance, coincidence, and spectacle rather than psychological motivation and realism (see Gaines, 1992). Although focusing on Bollywood, Sarkar (2008) makes note of melodrama's presence across Third-World cinema and television, which he attributes to the moral authority granted suffering in the good–evil antagonisms of melodramatic plots. For Sarkar (2008), the melodramatic structure of delay enables ambivalent desires for the modernization associated with globalization to be both sustained and moderated. On the one hand, Sarkar (2008) suggests, 'under the sign of capital, societies engage in fantasies of progress, they desire modernity, and they maintain these fantasies and desires through comparisons among and escalating demands on themselves' (p. 47). These fantasies find expression in the excessive displays of wealth and suffering in melodrama. On the other hand, the contradictions between universalist aspirations, distant economic systems, and local cultures and practices call modernization into question, thematized in the melodramas Sarkar (2008) discusses by the way 'class differences and/or economic exigencies keep a pair of lovers apart' (p. 41). Echoing the delays of a nation ambivalent about its own desires and frustrated about its relative powerlessness in relation to global capital, the lovers re-unite only when it is *too late* for them to be together: the fulfillment of the various conflicting desires is yet again *deferred*.

To understand why melodrama receives little scholarly attention or appreciation, it is worth turning to the European and American traditions, where melodrama is commonly misrecognized because judged under the terms of realism. Melodrama, cultural theorist Ien Ang (1982) states, is generally derided as 'a sentimental, artificially plotted drama that sacrifices characterization to extravagant incident, makes sensational appeals to the emotions of its audience, and ends on a happy or at least a morally assuring note' (pp. 61–62). Exaggerated, sensational, emotional, and clichéd rather than realistic, rational, and authentic, melodrama in its fictional forms is disparaged on the same grounds as popular approaches to humanitarianism, charity, and development aid, which tend to adopt its narrative and performative structures. As Ang (1982) notes, however, melodrama is a long-standing Western cultural form, popular, since the beginning of the nineteenth century, primarily among working classes, women, and others located on the social periphery. Melodrama is the mode of soap opera—the focus of Ang's (1982) study is the popularity of the soap opera *Dallas*. It is the mode of performance wrestling (Barthes, 2000). It is the mode of classic Hollywood film (Altman, 2012; Berlant, 2008; Gaines, 1992). Melodrama carries an inferior status because it emphasizes plot and public emotional display at the expense of character development and depth (Ang, 1982; Gaines, 1992; Williams, 1998). Realism, by contrast, is the mark of middle-class and middlebrow 'serious' art because it presents the individualized development of a psychologically rich interior life and an objectively rendered material world. In other words, realism prioritizes individuality and objectivity while melodrama prioritizes community and mythology—the existence of a *meaning-laden world*.

It is this communal and mythic orientation of melodrama that its detractors miss. The excessive expressions of melodrama provide mythic tableaux of unjust pain and suffering and the restoration of a just and moral world through revenge, foul play, or reversal of fortune (Barthes, 2000, pp. 17–25). Brooks (1976), in *The melodramatic imagination*, argues that a hyperbolic, excessive mode is adopted in melodrama to highlight the metaphoric nature of the actions. The melodrama's *irrealism* is underscored in order to make clear that it is pointing to another, spiritual or moral world *beyond the material one* in which we live, and the drama strives to make it—*this other world*—the more significant one. He provocatively suggests, 'We may legitimately claim that melodrama becomes the principal mode for uncovering, demonstrating, and making operative the essential moral universe in a post-sacred era' (Brooks, 1976, p. 15). Barthes (2000) emphasizes how melodrama is to be understood as a spectacle in the dramatic sense, in which sense-making is based on what is seen and displayed, and thus meaning is to be found on the surface of the body not in the interiority developed over a narrative (p. 17). Over dramatization and excessive gesture make injustice and pain, especially emotional pain, clearly and publicly visible (Ang, 1982, p. 63; Barthes, 2000, p. 17); 'human misery', Ang (1982) notes, 'is exposed in a very emphatic manner' in melodrama (p. 63).

Although pain and suffering is *embodied* in melodrama—enacted in the body of the person—it is *not privatized* to that individual; rather, the person re-enacts an archetypal situation, and it is to make clear and visible the moral situation that the drama undertakes. As Barthes (2000) explains in relation to wrestling spectacle, 'suffering appears as inflicted with emphasis and conviction, for everyone must not only see that the man suffers, but also and above all understand why he suffers' (pp. 19–20). The situation is shown to be 'intelligible' (Barthes, 2000, pp. 18, 20) or understandable by its dramatic location within a meaning-laden (not objectified) universe that encompasses the community as a whole. Suffering is given recognition in melodrama, but, as importantly, is explained and given a sense of meaning in relation to the values and identity of the collectivity to which the participants imagine themselves belonging.

What role melodrama might play in demonstrating or restoring a 'moral universe'—and what this might constitute—in a period of globalized media audiences has yet to be broached; even Sarkar's (2008) study remains focused on a national cinema. Intriguingly, however, Sarkar (2008) argues that the 'spectacular excesses' of contemporary melodrama point to fantasies of *material and personal fulfillment* as much as any moral framework, and these merge in the 'underdog' stance of melodrama: 'The neoliberal transitional model of development relegates the post-colonies to the peripheries of history, casting them as underdogs—even victims. But victimhood is a deeply ambivalent subject position, for it comes equipped with a remarkable moral authority' (p. 48). The fantasmatic excesses of Bollywood melodrama express *both* the desire for the material promises of modernization—located out of reach in that 'other', affluent world—*and* the 'wounded subjectivity' of the nation apparently stalled, unjustly, in 'the waiting room of history' (Sarkar, 2008, p. 48). It offers a consoling collective story for a nation, like India, 'caught between the "first world" and the "third world", the developed and the underdeveloped, the center and the periphery, the modern and the traditional, the global and the local' (Sarkar, 2008, p. 47). Sarkar's (2008) suggestion that this melodramatic structure may be common among Third-World cinemas points to the scholarly work still to be done on melodrama and globalization, especially how such melodramas travel and translate to different contexts and audiences and the politics of their production, distribution, and consumption.

Humanitarian Melodrama

Not surprisingly, though little discussed, Western humanitarian media spectacles tend to adopt a melodramatic mode in order to associate international humanitarian intervention with moral action. Humanitarianism emerges as a form of secular morality in the late nineteenth century (Barnett, 2011); its intertwining with international development, envisioned as poverty relief and economic growth, provides the central Western moral discourse of the post-1945 era, as Rist (2002) outlines in *The history of development*. It is, he suggests, part of the 'religion' of modernity: a 'collective task which, though constantly critiqued for its lack of success, appears to be justified beyond all dispute' (Rist, 2002, p. 1). De Waal (1997), in a Foucauldian reading of humanitarianism as a mode of power, similarly emphasizes the self-justifying dimension of humanitarianism as a global *moral* discourse: 'The exercise of the humanitarian mode of power not only involves dispensing large sums of money and becoming intimately involved in distressed foreign societies, but also defining what is moral and what is true' (p. 4). In the form of 'development assistance', this collective moral project was announced by US President Truman alongside the Marshall Plan, the UN, and NATO at the close of World War II (Escobar, 1995; Rist, 2002). In 1974, in the wake of famine in Bangladesh, the Sahel, and Ethiopia, Henry Kissinger reaffirmed it in his speech to the World Food Conference in Rome, where he famously declared—in a decidedly melodramatic tenor—that 'within a decade no child will go to bed hungry, that no family will fear for its next day's bread, and that no human being's future and capacities will be stunted by malnutrition' (qtd in Rist, 2002, p. 12). Voluntary organizations such as Save the Children, CARE, CONCERN, World Vision, and so on, as their names attest, do not only undertake aid and development but also sustain a moral vision, whether religious or secular. They mediate between the moral and real worlds by inserting seemingly exceptional places and events into everyday spaces and routines and, through their ongoing presence, providing confirming examples that transnational poverty relief is a shared moral aspiration that might yet be made real on earth. 'The strength of "development" discourse comes of its power to seduce', Rist (2002) notes, 'How could one possibly resist the idea that there is a way of eliminating the poverty by which one is so troubled?' (p. 1).

The relationship between humanitarianism and development is, of course, contentious: sometimes they are distinguished as short-term versus long-term strategies; other times, they are opposed on the grounds that humanitarianism is symbolically situated in the realm of moral belief or ethical action, while development involves professionals, policy, and politics (Payne & Phillips, 2010; Rist, 2002). I argue that the evident *contradiction* between humanitarian universalism and the extreme disparities of wealth, security, and opportunity of uneven development is managed through the temporal rhetoric of development: it is possible to *both* condemn *and* perpetuate global inequality because it will be remedied *over time*, a classic example of melodramatic deferral. The envisioned future will come, albeit *not yet*. When enacted melodramatically, this temporal narrative, as I explore below, also shows its cracks and the contingent, tenuous nature of these claims.

International development gives postcolonial British and American internationalism a moral tinge, especially when melodramatically presented as the transcendence of racial difference. While many scholars emphasize the *cosmopolitanism* of humanitarianism—the identification with others beyond one's particular identity (Appiah, 2006; Held, 1995)—its universalism is clearly fraught and complicated by the various forms of intermeshing of globalist geopolitics and humanitarianism in the post-1945 period. Both Gopal (2006) and Härting (2010) emphasize the similarities of the racial imagination that underlies global humanitarianism and the 'civilizing mission' of British Victorian imperial discourse. The humanitarian, a cosmopolite free to physically *and affectively* travel the world, appears as a universal subject of compassion by way of contrast with the racialized and limited others who must be helped (Härting, 2010).[2] The political agency of the 'other' remains, Härting (2010) concludes, 'unthinkable' in global humanitarianism (p. 172), precisely because a disavowed racial imaginary underlies the very conception of ethical autonomy. In the liberal framework of voluntary, disinterested ethics, ethical principles are best demonstrated as *universal* when applied to strangers: those one has no interests in or ties to. Humanitarianism fetishizes the figure of the other—the stranger is marked most visibly by racialized, class, and/or national difference—because a non-differentiated object of concern would appear narcissistic and particular, not universal. In the secular, postcolonial world of post-1945 internationalism, transnational poverty relief—the ethical concern for the other—came to emblemize morality itself, making this new form of globalism 'meaning-laden'.

The most spectacular staging of this global moral order was the transnational Live Aid concert on 13 July 1985, which drew at that time the estimated largest ever television audience for a single event. Live Aid has become the 'magical moment' when this moral aspiration was seemingly universally echoed, the capstone to eight months of popular support for African famine relief. Vaux (2001) writes, as an Oxfam relief manager, about how many aid workers consider the Ethiopian emergency of 1984–1985 'the golden age of humanitarianism', a time when humanitarian work seemed simple and uncontested and 'money poured into aid agencies as never before' (p. 43). Humanitarian aid workers are not alone in casting a special aura around the now anachronistic events of Ethiopia and Live Aid. The events retain a prominent place in British public memory, especially. The BBC produced commemorative broadcasts on the first, 10th, 15th, 20th, and 25th anniversaries. The 30th anniversary will fall in 2015. Other television networks have produced regular 'return to Ethiopia' programs, featuring the journalists who covered aspects of the original story. From the 1980s through the 2000s, memoirs have been published by expatriate doctors and nurses who worked in feeding camps, as well as by Dawit Wolde Giorgis, head of the Ethiopian Relief and Rehabilitation Commission, BBC television reporter Michael Buerk, and, not surprisingly, Band Aid and Live Aid organizer Bob Geldof.[3] In 2005, the audiovisual recording of Live Aid was also made commercially available for the first time. Memorabilia such as concert tickets, T-shirts, and autographed programs are auctioned on eBay, and fan memories are shared on web pages dedicated to either the famine or Live Aid. Even popular novelist Helen Fielding, author of *Bridget Jones's diary*, penned an early satirical novel, *Cause celeb*, about celebrities, aid workers, and African famine, based on her experiences as a producer with Comic Relief. Two 'mega-event' music concerts organized in the 2000s cited Live Aid in their names in order to situate themselves in its global moral imaginary: 'Live 8' in 2005 and 'Live Earth' in 2008. The retrospective glance of Live 8 to Live Aid was also repeated, as Gopal (2006) notes, in extensive cross-marketing materials that included a BBC television series on Geldof touring Africa, a glossy print book, and an 8-CD audiobook, *Geldof in Africa*.

Many development scholars, of course, wish that people would *not* remember Live Aid. The 'legacy of Live Aid'—to cite the title of a study of British perceptions of the 'developing world' (VSO, 2002)—is considered to be persisting and widespread stereotypes about poverty, blackness, and Africa, as documented in a stream of studies from 1987 to 2009.[4] Kapoor (2013) further decries Live Aid, Live 8, and the associated 2005 'Make Poverty History' campaign as examples of the 'logoization of poverty', a mimicry of corporate retail whereby simplified labels substitute for complex structural analysis (p. 31). 'The tendency', he notes, 'is to focus on "visible" and soundbite-friendly problems—sick children, weeping mothers, derelict housing—sidelining the often complex and not immediately perceptible structural inequality and domination that have often caused them' (Kapoor, 2013, p. 35). The criticism that humanitarian and development campaigns rely on simplified clichés that obscure structural causes and perpetuate condescending stereotypes is long standing. These disparaged aspects of Live Aid humanitarianism—visual spectacle and simplified cliché—are not unique to Live Aid and its legacies, but are indeed melodramatic devices, worth grasping at their formal level in order to more adequately understand and historicize their mode of meaning-making. When Kapoor (2013) argues for better representational practices, his concern is with the imperceptibility of systemic underlying causes such as structural adjustment and debt and colonial histories. Melodrama, by contrast, is concerned with the imperceptibility of a meaning system that would recognize and validate the pain, suffering, and disappointments of the material world.

Staging Poverty's History

In 2000, with the utopian symbolism of a new millennium, the UN adopted a set of eight Millennium Development Goals focused on alleviating extreme poverty and empowering impoverished people. The goals are significant for showing an international re-affirmation of development priorities in the post-1989 period. To pressure governments to follow through on their commitments—particularly the governments of the Group of 8 economically dominant countries with the power to relieve debt burdens and redress trade imbalances—an international alliance of anti-poverty, aid, and development groups formed in advance of the 2005 meeting of the Group of 8 leaders in Scotland. The British coalition developed a political campaign mobilizing grassroots supporters to target G8 leaders under the brand name 'Make Poverty History'—a slogan adopted by many other national coalitions as well. Its metaphorical appeal to a chronological progression such that poverty will, in the future, be located in the past seems, straightforwardly, to exhibit the developmentalist logic Chakrabarty (2009) describes.

Yet the campaign and slogan, with its ambitious focus on ending extreme poverty, also aimed to demonstrate a new approach to development: one that would address systemic causes and injustice rather than treat symptoms like hunger through humanitarian relief. The Live Aid concerts of 1985 represented the 'charity' approach; Live 8, organized to coincide with the G8 meeting, was to represent instead a 'justice' focus (Sireau, 2009). Live 8, however, deepened Live Aid's seminal intermeshing of development, marketing, and the entertainment industry, and the results of the 'Make Poverty History' campaign are controversial because high brand-recognition and participation were achieved but its core message of 'justice not charity' seemed to be lost once high-profile celebrities became involved (Gopal, 2006; Sireau, 2009). These celebrities, moreover, were also at the center of the performance of global humanitarianism as melodrama.

When celebrity campaigner Bob Geldof strode across the Live 8 stage in London, the giant side screens and background screen featured a magnified close-up still of Birhan Woldu at the age of three when she was filmed in 1984 by a Canadian Broadcasting Corporation news crew at a relief camp in Mekele, Ethiopia, on what seemed the verge of death. On stage, Geldof tells the story of this television broadcast in which a nurse touring the news crew examines the girl and says that she will die within 15 minutes. Her arrival, it seemed clear, had come *too late*. Adopting the melodramatic device of peripety, or sudden narrative reversal, Geldof then announces that 'this little girl' has recently graduated from agricultural college and invites her to join him on the stage. Not only has the anticipated death been reversed into life, a reversal of Birhan's fortune is also apparent in famine giving way to agricultural production, suffering to happiness, and poverty to wealth. Her Third-World past has led to a First-World future—just the chronological progression the project of international development promised.

Cue here a critical cringe at the naive arrogance of this uplifting message. No doubt my own reader is skeptical that this scene involves the ambivalence I argue can be usefully identified in humanitarian melodrama.

Melodrama's 'myth-making function' (Ang, 1982, p. 64) is the key to grasping the role celebrities as iconic personages play in humanitarian melodramas like Live 8. The contempt that media and development commentators often express about celebrity humanitarians is attributed to celebrities' superficial knowledge of the issues and inauthentic relation to the people involved; Live Aid, as music scholar Garofalo (1992) notes, featured celebrity artists 'singing about an issue they will never experience on behalf of a people most of them will never encounter' (p. 29). True to the melodramatic mode, however, pop star humanitarians do not aim to reveal deep personal insights or knowledge but, rather, to re-enact a well-known, mythic scenario where natural justice prevails: the wrongs of the world are righted. As a melodrama, the Live 8 scene enacted, amidst the decidedly secular and fallen world of pop culture, the end of poverty that is promised by 'development'. Geldof and Birhan Woldu were dramatizing, as if archetypal characters in a play, the 'end' of poverty—an end that is *obviously* not yet to found be in *this* world, but is the promised salvation in a shared moral world in which the suffering of poverty is judged to be wrong.

Birhan Woldu's peripatetic presence was a dramatization of the shift from Live Aid 'charity' to Live 8 'justice'. Her deathly ill face was part of a Canadian Broadcasting Corporation montage played during the 1985 Live Aid concert, and, dubbed the 'Face of Famine', she has been successively featured in the international media over the years as a 'miracle' child, returned from the dead.[5] When she joined Geldof on the London stage of Live 8, she performed this magic trick yet again, dramatizing the redemption story outlined by Geldof in his brief introductory speech: she is the sign that we should continue to believe in the possibility of miracles, in the possibility of a world without poverty. She stood before the two-dimensional image of her younger self and addressed the crowd in Amharic, performing with the juxtaposition of her body and her image the double narrative that poverty was 'history' (in the past) for her, and thus could be made history (in the future) for everyone. Pop icon Madonna then entered the stage and, holding Birhan's hand, began singing her top single 'Like a prayer', with the opening line, 'Life is a mystery'. The presence of Birhan Woldu—an embodied, speaking presence—was Geldof's response, as he said in his speech, to the cynics 'who question why we should even try'. Birhan's speaking presence was the sign that Africa had a future. Against all the negative representations of Africa, here was a positive, personalized image of hope. Against all the cynics who dismiss hope, here was this one miraculous life that should not have been but still was.

Cynicism, critique, and cliché are thus anticipated within the melodrama itself, becoming themselves the 'antagonists' to battle against. In melodramatically displaying her living body in front of the iconic, depersonalized image of the starving child, Birhan *re-animates* the cliché. In a now-classic essay, Orwell (1946) defines a cliché as a 'dying' metaphor that languishes in the 'huge dump of worn-out metaphors which have lost all evocative power' (np). This melodramatic spectacle was staged to overcome what many media and humanitarian commentators, in their concept of 'compassion fatigue', take to be the tiredness of spectators with an image, and thus the *tiredness* of the image of dying.[6] While Roland Barthes once suggested that the photographic appearance of a concrete individual functions in the contemporary era to give a myth its legitimacy and naturalness, here it is the spectacular display of the living person herself that legitimizes and re-naturalizes a now iconic photograph, placing it back within the progressive time of 'Third World development'. For there she is, the drama posits: How can representations of dying be dismissed as tired stereotypes and static repetitions when the individual yet lives, showing poverty has been overcome *with time*? The 20 years that have passed between the Live Aid concert and the Live 8 concert are given organic continuity as development progress when represented as the growth of this child into a woman, and the transformation of the static, dead image into vibrant, speaking life.

Past Futures, Old Globalisms

Postcolonial anthropologist David Scott (1999, 2004) suggests that narratives of the future—and associated struggles for the authority to imagine and shape a future—are pivotal in political thought. He points out that social and political movements may remain attached to particular narratives of futurity that have since lost their salience as historical conditions change. They become 'old utopian futures', or what Reinhart Koselleck calls 'past futures' (Scott, 2004, p. 1). Inspired by Scott (1999), I read the staged resurrection of Birhan Woldu and the iconic 'famine child' in the humanitarian melodrama of Live 8 as a nostalgic attachment to an 'old globalism': the moralized Euro-American hegemonic vision of universal development promised in post-1945 internationalism, and now superseded. On the stage at Live 8, Birhan's past represented not just 'poverty' but *Live Aid* as a shared global past, a now anachronistic staging of an imagined 'global community' that Live 8 strived to resuscitate.

The Live 8 concert offered a transnational equivalent to the experience of simultaneity Anderson (2006) identifies in the singing of national anthems: 'At precisely such moments, people wholly unknown to each other utter the same verses to the same melody. The image: unisonance' (p. 145). The Make Poverty History campaign enacted its imagined global community *as global* by staging the Live 8 concert on 1 day in 10 venues, in 9 countries, and on 4 continents, and broadcast to a claimed television audience of 3 billion people. Like any modern nation, the global these events reference is '*imagined* because the members ... will never know most of their fellow-members, meet them, or even hear of them, yet in the minds of each lives the image of their communion' (Anderson, 2006, p. 6, italics in original). That the Live 8 concerts involved common transnational participation among unknown people was highlighted by the country names listed on each stage (and thus on each television broadcast). The acknowledged national and geographical dispersion of the anonymous participants was crucial to the transcendent image of global communion—unisonance—their simultaneous mass participation generated.

The feeling of global unisonance is similar what is being remembered and celebrated in Live Aid commemorations and memorabilia. A two-part BBC program commemorating Live Aid produced in 2005 (and re-broadcast in 2010) featured interviews with people who had attended or watched the event on television, who recalled the 'fantastic feeling' of the day, when 'everyone was nice to each other' (BBC, 2005a). One British fan described her memory of leaving Wembley stadium and hearing the broadcast coming out of every window, on every street, likening it to the 1977 Jubilee Day commemorating the 25th anniversary of Queen Elizabeth II's ascension to the throne ('Rockin''). Included among the fans was Harry Potter author J.K. Rowling, who commented that 'everyone remembers where they were, everyone remembers what they were feeling' (BBC, 2005b). Many participants, including veteran television commentators, recall themselves and everyone else crying when the CBC montage of famine scenes was screened during the concert. For one woman, it was 'the most extreme set of emotions I'll ever experience' (BBC, 2005a). Similar comments can be found on Internet fan sites dedicated to Live Aid. One fan posted this comment: 'I looked round, and EVERYONE was crying— 74,000 people in tears. This was the total experience that will never be there ever again in our lifetime. We were one' ('Memories of Live Aid', 2005). Another, who watched the event on television from a US army base in Guam, wrote: 'It's the closest thing to world harmony I've ever experienced' ('Memories of Live Aid', 2005).[7]

The existence of this commodified culture of memory contradicts the assumptions implied by promoters of 'compassion fatigue' about the tiredness of the clichéd image and the associated indifference of spectators, but nor does it simply confirm, as Geldof would have it, that compassion still thrives and the moral community persists. Instead, it shows a strong affective and commercial investment in a 'mass normative fantasy' of compassionate globalism, drawing an analogy from Berlant's (2008, p. 12) work on national affect. Studies of nationalism highlight the conventional, sentimental structures of moments of strong national feeling, and, with some caution to avoid universalizing their premises, provide a useful beginning for considering structures of globally oriented identity and affect. Berlant (2008) suggests sentimental and melodramatic modes dominate popular culture because they performatively sustain a social imaginary in which the desire for a certain relation to the world can be lived and *felt* to be true.

The experience of unisonance described by the Live Aid fans was created through the staging of a transnational simultaneity enabled by the globalization of pop music marketing and nationally organized mass television broadcasting—a communications assemblage brokered by news information media—and then displaced with the shift to niche-market-based cable television networks and then the Internet in the 1990s. Organized in partnership with the BBC as a live concert with live television broadcast, Live Aid was, indeed, a 'globalist' echo of the British 1977 Jubilee celebrations, as well as the 1981 royal wedding, and the other rare events given official authorization as carrying national/imperial significance through their occupation of the airways. Dayan and Katz (1992), in their book *Media events*, suggest that these live broadcasts, usually with monopolistic coverage (so that all television channels are covering the same event), are distinct from regular television viewing because *staged* as social rituals and ceremonial events where the whole community gathers together *at the same time*: 'Audiences recognize them as an invitation—even a command—to stop their daily routines and join in a holiday experience' (p. 1). Although diffused across social space, including the domestic spaces where television is commonly viewed, rather than contained to special or sacred spaces, the *temporal exceptionalism* of these television events nevertheless allows them to play a ceremonial role in national culture. '"Ceremonial politics" expresses the yearning for togetherness, for fusion', they suggest, providing an experience of national cohesion amidst the fractured partisanship of parliamentary politics (p. viii): 'We think of media events as holidays that spotlight some central value or aspect of collective memory. Often such events portray an idealized version of society, reminding society of what it aspires to be rather than what it is' (p. ix).

Performing the Global, Suspending Time

Postcolonial literary scholar Homi Bhabha (1994) troubles the moment of simultaneity Anderson (2006) identifies in the visual spectacle of nationhood. He suggests that the repeated spatial performance of horizontal nationhood is a disruption of historical time, the way the nation as already existing entity must be represented in a narrative of succession from past to present. Bhabha (1994) writes, 'In the production of the nation as narration there is a split between the continuist, accumulative temporality of the pedagogical, and the repetitious, recursive strategy of the performative' (p. 145). The time of the nation is always already doubled, Bhabha (1994) points out; even during the spatial appearance of horizontal unisonance, there is the 'distracting presence of another temporality' (p. 143). The 'performative' suggests the citizens of the present, fully present, actively inventing and shaping an open future; the 'pedagogical' indicates the citizens as inheritors of a remembered, common past that instructs them on who they are to be in the present and into the future. These two temporalities—synchrony and succession—disclose the representational practices required for authorizing the nation. In their disjuncture, Bhabha (1994) suggests, they expose the anxieties and insecurities of a nation's claims to spatial integrity and temporal continuity, fissures through which marginal subjects may act and speak. Bhabha's (1994) concern lies with disrupting the apparent 'unisonance' of the nation in synchronous time; my interest lies in how something so easily disputed as global unisonance might be staged, felt, and dreamt—and thereby have material effects. Bhabha's (1994) elaboration of the temporal dimensions of the enunciation of collective spirit is useful, nevertheless, because of the priority given to *time* in the slogan 'Make Poverty History', a temporal gesture, I argue, that demonstrates how global subjects are interpellated through more than the performative staging of global simultaneity alone.

The melodramatic staging of Birhan's presence, confirmed by the gathered transnational audience who witness her transformation, involves the same doubling of temporalities that Bhabha (1994) associates with narrating the nation. She embodies hope—this pedagogical narrative of progress and succession—by way of her juxtaposition with an earlier time. The biographical narrative of the maturing individual provides the sense of time as progression that can be extended across global space and time to anticipate the better future. Her 'past', represented by the globally circulating image, becomes 'our' past at Live Aid, with the memory *of the image* called up to constitute a remembered collectivity of shared sentiment, a past shared by all who contributed to famine relief. Birhan is here today, Geldof says,

> because we did a concert in this city and in Philadelphia, and all of you came and some of you weren't born and because we did that ... She's here tonight, this little girl, Birhan. Don't let them tell us that this doesn't work.

The temporal disjuncture of an effect preceding its cause—she is here because of the participation that could not have happened by those who did not yet exist—is readily understood as an indication that Geldof's words are not to be taken literally. But rather, like the deliberate temporal slippage between 'this little girl' of *then* being present *now* (and still a 'little girl'), they function to hold together the collectivity *now* gathered as part of a continuum with an earlier collectivity, and thus gesture toward its continuity in the future. With Geldof's speech (and in the citation of Live Aid in Live 8), the 'we' performatively enacted in the mass participation at Live Aid and the 'we' performatively enacted in the mass participation at Live 8 are sutured together into one collective capable of making change in historical time. The enemies—the 'them' that must be disregarded—are those who deny the strength and force of moral will and collective action.

And yet, Birhan's uncannily doubled presence belies the spectacle's pedagogical or successive narrative of progress and redemption, from starvation to health, from poverty to wealth, from humiliating to dignified image. The giant, ghostly image of her dying child self dwarfed Birhan on the stage; the icon, frozen outside time, overshadows the living person, with her all-too-human mortal time. Precisely in being summoned up to dramatize transcendence (the past will be put behind us, poverty overcome), the past is *not* contained to history, but spectrally lives or—more properly—*dies on* within the present. Alongside the synchronous time of the gathered collectives and the successive time of the individual and collective's historical actions, we find yet another temporality, which seems to be precisely that of the haunting—the dead *suspended in the moment of their dying*. The return of the clichéd figure of poverty in 1984—and 1985, 1995, 2005, and each successive commemorative year—actually belies the post-war narrative of development as the temporal progression of a now globalized humanity. It *ruptures* the pedagogical narrative of developmentalist globalism. If the progressive narrative of globalization achieves hegemony by suspending time, as Cazdyn and Szeman (2011) note, then the melodramatic display of suspended dying troubles its certainty. This melodramatic scene is strikingly ambivalent, offering *both* the fantasy of 'just-in-time' rescue, since death might yet be forestalled, and *also* a vision of failure in the missed chance, the rescue that might have been but did *not* happen in time. The suspension of time holds both options open without resolving their contradictory assumptions.

The 'Too Late' Global Community

Moretti (1983) suggests that melodrama's affective effects are organized around this rhetoric of 'the too late' (p. 159). In particular, the reader begins to *cry* at the narrative point when a new point of view or newly received information reveals love or goodness but it comes too late to change the situation. As Moretti (1983) notes, 'to express the sense of being "too late" the easiest course is obviously ... the moment when the character is on the point of dying' (p. 160). In a parallel analysis, famine theorist Jenny Edkins (2000) suggests that the voyeuristic place of the television spectator to distant dying intensifies an experience of helplessness for the spectator because implicitly 'too late' to intervene in the scene. The spectator is a voyeur: able to see without being seen and empowered because able to see intimate acts or remote places without even leaving the home. But this voyeurism in Edkins's (2000) view, contrary to Sontag's (1977) classic stance, *implicates* the spectator as much as it distances: we are called on but cannot respond; our position of power suggests we can act, though in the immediate sense we cannot. We especially cannot help these *particular* people who look at us, seemingly asking for our help. For them, we have arrived *too late*. A message commonly repeated in news reports about famine is that those filmed are likely *already dead* by the time we see them—hence the fixation on the 'miracle' of Birhan Woldu's recovery.

Berger (1980), in *About looking*, also links humanitarian responses to feelings of powerlessness and inadequacy. He suggests that photographs of agony overwhelm spectators due to their rupture of quotidian time and space:

> As we look at them, the moment of the other's suffering engulfs us ... We try to emerge from the moment of the photograph back into our lives. As we do so, the contrast is such that the resumption of our lives appears to be a hopelessly inadequate response to what we have just seen. (p. 38)

Berger (1980) concludes that there are two possible responses: to 'shrug off' the sense of inadequacy 'as being only too familiar' or to 'perform a kind of penance—of which the purest example would be to make a contribution to OXFAM or UNICEF' (p. 40). Sontag (2003) similarly writes, 'There is shame as well as shock in looking at the close-up of a real horror' (p. 42). For Moretti (1983), the effect of the 'too late' device is to confirm a shared set of values but to cast doubt on the possibility of their materialization in the world: 'Only then is the original truth-morality restored and the discrepancy in points of view reconciled. But it is too late. A universal consensus has been re-established, but to no avail' (p. 163). The melodramatic narrative thus recuperates a moral consensus by placing the tragedy in the irreversibility of time—that all *would have been* fine, if only the news had come 'in time'.

The effect, Morretti suggests, is to heighten the sense of powerlessness of the too-late survivor, repeated and amplified in the powerlessness of the too-late reader or spectator, who has no capacity to change the course of narrated events (see also Sontag, 2003, pp. 42, 117). The spectator experience that Berger (1980) and Edkins (2000) recount follows this highly familiar structure of melodrama where loss and injustice are *recognized* but immediately recuperated as redemptions of the moral order:

> Being moved—and crying, which is its most complete manifestation—is the exact opposite of being angry. Anger divides; tears *unite*. But to whom do they unite us? Not to the protagonist-victim. .... Our identification slides, imperceptibly yet inexorably, towards the others, the survivors. As at a funeral, the death of the protagonist manages to rebuild the community of those who remain. Through communal weeping, all rancour, all injustice, all blame is abolished. It is a ritual of reciprocal collective absolution. (Moretti, 1983, 173, italics in original)

Live Aid, in its euphoric staging of global love and togetherness, offered this cathartic release from the personal shame of arriving 'too late' to help. As 'Band Aid' explicitly symbolized in the pun of its name, charity could only be an inadequate gesture—yet some expressive gesture of care had to be made in order to *reaffirm* the goodness of the First-World self in the face of its utter failure. It is a reaffirmation anxiously repeated with each Live Aid commemoration.

Berlant (2008) notes that this melodramatic loss-redemption structure is *pleasurable* to repeat, as shown by the pervasive popularity of melodramatic narrative in soap opera and film. The persistence of the clichéd figure of the always dying child, despite so many critical efforts to expel it, also suggests that there is a certain pleasure associated with it: a melancholic attachment to the loss-redemption feelings of the moment of being too late. Freud (1957) described the melancholic as remaining attached to the *feeling* of love and affective investment itself; a love that remains—that the melancholic stubbornly will not let go of—even though the object of that love has long since died, been lost, left, or grown up. The melancholic keeps alive an internalized, ghostly version of the beloved object, which does not function as a sign or reminder of the real original, but keeps the beloved proximate in order to sustain the feelings of the love that once existed in their name. In this sense, the physical presence of Birhan Woldu at Live 8 could *re-animate* global moral sentiment not only because she signified hope and transcendence, but also because her appearance keeps present or alive a 'global love' that melancholic spectators will not let die.[8]

The insistent, melodramatic, and anachronistic flourishing of Live Aid commemorative events and commodities in the twenty-first century suggests that there is a melancholic attachment to Euro-American global hegemony, retroactively and repetitively constructed as a missed chance to do good that always meant well. The melodramatic enactment at Live 8 of the 'end' of poverty promised by Live Aid patches over the *discontinuities* between the era of development internationalism and neoliberal globalization, creating a moralized image of Euro-American globalization as a 'long-standing' form of humanitarian power that can be lamented in place of confronting the absence of any alternative explanatory framework for escalating processes of uneven development. The humanitarian melodrama of Birhan Woldu's peripatetic return from starvation confirms the existence of a globally meaningful moral vision. The melancholic attachment to the 'past future' of 'just-in-time' humanitarian rescue retains the assurance of a universal promise—that a better future lies in store for all—as that promise is being abandoned, nation by nation, for many working and middle classes in the Global North, as well as in the Global South. For all that humanitarian melodramas, as spectacles of a global media–celebrity industry, confirm and consolidate elite power networks, they retain, nevertheless, a kernel of ambivalence about globalization. The way that prosperity for all *has been deferred* is recognized and given collective expression in these performances of the suspended time of globalization. This complex, affective mix of pleasure, nostalgia, frustration, loss, and aspiration belies efforts to make melodramatic performances simple, efficient devices for humanitarian results; their very popularity suggests that humanitarianism is only one part of the meaningful worlds they create for audiences.

Disclosure Statement

No potential conflict of interest was reported by the author.

Funding

This work was supported by the Rachel Carson Center for Environment and Society, Munich, Germany, under a Carson Fellowship and the Social Sciences and Humanities Research Council of Canada under a Postdoctoral Fellowship.

Notes

1 Barnett (2011) usefully outlines three distinct ages of humanitarianism: 'imperial humanitarianism', extending from the late eighteenth century to World War II, and which involved colonialism, commerce, and the civilizing mission; 'neo-humanitarianism', which lasted from the end of World War II to the end of the Cold War, and which involved nationalism, development, and sovereignty; and 'liberal humanitarianism', extending from the end of the Cold War to the present, and which involves liberal peace, globalization, and human rights (p. 7).

2 See also Sontag's (2003) note on how humanitarian images of suffering in Africa tend to 'confirm that this is the sort of thing which happens in that place ... [and] nourish belief in the inevitability of tragedy in the benighted or backward—that is, poor—parts of the world' (p. 71).

3 See Lousley (2013) for further discussion of these Live Aid memoirs.

4 Major British audience perception studies on development include Van der Gaag and Nash (1987); VSO (2002); and the Public Perceptions of Poverty reports. Sireau presents a participant study of the 2005 British Make Poverty History campaign, with which Live 8 was associated. Although many aid critics take Band Aid and Live Aid to be the origin of such stereotypes, it is important to note that the image of the starving child was already a cliché by 1984. As BBC journalist Michael Buerk discusses in his 2004 memoir, the market for such images was thought to be already in decline by 1984 when he broke the story of the Ethiopian famine. It was, however,

considered to be still sizable enough that the BBC did not want to miss out on the anticipated spin-off interest to be generated by a British humanitarian appeal campaign (which was centered on African famine relief as a product tie-in to the documentary *Seeds of Despair* produced by BBC domestic competitor ITV).

5   'The Face of Famine' was commonly used as a caption during CBC's coverage of the 1984 Ethiopian famine, and appears as the caption to the image of Birhan Woldu on the CBC web page dedicated to remembering the 1984 news coverage: http://www.cbc.ca/news/background/ethiopia/; Brian Stewart's accompanying article, 'Strange Destiny', describes her as the 'miracle girl' and discusses her various media re-appearances. The first news report on Birhan Woldu was broadcast on 7 November 1984 on CBC's flagship evening news program *The National*. *The National* presented a follow-up program on her recovery on 26 November 1984, under the title 'Bertani Healthy'.

6   Susan Moeller's (1999) *Compassion fatigue* is the most elaborate account of this concept, but the term predates her book considerably, and was widely used in journalist commentary during the 1984 Ethiopian famine. Precisely at the moment when the levels of popular response were unexpectedly high, journalists would speculate on when the inevitable 'compassion fatigue' would set in. An edition of the Canadian Broadcasting Corporation's program *Man Alive* on 28 November 1984, dedicated to famine relief, closes with the host posing the familiar question: 'How long will generosity continue? Is it realistic to expect the cheques to keep coming month after month . . . will we develop compassion fatigue'? Sontag (2003) notably re-evaluates and questions her earlier, classic argument that photographs of suffering lose their shock power and 'emotional charge' over time as aesthetic distance replaces ethical concern (Sontag 1977, p. 21).

7   This paragraph is also included in Lousley (2014).

8   See Lousley (2013, 2014) for further critical discussion of Live Aid and Band Aid as forms of 'global love'.

References

Altman, R. (2012). A semantic/syntactic approach to film genre. In B. K. Grant (Ed.), *Film genre reader IV* (pp. 159–177). Austin: University of Texas Press.

Anderson, B. (2006). *Imagined communities: Reflections on the origin and spread of nationalism*. London: Verso.

Ang, I. (1982). *Watching Dallas: Soap opera and the melodramatic imagination*. London: Methuen.

Appiah, K. A. (2006). *Cosmopolitanism: Ethics in a world of strangers*. New York, NY: Norton.

Barnett, M. (2011). *Empire of humanity: A history of humanitarianism*. Ithaca: Cornell University Press.

Barnett, M. N., & Weiss, T. G. (Eds.). (2008). *Humanitarianism in question: Politics, power, ethics*. Ithaca, NY: Cornell University Press.

Barthes, R. (2000). *Mythologies*. London: Vintage.

Bauman, Z. (1998). *Globalization: The human consequences*. New York: John Wiley & Sons.

BBC. (2005a, June 18). Live aid, Rockin' all over the world. BBC. Retrieved from http://www.bbc.co.uk/programmes/b0078×3p

BBC. (2005b, June 18). Live aid, against all odds. BBC2. Retrieved from http://www.bbc.co.uk/programmes/b0078×3n

Berger, J. (1980). *About looking*. London: Pantheon.

Berger, M. T., & Weber, H. (2007). Introduction: Beyond international development. *Globalizations*, 4(4), 423–428. doi:10.1080/14747730701695612

Berlant, L. (2008). *The female complaint: The unfinished business of sentimentality in American culture*. Durham, NC: Duke University Press.

Bhabha, H. K. (1994). *The location of culture*. London: Routledge.

Brockington, D. (2014). *Celebrity advocacy and international development*. New York: Routledge.

Brooks, P. (1976). *The melodramatic imagination: Balzac, Henry James, melodrama, and the mode of excess*. New Haven, CT: Yale University Press.

Buerk, M. (2004). *The road taken*. London: Hutchinson.

Castells, M. (2010). *The rise of the network society* (2nd ed., with a new pref.). Chichester: Wiley-Blackwell.

Cazdyn, E., & Szeman, I. (2011). *After globalization*. Malden: Wiley-Blackwell.

Chakrabarty, D. (2009). *Provincializing Europe: Postcolonial thought and historical difference* (new ed.). Princeton, NJ: Princeton University Press.

Cheah, P. (2003). *Spectral nationality: Passages of freedom from Kant to postcolonial literatures of liberation*. New York, NY: Columbia University Press.

Davis, M. (2007). *Planet of slums*. London: Verso.

Dayan, D., & Katz, E. (1992). *Media events: The live broadcasting of history*. Cambridge, MA: Harvard University Press.

De Waal, A. (1997). *Famine crimes: Politics & the disaster relief industry in Africa*. London: African Rights & the International African Institute in association with James Currey, Oxford & Indiana University Press.

De Waal, A. (2008). The humanitarian carnival: A celebrity vogue. *World Affairs, 171*(2), 43–56.

Dirlik, A. (2007). *Global modernity: Modernity in the age of global capitalism*. Boulder: Paradigm.

Douzinas, C. (2007). *Human rights and empire: The political philosophy of cosmopolitanism*. New York, NY: Routledge-Cavendish.

Duffield, M. (2001). Governing the borderlands: Decoding the power of aid. *Disasters, 25*(4), 308–320. doi:10.1111/1467-7717.00180

Edkins, J. (2000). *Whose hunger? Concepts of famine, practices of aid*. Minneapolis: University of Minnesota Press.

Escobar, A. (1995). *Encountering development: The making and unmaking of the third world*. Princeton, NJ: Princeton University Press.

Fabian, J. (1983). *Time and the other: How anthropology makes its object*. New York, NY: Columbia University Press.

Ferguson, J. (2006). *Global shadows: Africa in the neoliberal world order*. London: Duke University Press.

Freud, S. (1957). Mourning and melancholia. In J. Strachey (Ed. and trans.), *The standard edition of the complete psychological works of Sigmund Freud, volume XIV (1914–1916): On the history of the psycho-analytic movement, papers on metapsychology and other works* (pp. 243–258). London: Hogarth.

Gaines, J. M. (1992). Introduction: The family melodrama of classical narrative cinema. In J. M. Gaines (Ed.), *Classical hollywood narrative: The paradigm wars* (pp. 1–8). Durham: Duke University Press.

Garofalo, R. (1992). *Rockin' the boat: Mass music and mass movements*. Boston, MA: South End Press.

Goodman, M. K. (2010). The mirror of consumption: Celebritization, developmental consumption and the shifting cultural politics of fair trade. *Geoforum, 41*(1), 104–116. doi:10.1016/j.geoforum.2009.08.003

Gopal, P. (2006). The 'moral empire': Africa, globalisation and the politics of conscience. *New Formations, 59*, 81–97.

Hardt, M., & Negri, A. (2000). *Empire*. Cambridge, MA: Harvard University Press.

Härting, H. (2010). Global humanitarianism and racial autonomy in Roméo Dallaire's shake hands with the devil. In W. D. Coleman, P. Rethmann, & I. Szeman (Eds.), *Cultural autonomy: Frictions and connections* (pp. 156–177). Vancouver: UBC Press.

Harvey, D. (1990). *The condition of postmodernity*. Cambridge, MA: Blackwell.

Held, D. (1995). *Democracy and the global order: From the modern state to cosmopolitan governance*. Stanford, CA: Stanford University Press.

Jameson, F. (1991). *Postmodernism, or, the cultural logic of late capitalism*. Durham, NC: Duke University Press.

Kapoor, I. (2013). *Celebrity humanitarianism: The ideology of global charity*. New York, NY: Routledge.

Kennedy, D. (2004). *The dark sides of virtue: Reassessing international humanitarianism*. Princeton, NJ: Princeton University Press.

King, S. (2006). *Pink ribbons, inc: Breast cancer and the politics of philanthropy*. Minneapolis: University of Minnesota Press.

Littler, J. (2008). 'I feel your pain': Cosmopolitan charity and the public fashioning of the celebrity soul. *Social Semiotics, 18*(2), 237–251.

Lousley, C. (2013). Band aid reconsidered: Sentimental cultures and populist humanitarianism. In D. Lewis, D. Rodgers, & M. Woolcock (Eds.), *Popular representations of development: Insights from novels, films, television, and social media* (pp. 174–192). London: Routledge.

Lousley, C. (2014). 'With love from band aid': Sentimental exchange, affective economies, and popular globalism. *Emotion, Space and Society, 10*, 7–17. doi:10.1016/j.emospa.2013.02.009

Mbembe, A. (2001). *On the postcolony*. Berkeley: University of California Press.

Memories of Live Aid. (2005). *Live Aid*. Retrieved May 31, 2011, from http://www.herald.co.uk/local_info/la_memories.html

Moeller, S. D. (1999). *Compassion fatigue: How the media sell disease, famine, war and death*. New York, NY: Routledge.

Moretti, F. (1983). *Signs taken for wonders: Essays in the sociology of literary forms*. London: Verso Editions.

Nixon, R. (2011). *Slow violence and the environmentalism of the poor*. Cambridge, MA: Harvard University Press.

Orwell, G. (1946). Politics and the English Language. *Horizon*. Retrieved from http://www.mtholyoke.edu/acad/intrel/orwell46.htm

Payne, A., & Phillips, N. (2010). *Development*. London: Polity.

Rist, G. (2002). *The history of development: From Western origins to global faith*. London: Zed Books.

Robbins, B. (1999). *Feeling global: Internationalism in distress*. New York: New York University Press.

Saldaña-Portillo, M. J. (2003). *The revolutionary imagination in the Americas and the age of development*. Durham, NC: Duke University Press.

Sarkar, B. (2008). The melodramas of globalization. *Cultural Dynamics, 20*(1), 31–51.

Sassen, S. (2008). *Territory, authority, rights: From medieval to global assemblages*. Princeton, NJ: Princeton University Press.

Scott, D. (2004). *Conscripts of modernity: The tragedy of colonial enlightenment*. Durham, NC: Duke University Press.

Scott, D. (1999). *Refashioning futures: Criticism after postcoloniality*. Princeton: Princeton University Press.

Sireau, N. (2009). *Make poverty history: Political communication in action*. Basingstoke: Palgrave Macmillan.

Smith, N. (2008). *Uneven development: Nature, capital, and the production of space*. Athens: University of Georgia Press.

Sontag, S. (1977). *On photography*. London: Penguin.

Sontag, S. (2003). *Regarding the pain of others*. New York, NY: Picador.

Tsing, A. L. (2005). *Friction*. Princeton, NJ: Princeton University Press.

Van der Gaag, N., & Nash, C. (1987). *Images of Africa: UK report*. Oxford: Oxfam. Retrieved from http://www.imaging-famine.org/papers/UK_Report_Section_1.pdf

Vaux, T. (2001). *The selfish altruist: Relief work in famine and war*. London: Earthscan.

VSO. (2002). *The live aid legacy: The developing world through British eyes—A research report*. London: Author.

Wenzel, J. (2006). Remembering the past's future: Anti-imperialist nostalgia and some versions of the Third World. *Cultural Critique, 62*(1), 1–32. doi:10.1353/cul.2006.0011

Williams, L. (1998). Melodrama revisited. In N. Browne (Ed.), *Refiguring American film genres: History and theory* (pp. 42–88). Berkeley: University of California Press.

'We Thought the World Was Makeable': Scenario Planning and Postcolonial Fiction

SUSIE O'BRIEN

McMaster University, Hamilton, ON, Canada

ABSTRACT *This essay uses Indra Sinha's 2007 novel,* Animal's People, *as a critical lens to analyse the discourse of scenario planning. I argue that scenario planning, a strategy of speculation about possible futures, elides history—specifically the intertwined processes of colonialism and capitalism—in favour of the idea of globalization as an inexorable unfolding of the world as a complex system. Following a brief genealogy of the discourse of scenario planning that highlights its Cold War origins, and ongoing function in imagining, and helping to secure, the future of global capitalism, I offer as counterpoint a postcolonial reading of* Animal's People. *A fictional exploration of the aftermath of the 1984 Union Carbide factory gas leak in Bhopal, India, the novel contests (thematically and formally) the hegemonic temporality of globalization that informs scenario planning and the model of risk management it inspires.*

A third of the way into Indra Sinha's 2007 novel *Animal's People*, a fictional exploration of the aftermath of the1984 Union Carbide factory gas leak in Bhopal, India,[1] the narrative focus shifts briefly from the town of Khaufpur where the explosion occurred, to the distant offices of the company headquarters in the USA.[2] There, the Khaufpuris learn, officials have conducted a simulation exercise, planning for the possibility of a terrorist attack launched by the victims of the disaster. The narrator, Animal, and his friends are greatly amused by news of this event, and elaborate it with imagined details of their own: 'In the Kampani's fantasy', Animal's friend Zafar tells the group,

> 'the Khaufpuris took hostages and demanded coffee, then executed one of the hostages because the coffee was not to their liking.'
>
>   'What was wrong with it?' someone asks.
>
>   'Not enough cardamom, probably,' says someone else.

> In typical Khaufpuri fashion a debate starts about how much cardamom or clove should be used in coffee, and whether a few grains of salt improves the flavour.
>
> 'It was not hot enough,' says Zafar.
>
> Silence, a moment's incredulity, then a rose of laughter blossoms in the room. (Sinha, 2007, p. 283)

These embellishments underline the absurdity of the initial premise, which characterizes the Kampani as a virtuous corporate citizen, and its victims as terrorists. The context of the story's appearance, in a larger narrative about the Khaufpuris' interminable search for justice, also illustrates the limitations of the Kampani's imagination of the future, by locating it, and the associated conception of risk, in a more complex historical landscape, defined by the legacies of colonialism, sharpened by economic globalization. I begin with this brief story-within-a-story as a way into an examination of scenario planning, of which the Kampani's exercise serves as a crude example. Following a brief genealogy of the discourse of scenario planning that highlights its function in imagining, and helping to secure, the future of global capitalism, I offer as counterpoint a postcolonial reading of *Animal's People*. In both its theme and its form, I suggest, the novel contests the hegemonic temporality of globalization that informs the world-view of scenario planning.

In the discourse of scenario planning, a scenario is 'an account of a plausible future', an 'alternative, dynamic stor[y] that capture[s] key ingredients of our uncertainty about the future of a study system' (Peterson, Cumming, & Carpenter, 2003, p. 360). Employed by a diverse range of groups, including military strategists, corporations, educational institutions, and public policy-makers, scenario planning encompasses a variety of practices, including simulations of future crisis situations to demonstrate the capacities and limits of systems and equipment, and the construction, often by multiple agencies and stakeholders, of complex narratives of possible futures. Combining elements deemed to be predetermined or inevitable with a variety of unpredictable circumstances, scenarios of this latter type imaginatively play out the storylines suggested by these combinations, producing alternative future worlds. Such exercises are not designed to be predictive: 'the point', as pioneering scenario planner Pierre Wack notes:

> is not so much to have one scenario that 'gets it right' as to have a set of scenarios that illuminates the major forces driving the system, their interrelationships, and the critical uncertainties. The users can then sharpen their focus on key environmental questions, aided by new concepts and a richer language system through which they exchange ideas and data. (Wack, 1985b, p. 146)

Hailed for its capacity to help organizations plot a course through a global landscape of increasingly complex and rapid change, scenario planning has become, in the words of Melinda Cooper, 'the most ubiquitous and most consequential of epistemologies in contemporary politics' (2010, p. 171).

It might seem counterintuitive to read the discourse of scenario planning through the lens of postcolonial theory, a field that some see as increasingly *in*consequential: in the last couple of decades, a chorus of critics has argued that postcolonialism, focused on 'combat[ting] the remnants of colonialist thinking' (Hardt & Negri, 2000, p. 137), 'throws limited light on the world we now face' (Fernando Coronil, in Yaeger, 2007, p. 636). Contra arguments for its obsolescence, I work from a conviction in the continued usefulness of postcolonialism as a mode of critical analysis that works to 'challenge the failures of imagination that led to colonialism and its aftermath, a failure that continues with globalization, but is now assuming horrific new forms' (Brydon, 2006, n.p.).

Noting the persistence of 'domination by nondemocratic forces (often exercised on others by Western democracies, as in the past) ... albeit in contemporary forms such as economic globalization', Robert Young argues that:

> analysis of such phenomena requires shifting conceptualizations, but it does not necessarily require the regular production of new theoretical paradigms: the issue is rather to locate the hidden rhizomes of colonialism's historical reach, of what remains invisible, unseen, silent, or unspoken. In a sense, postcolonialism has always been about the ongoing life of residues, living remains, lingering legacies. (2012, pp. 20–21)

Postcolonialism is therefore well equipped to complicate the temporal framework of scenario planning, which is based on the logic of risk and corresponding imperative to manage future turbulence. The scene from *Animal's People* cited above highlights the ludicrous quality of future speculations that fail to take account of the historical violence that undergirds the present and, by extension, the place from which the speculation unfolds. This point speaks to an important feature of postcolonial thinking, which is the self-conscious demarcation of the location from which a story is told, and the excavation of the ground of narrative authority. Postcolonialism highlights, in Leela Gandhi's words, the 'vexed colonial history of the concept of universalism' and 'the failure of its agents consistently to transcend their own interests' (2011, p. 30, 34).

A brief history of scenario planning since its incarnation in Cold War military strategy and 1970s petro-politics highlights its unacknowledged alignment with aggressive projects of neoliberal world-making. This history troubles one of scenario planning's most compelling claims: that its commitment to diversity and emphasis on multi-stakeholder consultation translates into an enlightened and democratic approach to shaping the future. Read from the perspective of the casualties of globalization, recast as terrorists, the purview of scenario planning reflected in the Kampani's simulation exercise is an exclusionary one. Returning to the theme of time, I contend that the discourse of scenario planning elides history—specifically the intertwined processes of colonialism and capitalism—in favour of the idea of globalization as an inexorable unfolding of the world as a complex system. If, as I will argue, the overarching goal of scenario planning is to optimize the operation of that system, then postcolonial fiction may function to introduce some friction,[3] to raise questions of who is planning, for what and for whom.

The World According to Scenario Planning

As the foregoing discussion suggests, my critique of scenario planning does not proceed from an analysis of the viability of this or that specific scenario; my argument proceeds rather from an understanding of scenario planning as an 'epistemology', as suggested by Cooper (2010, p. 171), developed in a specific historical conjuncture, in association with a particular deployment of power. That is to say, scenario planning operates as a field of knowledge, a discourse, in Foucault's sense, whose production is '[i]n every society ... at once controlled, selected, organized and redistributed according to a certain number of procedures, whose role is to avert its powers and dangers, to cope with chance events, to evade its ponderous, awesome materiality' (1972, p. 216). While proponents might dispute this characterization of scenario planning, arguing that its hallmarks, such as its multidisciplinary allegiances (it draws on economics, systems theory, psychology, and risk management); its acceptance of uncertainty and turbulence as fundamental operating conditions; and its incorporation of diverse (lay and expert) perspectives actually make it *post* or *anti*-discursive, I would argue the opposite: it is precisely those elements that make scenario planning seem like a common-sense approach to globalization that constitute its political—its discursive—force.

Scenario planning proponents attribute its increasing popularity since the 1990s to the rise of uncertainties, particularly in the realms of finance, environment, and security. From a systems-analysis perspective, 'our global supernetwork is what is called a dynamically unstable system, or one so responsive and interconnected (i.e. tightly coupled), that it is prone to operating in an uncontrolled manner' (Robb, 2009). In sociological terms, following Beck (1992), globalization is frequently cited as the major force behind the proliferation of risks, as well as a weakening—in practical and social terms—of conventional forms of knowledge. Geographer and scenario planning expert Barbara Heinzen puts it simply:

> [Scenario planning exercises] have come into being thanks to two important factors: first we are living in very changeable and uncertain times, leading all societies, everywhere, to grope for new answers. Second, this need for new understanding and direction comes at a time when governments and politicians are mistrusted. (2004, p. 6)

Scenario planning thus aims to address two key weaknesses in knowledge that affect our ability to plan for the future: (1) increasing turbulence; (2) decreasing trust in traditional sources of authority for information and leadership. The collaborative nature of scenario planning purports to address both these weaknesses: including a broad group of 'stakeholders' in the scenario-creation process expands and nuances the knowledge base, as well as gesturing towards more democratic decision-making processes. Questions about the nature and extent of that democratic element are particularly pertinent to this discussion, and will be addressed below. First, however, a brief and selective history of the practice will be useful, both for establishing the key moments to which its proponents often refer as evidence of its legitimacy, and also to highlight the historical conditions of its emergence that tend to get left out of the official story.

'From Corporate Survival Strategy to Social Contract Parable': A Brief History of Scenario Planning

The story of scenario planning's emergence usually begins with Herman Kahn. A military strategist employed by the RAND Institute in the 1950s, Kahn drew on systems theory and game theory to generate what he called scenario planning—'a collective thought-experiment in which specialists from different disciplines are asked to establish and unfold a series of alternative futures from a position of present uncertainty' (Cooper, 2010, p. 172). Kahn departed from conventional Cold War assumptions by 'thinking about the unthinkable'—the possibility of various survival scenarios, post-nuclear war (Kahn, 2007, p. 211).[4] Kahn went on to establish the Hudson Institute, a conservative think tank that popularized the use of scenarios as a policy-planning tool, with a particular focus on economics.

Among the institute's corporate sponsors, and early adopters of scenario planning, was the petroleum company Royal Dutch Shell. Employment of the strategy in the early 1970s allowed the company to move outside conventional assumptions of continued price falls and anticipate the formation of OPEC and associated worldwide shortage of oil. Shell's success with scenario planning (which has become a permanent part of its corporate strategy) is routinely invoked as a case study for the usefulness of the practice as a way of navigating a crisis-laden future. Shell executives helped to translate scenario planning into a variety of different contexts, including the Mont Fleur Scenarios, developed in South Africa in 1992 to explore 'the dangers and opportunities that lurked in the transition' to democracy (Peterson et al., 2003, p. 363). The latter example in particular, is often cited in support of scenario planning's value as a tool not just of economic risk management but also of social and political emancipation (Kahane, n.d.; Marcus & Flowers, 1998).

A more detailed look at the historical context of these early chapters in scenario planning's development complicates the picture, highlighting its geopolitical contours. A key reason cited for scenario planning's appropriateness to current circumstances is the failure of conventional forms of planning in an era of unprecedented volatility. Where the science of prediction traditionally drew on the past to forecast the future, this model was inadequate to the Cold War climate in which Herman Kahn was working: 'The wisdom of experience was useless in the atomic era, because no one had ever participated in a nuclear exchange' (Menand, 2005, n.p.). Exacerbating the unknown consequences of nuclear war were the long-term, unpredictable and irreversible effects of radiation on humans and other life forms. The spectre of nuclear catastrophe loomed large in the modern global landscape that, after Beck (1992), has come to be characterized as 'risk society'. One possible response to the uncertainties of nuclear and other technologies, outlined by Barbara Adam in *Timescapes of modernity: The environment and invisible hazards*, is to proceed with care: 'On the basis of [irreducible uncertainty], ... we have no option but to live cautiously and precautionarily, cognisant of the fundamental limits to our contextual, perspectival knowledge and of the time-space indeterminacy of our actions' impacts' (1998, p. 35). Kahn's work on scenarios opened up another option: to proceed, not by ignoring or downplaying the possibility of catastrophe, which is how Adam characterizes the approach of policy-makers wedded to outmoded scientific models (1998, p. 41), but rather by *imagining* in detail worst-case scenarios and rationally weighing their cost–benefit ratios. By presenting plausible scenarios of survivability, Kahn advances the premise that *'even though the amount of human tragedy would be greatly increased in the postwar world, the increase would not preclude normal and happy lives for the majority of survivors and their descendants'* (Kahn, 2007, p. 21, italics in original). Debate persists over whether, by 'normalizing the unthinkable', Kahn sought to legitimate nuclear war (Peattie, 1984),[5] or to avoid, or at least, limit it (Jones, 2007, p. xi). What is certain is that Kahn, and the members of the Hudson Institute who shared his vision, saw what they were doing as a radical departure from the thinking of the time.

One key element of their perspective, which was to emerge in force over the next two decades, was a confident belief in a prosperous global future, with corporations at the helm. Multinationals, as Kahn and his colleagues saw it, would be 'playing the central role in the development of an interdependent world economy', heralding an era of peace, because 'No one will kill or die for General Motors' (Kahn & Briggs, 1972, p. 60). They would also serve as 'intensive laboratories for productivity', whose competition would conquer 'the bureaucratic mind-set of current management' (Kahn and Briggs, as cited in Kleiner, 2008, p. 252).

From the Hudson Institute perspective, pessimistic prognostications like the Club of Rome's 1972 *Limits to growth*, a document that played a significant role in the burgeoning environmental movement, exemplified the general problems with bureaucratic efforts to manage complex systems. The Hudson Institute shared the philosophy of Friedrich Hayek, whose rejection of the Club of Rome's analysis of population growth, along with Keynesian economic policy, reflected his long held belief that 'central planning' constituted a misguided and ultimately dangerous attempt to control the natural flows of the market. Scenario planning draws from this well of suspicion of traditional forecasting methods, in conjunction with an unquestioning faith in the inexorable forward pull of economic currents. The scenario planners even drew from the same well of hydrological metaphors as neoliberal economists: in his 1981 address to the London School of Economics, Hayek described 'multiple "streams" of value, ebbing and flowing into a river of liquid capital, constantly readjusting the production process, coursing down an ever-changing river bed' (Hayek, as cited in Walker & Cooper, 2011, p. 149). Pierre Wack's frequent use of the phrase 'shooting the rapids' to describe the context of corporate scenario planning (e.g. it is the title of his seminal 1985a article in Harvard Business Review, followed by another titled 'Uncharted waters ahead') confirms both a sense of the market as a natural ecology, and an assumption of turmoil ahead.

As the whitewater rafting metaphor suggests, the economic optimism of scenario planning advocates like Wack was tempered with wariness of encroaching danger. Forged in the environment of Cold War anti-communism, scenario planning, as developed by Shell and other multinationals through the 1970s, addressed new worries of a developing world beset by economic weakness and growing militancy. The discourse echoed Kahn's conception of the world as a complex, non-linear system, whose turbulence embodied both the exuberance of economic growth and the resistant force of postcolonial nationalist movements, which threatened to derail the Western project of ever-expanding market freedom. The language of corporate planning also retained a military flavour: when presenting the rationale for coming up with multiple scenarios of the future to Shell's managing directors, Wack explained: 'Sometimes you have to prepare for a nuclear war and a guerrilla war, two wars that are completely different, and you have to do it at the same time because both may come' (as cited in Kleiner, 2008, p. 147). The metaphor, which informed the scenario that imagined an oil crisis (something no other oil company predicted), proved prescient. The oil embargo imposed by OPEC nations in response to the USA and European support for Israel in the 1967 Arab–Israeli war registered as a threat, not just to the global economy, but also to a Western world order still struggling to come to terms with the end of colonialism. As Art Kleiner puts it in his largely admiring account of the 'radical thinkers' at Shell: 'To the oil executives (and to most American citizens), it was as if a gang of belligerent street thugs had suddenly gained the power to dominate the world' (Kleiner, 2008, p. 140). Shell's scenario plans are credited with the company's success in outwitting the thugs, and thereby contributing to the larger project of securing Western interests amidst the turmoil of globalization.[6]

If Shell's example is often cited as evidence of scenario planning's effectiveness, Mont Fleur imbues it with a quality of social legitimacy. Not the first scenario planning exercise in South Africa, Mont Fleur, facilitated by Shell executive Adam Kahane, is most widely cited, based partly on the diversity of participants (a group of 22, including 'political office bearers, academics, trade unionists and business people' [le Roux et al. n.d., p. 7]), with consultation from the ANC and PAC. The group came up with four different scenarios that became the basis for public consultation.

Notwithstanding Wack's claim that the goal of scenario planning is not to arrive at a single, winning scenario that 'gets it right' (1985b, p. 146), most scenario-planning exercises have a normative element; that is, one narrative encompasses the combination of circumstances and decisions that seem conducive to the long-term goals of the organization. In the South African case, the scenario the planners called 'Flight of the Flamingoes', which described a path of a decisive political settlement and 'sound economic and social policies' (le Roux et al., n.d., p. 17), leading to slow but ever-growing prosperity, fulfilled this mandate. The other stories sketched out very different futures. 'Flight of Icarus', for example, described a dizzying ascent, followed by a crash, while 'Ostrich' described a 'head-in-the-sand' approach by the ruling white government. The virtues of the preferred narrative are cogently summarized by the mythologized habits of its principal character: 'flamingoes characteristically take off slowly, fly high and fly together' (le Roux et al., n.d., p. 4).

The ornithological names of the scenarios were chosen to be 'accessible' (le Roux et al., n.d., p. 10) and 'unthreatening' (Marcus & Flowers, 1998). Read more critically, they help to convey scenario planning's odd mix of economic theory and mythology, whose metaphorical form is thought to make the stories both compelling and universally intelligible. Concepts loosely borrowed from evolution science help to suture the elements of myth and neoliberal economics into a framework of progress based on the logic: adapt or die. 'From studying evolution', Wack says, 'we learn how an animal suited to one environment must become a new animal to survive when the environment undergoes severe change' (1985a, p. 73). It is unclear in this formulation whether 'animal' refers to a species or an individual. Scenario planning, Wack asserts, 'aims to rediscover the original entrepreneurial power of foresight in contexts of change, complexity and uncertainty' (1985b, p. 150). The ambiguous invocation of animals and evolution illuminates the spectre of race that haunts both postcolonial economics and the 'universal' mythical imagination to which scenario planning purports to speak.

We should not be surprised that the animating vision of the Mont Fleur scenarios, which were funded by Germany's Friedrich Ebert Stiftung and the Swiss Development Agency, tied social democracy to economic development and the need for South Africa to evolve into a solid player in the global economy. The neoliberal orientation of the exercise is confirmed in the association of the 'populist' scenario—which described a substantive response to black demands for fair income distribution—with the doomed 'Icarus'. By contrast, the 'Flight of the Flamingoes' scenario 'combined strategies that le[d] to significant improvements of social delivery with policies that create[d] confidence in the economy' (le Roux et al., n.d., p. 17). The choice of this as the most plausible/desirable narrative derived validation from the much-touted democratic character of the process, in which the ANC's involvement was seen to be critical. Graham Galer explains: 'it took 3–4 months to convince relevant people of the value of this approach, and then 6–9 months to get the right people together (many of those involved are now in government)' (2004, p. 30). Getting the 'right' and 'relevant' people clearly played an important role in the planning exercise's effectiveness. While the ANC imprimatur was critical to the project's credibility, the 'right' people were those whose eventual election to power would retroactively confirm their qualifications for devising plausible futures. South African political economist Patrick Bond comments sceptically on the 'evolution of the scenario plan from corporate survival strategy to social contract parable' (1993, p. 1). Noting the tendency, borrowed from the corporate model, to construct scenario planning teams made up of 'semi-charismatic individuals',[7] he suggests that in the South African transition context, 'the scenario exercises reflected a desire of the masters and carefully hand-picked participants to come up with a *deal*—rather than with good analysis' (1993, p. 2).[8]

In line with the mandate for consensus, which, along with the selection of the most 'plausible' scenario, is essential for investor confidence, it is significant that, as one commentator notes approvingly:

> none of [the Mont Fleur] scenarios focuses on the divisive issues of black-white antagonism. Rather, they keep their sights on the long term economic prosperity of the nation as a whole. The word *apartheid*, for example, is only mentioned once. This was intentional, and is one of the great benefits of the scenario process: scenarios shift the focus from specifically opposed political positions to a broader look at *what will work—or fail—in the long run*. (Marcus & Flowers, 1998, note 2)

The rejection of 'political positions' in favour of pragmatics defines the seamless narrative of scenario planning as an activity that, while it claims to serve both corporate strategies to secure future profits *and* the efforts of citizen groups to create diverse, sustainable communities, actually *conflates* these activities in the name of a global future in which diverse groups of people work harmoniously to secure the conditions for sustainable capitalism.

The capitalist scaffolding sometimes intrudes awkwardly in scenario-planning literature; for example, a long laudatory interview with an editor with the Shell project omits details about the actual scenarios, because at the time these were considered to be proprietary information (Marcus & Flowers, 1998). The issue of private ownership is of critical significance, given the drive and the capacity of scenario planning to shape events on a global scale. Melinda Cooper elaborates this aspect of scenario planning, suggesting that, '[i]n its globalizing scope, scenario planning might be characterized as the practical, methodological counterpart to the power relations described by world systems theory' (2010, pp. 170–171). Linking the speculative nature of scenario planning to finance, in which, she suggests, the derivative (a wager on future uncertainty), works as a kind of shorthand for a scenario, Cooper highlights the capacity for such speculative activity to bring about the conditions it forecasts; indeed, this is an explicit goal of scenario planning. As in finance, the wager is not on the likelihood of this or that event, but rather on the proliferation of unpredictable events, whose volatility itself creates the climate for profit. When scenario planners invoke Mont Fleur, they lend an aura of democracy to this process—but it is just an aura, confirming Wendy Brown's argument that 'neo-liberal policies and actions' often work 'under the legitimating cloth of a liberal democratic discourse increasingly void of substance' (2003, p. 25).

The hollowing out of democracy into a shell for neo-liberalism is hastened, and given sanction, by a post 9/11 security climate, in which terrorism joins financial crisis and climate change as a source of incalculable turmoil. Though these challenges are represented as unprecedented in kind and scope, their narrativization echoes the early days of scenario planning. Then as now, the racist and nationalist underpinnings of visions of increasing turbulence are masked by references to impersonal forces. In an interview, Kees van der Heijden, one of the pioneers of scenario planning at Shell nostalgically recalls the time when, 'we thought the world was makeable' (Heinzen, Maliro, van der Heijden, & Collyns, 2004, p. 9), and attributes the end of this period to the burgeoning of computer technology and the oil politics of the 1970s. Heijden describes the defining moment as a visit to the office of a Shell manager in the Philippines to gather data, including five-year forecasts for the price of gas:

> The guy … thought it was a totally ridiculous question. How could he possibly know this? He understood there were some things not predictable in this world. This was the first time that I was confronted with the notion that a makeable world was a bit of an illusion. Anyway … it happened and I think it happened in Shell much earlier than in most other places for some reason … . (2004, p. 10)

A couple of things are notable in van der Heijden's account; first: the unexamined nostalgia for a time when 'we thought the world was makeable' (Heinzen et al., 2004, p. 9), a 'we' he later characterizes vaguely but tellingly as 'a fraternity' (Heinzen et al., 2004, p. 12). Second: the identification of the late 1960s–early 1970s as the time when this authority began to wane—without providing any historical context for this development. In his account of the meeting with the Filipino office manager, van der Heijden, credits, not the manager, whose residency in a country historically subject to the upheaval of repeated imperial incursions might have informed his insights into unpredictability, but Shell, for its prescient view of the future. What's missing here, aside from historical perspective, is any sense of reflexivity about the temporal framework scenario planning depends on, a framework whose claims to universality masks the unequal power relations that inflect conventional understandings of time, including concepts of event, evolution, past, present, and future.

The Scenario of 'Slow Violence'

In the space remaining, I want to suggest, through a reading of *Animal's People*, that postcolonial literature might offer a useful corrective—a repertoire of counter-scenarios you could say—to the world according to scenario planning. Sinha's novel challenges the temporal and geopolitical foundations of dominant constructions of a 'plausible future' by embedding them in a denser historical picture. Narrated by 19-year-old Animal, so-called because toxins from the factory explosion left him with scoliosis so severe that he walks on all fours, *Animal's People* tells the story of the Khaufpuris' long journey to bring the Kampani's American CEO to face justice in the Indian court. The novel confounds the temporality of scenario planning in several ways: first, the conventional narrative of unpredictable events, in which 9/11 assumes central, global significance,[9] is upended by the focus on the earlier more devastating disaster of Bhopal; second, the concept of the event itself gives way in the face of what Nixon (2011) terms the 'slow violence' represented by Bhopal. Finally, the novel supports scenario planners' assumption of an uncertain future, but is attuned to the unequal distribution of turbulence and, by extension, the power to create and to realize scenarios.

9/11 has come to assume iconic status in scenario planning literature. Not only has the popularity of scenario planning burgeoned since 9/11, particularly in the USA; the war on terror has become the model for dealing with all kinds of disasters.[10] In *Animal's People*, 9/11 assumes a different significance. Ma Franci, Animal's adopted mother, understands the event in the context of her idiosyncratic religious eschatology, confirming that:

> the Apokalis has already begun ... It started on that night in Khaufpur ... It has begun again, and will not stop. Round the world it will go. Right now it's in Amrika but it will return to Khaufpur. Terror will return to this city. It began here, here it will end. (Sinha, 2007, pp. 63 64)

In addition to shifting the perspective (historical and geographical) from which terror is conventionally defined, this reading alters the temporal framework that supports scenario planning. For Ma Franci, as for many Khaufpuris, 9/11 is not a unique event, but one moment in an unfolding cycle of violence dating back centuries, and culminating in the factory explosion to which it serves as a faint echo. In more pragmatic terms, the ongoing tragedy of 'that night' in Khaufpur redirects the anticipatory energy of scenario planning backward into the past conditional: ' ... if this pipe had been mended, that wheel tightened, I might have had a mother and father, I might still be a human being' (2007, p. 32). Thwarting the sentiments professed by officials claiming that 'citizens, city council, chamber of commerce, everyone, we all want to move on' (2007, p. 153), the insistent retrospective glance illuminates the costs of accepting the inevitability of what sociologist Perrow (1984) calls the 'normal accidents' of high-risk technology.

These costs are unequally distributed, as Rob Nixon points out:

> Discrimination predates disaster: in failures to maintain protective structures, failures at pre-emergency hazard mitigation, failures to maintain infrastructure, failures to organize evacuation plans for those who lack private transport, all of which make the poor and racial minorities disproportionately vulnerable to catastrophe. (2011, p. 59)

Nixon looks at *Animal's People* in the context of a discussion of the difficulties of representing what he calls 'slow violence'. Refocusing and overflowing the conceptualization of 'events' that constitutes even the most sophisticated discourses of scenario planning, slow violence, in Nixon's formulation, constitutes 'political violence both intimate and distant, unfolding over time and space on a variety of scales, from the cellular to the transnational, the corporeal to the global corporate' (2011, p. 46). The slow diffusion of violence makes it possible for responsible parties strategically to underestimate and obfuscate liability; it becomes possible to conclude, along with a cynical Khaufpuri doctor: 'those poor people never had a chance. If it had not been the factory it would have been cholera, TB, exhaustion, hunger. They would have died anyway' (Sinha, 2007, p. 153). The non-linearity and uncertainty of cumulative effects exacerbate the suffering of victims on a multi-generational scale, while confounding the efforts of victims to seek legal redress.

In some respects, the world in *Animal's People* does not look that different from the world according to scenario planners: turbulence is the norm and the future is uncertain. It only the well-meaning but naïve American character, Elli, who cleaves earnestly to the old-fashioned notion that 'the world is made of promises' (2007, p. 200). The Khaufpuris, by contrast, are intimately familiar with the volatile fallout of the fantasy of the 'makeable' world. The pesticide factory where the accident occurred was part of the Green Revolution, a post Second World War initiative funded by the Ford and Rockefeller Foundations designed to free farmers from India and other developing countries from the 'shackles of the past' by introducing methods of intensive agriculture that were highly dependent on synthetic fertilizers, herbicides, and pesticides (A.A. Johnson, as cited in Shiva, 1991, p. 35). 'You were making poisons to kill insects but you killed us instead', an elderly Khaufpuri woman tells the Kampani lawyers; 'I would like to ask, was there ever much difference, to you?' (Sinha, 2007, p. 306). Her comments locate the roots of the disaster in a development programme steeped in the values of colonialism, and translate the socio-scientific concept of risk into the discourse of social justice. The dimensions of the post-disaster landscape confound representation, let alone reduction. Writing about the challenge of advocating for Bhopal victims, anthropologist Kim Fortun notes:

> [The Union Carbide accident] is a disaster that has persisted, and operated cumulatively, drawing in a spectrum of issues that can't be contained by old blueprints for social change ... Technoscience must be condemned, while it is relied on. Legality must be pursued, while acknowledged as an insufficient remedy. (2001, p. xvii)

Fortun's observations are important in the way they articulate the limits of knowledge—a key premise of scenario planning—not with economics but with ethics: legal restitution is inadequate but *must be pursued*.

The climactic moments in Sinha's novel arise in the context of a protest over a proposed negotiated settlement between the Kampani and the Indian government, in which the Khaufpuri people greet the arrival of American negotiators with chanted protests 'NO DEAL! NO DEAL, NO DEAL!' (Sinha, 2007, p. 306): the demands of justice must exceed those of economics. It is notable, moreover, that the 'divisiveness' that Mont Fleur scenarios sought to avoid in their scenarios (by not mentioning 'apartheid') is constitutive of the relationship between the people and the Kampani; the terrain on which they meet is first and foremost political. The court offers one (admittedly insufficient, provisional) arena from which their turbulent future will be planned. Access to that arena—let alone the obtainment of justice within it—is not assured, but must be won through struggle.

What finally sabotages Kampani executives' bid to negotiate a settlement is not the protest, or even the hunger strike conducted by Animal's friends, but rather a caricatured version of the anti-terrorist planning scenario conducted back in the USA. Disguised as a cleaner, wearing a burqa and carrying a broom, the American woman Elli, enters the hotel where the lawyers are meeting and empties a bottle of stink bomb juice into the air conditioner (2007, pp. 360–361). The lawyers run frantically from the hotel; in Animal's words,

> these Kampani heroes, these politicians, they were shitting themselves, they thought they were dying, they thought they'd been attacked with the same gas that leaked on that night, and every man there knew exactly how horrible were the deaths of those who breathed the Kampani's poisons. (2007, p. 360)

To recall Cooper's observation (2010), scenarios have a way of bringing about the events they forecast. However, they do not always transpire in the way planners conceived them; the subjects of this scenario—the Khaufpuri 'terrorists'—turn out to possess agency and imagination that exceed the speculative abilities of the Kampani's planners. Their agency is limited, though, by a global system that operates on the basis of their exploitation: the 'Kampani heroes' actually have no idea of the horror of the deaths of those who breathed the factory's poisons, and the energies of prevailing economic and political orders are directed to ensuring that they never will.

The novel ends with a partial victory; a hearing has again been postponed, but there is some confidence that the Kampani will finally be brought to justice. It also ends with the resolution of a parallel narrative that has bearing on the authority of scenario planning. Animal's driving desire throughout the novel is to go to Amrika [sic] and have surgery to straighten his spine, to make him human (and—most importantly by his reckoning—attractive to women). Finally, the money is raised, and the long-awaited operation scheduled. In the end, Animal changes his mind, using the money to buy a friend out of prostitution and marry her. In declining the opportunity to elevate his stature—literally and metaphorically—to become human, Animal confounds the evolutionary logic that Wack claims informs scenario planning. His non-human status also affects the meaning and the ownership of his story, with implications for how we understand the 'plausibility' of scenario planning. According to one account, scenario planning projects often come about 'when an individual [takes] a personal risk and [draws] on his personal networks to open a new dialogue' (Heinzen, 2004, p. 5). Resonating with the description cited earlier of 'semi-charismatic individuals' and 'remarkable people', scenario planning, however much diversity is figured into it, is the province of 'leaders' and 'visionaries', whose representative authority is assumed rather than examined. Animal's status is strikingly different. On the one hand, as the title suggest, he is explicitly positioned as an advocate for the people of Khaufpur rather than simply an exemplary member of the community; he possesses special gifts (including multilingualism and modest psychic abilities), and is unapologetic in his use of them to achieve specific ends. On the other hand, as an 'animal', he can make no claim to representative status or authority; constitutively excluded from the realm of intelligibility, he speaks for those who have no voice. Rather than lending authenticity to the story (which is putatively composed of tapes made by Animal and transcribed and translated by a journalist), Animal's status casts doubt on its truthfulness and our capacity to understand it. The shadow of untranslatability looms over the whole story, encapsulated in Elli's frustrated complaint: 'Animal's People! I don't fucking understand you!' (Sinha, 2007, p. 177). *Animal's People* explores the ground of that misunderstanding, a terrain whose vast unevenness shaped the disaster and its aftermath, including the Khaufpuris' interminable wait for justice, and the Kampani's preparation for a future beset by the threat of terrorism.

Scenarios 'After Globalization'

I have suggested that the satirical light *Animal's People* sheds on the Kampani's simulation exercise can be productively enlarged to consider the problems with scenario planning more generally. These can be summarized as follows.

The Temporality of Scenario Planning

Scenario planning works according to a spatio-temporal logic whose principles are unquestioned. As one group of scholars puts it, 'To be plausible, each scenario should be clearly anchored in the past, with the future emerging from the past and present in a seamless way' (Peterson et al., 2003, p. 362). For all its sophisticated modelling of uncertainty, scenario planning according to this formula adheres to a simplistic conception of time–space dynamics. Contrary to scenario planners' vision of a future in which space and time blur together via the metaphor of turbulence, the scenario plan itself conforms to a straightforwardly linear framework. It also posits, paradoxically and anachronistically, a stable ground from which a 'plausible scenario' can be constructed.

Postcolonial literature, by contrast, while insistent on the material consequences of history, is not invested in the concepts of linearity. To the contrary, by focusing on the ongoing trauma of colonialism, it represents time as always-already fractured (as Animal explains to Elli, 'I don't need a watch because I know what time it is. It's now o'clock, always now o'clock. In the Kingdom of the poor, time doesn't exist' [2007, p. 185]). Without recourse to a (fictional) past from which 'the world was makeable', and the future apparently secure, the postcolonial subject grasps the effects of chaos and contingency on a visceral as well as an intellectual level. The negative consequences of this instability are profound: Animal suggests that 'hope dies in places like this, because hope lives in the future and there's no future here, how can you think about tomorrow when all your strength is used up trying to get through today' (2007, p. 185). However, without offering compensation for the theft of hope, the absence of any solid stake in contemporary constructions of futurity make it possible to see its limits, and might create space for more radical possibilities,[11] a point I elaborate below.

The World of Scenario Planning

Melinda Cooper links scenario planning to Emmanuel Wallerstein's world systems theory, with the key difference that 'while world systems theory is critical, historical and analytic in perspective, scenario planning is pragmatic and strategic' (2010, p. 185, n. 3). Scenario planning takes an uncritical view of globalization as a collection of processes by which the world system is elaborated, its networks extended, as links between them are tightened and multiplied. While postcolonial literature and theory does not necessarily refute this view of the enactment of globalization, it tends to evoke the concept of 'world' in a different context, indebted to the work of Edward Said. For Said, the 'worldliness' of texts refers to their non-innocence, their embeddedness in material conditions and circuits of power. '[T]exts are worldly', he explains, 'to some degree they are events, and, even when they appear to deny it, they are nevertheless a part of the social world, human life, and of course the historical moments in which they are located and interpreted' (1983, p. 4). Though Said is speaking explicitly about literary texts, we can extend his theory to talk about scenarios. While there is of course a sense in which scenarios are explicably worldly—they aim to affect the actions of decision makers and thereby to intervene actively in the world, there is a sense in which their worldliness is denied; that is, grounded in the totalizing authority of neoliberal economics, interlaced with myth, they purport to be, not worldly, but global, coming from no place in particular. They thus provide an exemplary instance of the situation, trenchantly described by Eric Cazdyn and Imre Szeman, whereby the almost total concealment of capitalism by the idea of 'globalization'—a process that is both inexorable and unending—makes it almost possible to imagine an *after* to capitalism (2013, p. 7).

In contrast, by foregrounding the conditions of the story's production and interpretation, post-colonial literature insists on both their materiality (including the presence of unassimilable traces of the past) and their partiality. Said notes further: 'Words and texts are so much of the world that their effectiveness, in some cases even their use, are matters having to do with ownership, authority, power, and the imposition of force' (1983, p. 48). This brings us to the final issue in scenario planning, which concerns the politics of story making: whose future is being planned, by whom, for whom and to what ultimate end?

The Politics of Scenario Planning

A key part of the scenario planning process is the identification of which elements of the future are predetermined, as distinct from uncertainties. The one element in the philosophy of scenario planning that is 'predetermined' or seemingly inevitable is capitalism: thus, whatever structures, social forms and institutions come undone in the course of future events, the dynamic of the market, and the rule of property will prevail. That there will be winners and losers in the future is a foregone conclusion in scenario planning, the consolation being that resilient markets will generate optimal outcomes for society as a whole. Thus, in scenario-planning discourse, there is no apparent disconnect between the structure of the Shell scenarios, which for a time remained secret, and over which Shell retains ownership, and the Mont Fleur scenarios, which were conducted in an ostensibly public way in the interests of fostering democracy. Scenario plans work, that is, they are 'plausible', to use the jargon, to the extent that they focus on the robustness of the story and the world it supports, and not on the inevitable individual casualties of those worlds—the unemployed, refugees, the elderly, the homeless, the non-human, and so on. Postcolonial literature accomplishes the opposite task, in its illumination of those invisible lives, their forgotten pasts and possible futures, and the structures that constrain them. *Animal's People* concludes with a simple scenario: 'All things pass, but the poor remain. We are the people of the Apokalis. Tomorrow there will be more of us' (Sinha, 2007, p. 366). Contrary to the speculative openness of scenario planning, this is a bald statement, a stark description of future certainty. But in its illumination of the fundamental reality of neoliberalism, the system that sets the imaginary limits for the practice of scenario planning, it might enable a different kind of opening, to the possibility of something 'after globalization' (Cazdyn & Szeman, 2013).

Acknowledgements

I am grateful to participants in the Time and Globalization Workshops, held at McMaster University in 2012 and 2013 for their insights, and for helpful comments on earlier drafts of this paper. Thanks are also due to the two anonymous reviewers, whose critiques and suggestions were very helpful for crafting the final version.

Disclosure Statement

No potential conflict of interest was reported by the author.

Funding

This work was supported by the Social Sciences and Research Council of Canada under [grant number 865-2008-0068].

Notes

1 In what has been labelled the world's worst industrial accident (Biswas, 2009), methyl isocyanate gas and other chemicals escaped into the atmosphere around the Union Carbide factory in Bhopal, killing several thousand people instantly, and disabling many more. The ensuing decades saw a protracted struggle for justice, culminating in the eventual provision of small compensation to victims, and the conviction, in 2010, of eight employees.
2 The city in the novel is called Khaufpur; the company that owns the factory is known simply as the 'Kampani'.
3 My designation of *Animal's People* as 'postcolonial fiction' although it does not represent colonialism per se stems not just from its setting and the author's origins in the postcolonial South, but also from its preoccupation with what Young (qtd. above) describes as 'the hidden rhizomes of colonialism's historical reach'.
4 Kahn borrowed the word 'scenario' from an earlier vocabulary of filmmaking, where it referred to the storyline for a movie in early stages of production. Kahn in turn provided fodder for Hollywood, as the inspiration for Stanley Kubrick's film *Dr Strangelove* (Ghamari-Tabrizi, 2009, p. 275).
5 Among the more scandalous aspects of Kahn's work was his calm weighing of options, allowing, for example, that

> it might well turn out that U.S. decision makers would be willing, among other things, to accept the high risk of an additional one percent of our children being born deformed *if that meant not giving up Europe to Soviet Russia*. (2007, p. 46, italics in the original)

6 Evidence of Shell's involvement in this project can be adduced by the company's close connections with the Bilderberg group, a coalition of government and business leaders established in 1954 to 'defend Western ethical and cultural values' (Retinger, as cited in Thompson, 1980, p. 168). Bilderberg's annual meeting has been described as 'the most important international policy conference in the world' (Skelton, 2013). Shell has been closely aligned with Bilderberg since the group's early days under the leadership of Prince Bernhard of the Netherlands. The Dutch royal family holds significant shares in Shell (an estimated 25% of the company at one time [Pitman, 2001]), while Princess Beatrix (former Queen of the Netherlands), along with Shell CEO, are current members of Bilderberg.
7 This approach echoed Pierre Wack's method at Shell, of cultivating a network of 'remarkable people' to inform planners' sense of what was going on (Kleiner, 2008, p. 135).
8 Sampie Terreblanche takes a similar view, suggesting that the exercises were 'aimed at formulating an economic-strategy that would be business-friendly and would perpetuate its position of power and privilege in a fully democratic South Africa' (2002, p. 80).
9 It is worth noting that 9/11, like the oil crisis of the 1970s, was neither as global in magnitude, nor as unpredictable, as dominant accounts suggest.
10 The subsumption of the activities of the US Federal Emergency Management Agency (FEMA) into the Department of Homeland Security after 9/11 consolidated the dominance of terrorism preparedness as the model for different kinds of disaster planning (see Lakoff, 2007).
11 While dwelling in contingency can post a practical obstacle for groups engaged in on-the-ground political action, a point Kamilla Petrick clearly demonstrates in her essay in this issue, interrogating conventional conceptions of futurity is a vital step in linking the activity of speculation with the goals of social justice.

References

Adam, B. (1998). *Timescapes of modernity: The environment and invisible hazards*. New York: Routledge.
Beck, U. (1992). *Risk society: Towards a new modernity*. London: Sage.

Biswas, S. (2009). The unending tragedy of Bhopal. *BBC News*. Retrieved from http://www.bbc.co.uk/blogs/legacy/thereporters/soutikbiswas/2009/12/twenty_five_years_and_several.html

Bond, P. (1993, July/August). Scenario plundering. *Southern African Review of Books*. Retrieved from http://web.archive.org/web/20010723031908/www.uni-ulm.de/~rturrell/antho4html/Bond.html

Brown, W. (2003). Neo-liberalism and the end of liberal democracy. *Theory & Event*, *7*(1), n.p.

Brydon, D. (2006). Is there a politics of postcoloniality?' *Postcolonial Text*, *2*(1). n.p.

Cazdyn, E., & Szeman, I. (2013). *After globalization*. Malden, MA: Wiley-Blackwell.

Cooper, M. (2010). Turbulent worlds: Financial markets and environmental crisis. *Theory, Culture & Society*, *27*(2–3), 167–190.

Fortun, K. (2001). *Advocacy after Bhopal*. Chicago, IL: University of Chicago Press.

Foucault, M. (1972). *The archeology of knowledge*. New York, NY: Parthenon.

Galer, G. (2004). Preparing the ground? Scenarios and political change in South Africa. *Development*, *47*(4), 26–34.

Gandhi, L. (2011). The pauper's gift: Postcolonial theory and the new democratic dispensation. *Public Culture*, *23*(1), 27–38.

Ghamari-Tabrizi, S. (2009). *The worlds of Herman Kahn: The intuitive science of thermonuclear war*. Cambridge, MA: Harvard University Press.

Hardt, M., & Negri, A. (2000). *Empire*. Cambridge, MA: Harvard University Press.

Heinzen, B. (2004). Introduction: Surviving uncertainty. *Development*, *47*(4), 4–8.

Heinzen, B., Maliro, A. (Interviewers), van der Heijden, K., & Collyns Napier (Interviewees). (2004). The world is not makeable. [Interview transcript]. *Development 47*(4), 9–14. Retrieved from http://www.palgrave-journals.com. [institutional_identifier]/development/journal/v47/n4/pdf/1100098a.pdf

Jones, E. (2007). Introduction to the transaction edition. In H. Kahn (Ed.), *On thermonuclear war* (pp. xi–xii). New Brunswick, NJ: Transaction. (Original work published 1960).

Kahane, A. (n.d.). Learning from Mont Fleur: Introduction. *Deeper News*, *7*(1), 1–4.

Kahn, H. (2007). *On thermonuclear war*. New Brunswick, NJ: Transaction. (Original work published 1960).

Kahn, H., & Briggs, B. (1972). *Things to come: Thinking about the seventies and eighties*. New York, NY: Macmillan.

Kleiner, A. (2008). *The age of heretics: A history of the radical thinkers who reinvented corporate management* (2nd ed.). San Francisco, CA: Jossey-Bass.

Lakoff, A. (2007). Preparing for the next emergency. *Public Culture*, *19*(2), 247–271.

Marcus, G. (Interviewer) & Flowers, B. S. (Interviewee). (1998). Storying corporate futures: The Shell scenarios [Interview transcript]. In G. Marcus (Ed.), *Corporate futures* (Vol. V). Chicago, IL: Chicago University Press. Retrieved from http://www.davis-floydpresents.com/uncategorized/storying-corporate-futures-the-shell-scenarios/

Menand, L. (2005, June 27). Fat man: Herman Kahn and the nuclear age. *The New Yorker*. Retrieved from http://www.newyorker.com/archive/2005/06/27/050627crbo_books?currentPage=all

Nixon, R. (2011). *Slow violence and the environmentalism of the poor*. Cambridge, MA: Harvard University Press.

Peattie, L. (1984, March). Normalizing the unthinkable. *Bulletin of Atomic Scientists*, *40*(3), 32–36.

Perrow, C. (1984). *Normal accidents: Living with high-risk technologies*. New York, NY: Basic Books.

Peterson, G. D., Cumming, G. S., & Carpenter, S. R. (2003). Scenario planning: A tool for conservation in an uncertain world. *Conservation Biology*, *17*(2), 358–366.

Petrick, K. (in press). Strategic planning in the 'empire of speed'. *Globalizations*. doi:10.1080/14747731.2015.1056496

Pitman, J. (2001, June 26). How much is Queen Elizabeth Worth? *Forbes*, *6*. Retrieved from http://www.forbes.com/2001/06/26/0626queens.html

Robb, J. (2009, August 17). Risk and resilience in a globalized age: Containing chaos. *World Politics Review*. Retrieved from http://www.worldpoliticsreview.com/articles/4203/risk-and-resilience-in-a-globalized-age-containing-chaos

le Roux, P., Maphai, V., Boesak, D., Davies, R., Gabriels, H., Khane, A., … Wiese, C., n.d. The Mont Fleur scenarios: What will South Africa be like in the year 2002? *Deeper News*, *7*(1), 1–22.

Said, E. W. (1983). *The world, the text, and the critic*. Cambridge, MA: Harvard University Press.

Shiva, V. (1991). *The violence of the Green Revolution: Third World agriculture, ecology and politics*. London: Zed Books.

Sinha, I. (2007). *Animal's people*. New York, NY: Simon and Schuster.

Skelton, C. (2013, June 6). Bilderberg 2013: Friendly policeman, a press zone and the One Show. *The Guardian*. Retrieved from http://www.theguardian.com/world/2013/jun/06/bilderberg-2013-day-one

Terreblanche, S. (2002) *A history of inequality in South Africa, 1652–2002*. Pietermartizburg: University of Natal Press.

Thompson, P. (1980). Bilderberg and the West. In H. Sklar (Ed.), *Trilateralism: The Trilateral Commission and elite planning for world management* (pp. 157–189). Boston, MA: South End Press.

Wack, P. (1985a, September) Scenarios: Uncharted waters ahead. *Harvard Business Review*, 73–89.

Wack, P. (1985b, November) Scenarios: Shooting the rapids. *Harvard Business Review*, 139–150.

Walker, J., & Cooper, M. (2011). Genealogies of resilience: From systems ecology to the political economy of crisis adaptation. *Security Dialogue*, *42*(2), 143–161. Retrieved from http://journals2.scholarsportal.info.[institutional_identifier]/tmp/8371516184136214228.pdf

Yaeger, P. (2007) Editor's column: The end of postcolonial theory? A roundtable with Sunil Agnani, Fernando Coronil, Gaurav Desai, Mamadou Diouf, Simon Gikandi, Susie Tharu, and Jennifer Wenzel. *PMLA*, *122*(3), 633–651.

Young, R. J. C. (2012) Postcolonial remains. *New Literary History*, *43*(1), 19–42.

Strategic Planning in the 'Empire of Speed'

KAMILLA PETRICK

York University, Toronto, Canada

ABSTRACT   *This article examines the impact of the latest wave of the social acceleration of time on the capacity for long-term strategic planning within contemporary global justice movements. Drawing upon the interdisciplinary body of literature on time and temporality, the article begins by delineating the changes to the future time perspective wrought by the shift from the modern 'age of progress' ruled by 'clock time', to a global 'network society' characterized by speed, risk, and uncertainty. In the second, substantive part, the article draws upon several dozen semi-structured interviews with social activists in order to shed light upon the challenges to contemporary social justice movements posed by the pervasive sense of precarity and futurelessness associated with life in high-speed, global risk society.*

'The future ain't what it used to be', as the famous saying goes. It is certainly true that popular conceptualizations of the future have changed dramatically over the past several hundred years. This article traces the evolution of 'futurity', the pervasive way in which the future is conceptualized and organized—specifically in the West—to suggest that recent changes to our sense of the future undermine the struggles to imagine and bring about a future radically different from the status quo, by oppositional social movements, despite the role that these movements are often thought to play in imagining a different future.

To begin, the paper delineates the changes to the *future time perspective* wrought by the shift from the modern 'age of progress' ruled by 'clock time', to the short-termism of advanced capitalist, postmodern risk society, characterized by speed, volatility, and radical future uncertainty. Informed by the insights of critical political economy and a growing body of literature on time and temporality, the second part of the paper investigates the implications of shifting temporal conceptions and relations for the capacity of social actors—Canadian social movement actors in particular—to engage in long-term strategic planning. Drawing on interviews with several dozen activists associated with the 'anti' or better yet 'alter-globalization' movement in Canada, this article suggests that, thanks to the latest wave of social acceleration, the cultural conditions in a high-speed, advanced capitalist society like Canada tend to conduce to short-term *mobilization*, to the detriment of long-term *organization*, future thinking, and the *longue duree*. The article's conclusion offers some thoughts on how the capacity for social movements to engage in long-term thinking and planning might be improved.

Modernity and the Future Time Perspective

As sociologists, anthropologists, and other scholars interested in time have noted long ago, the ways in which human beings conceptualize and organize time and space are not static; rather, the dominant temporality within a given society evolves in response to changes in the broader socio-economic context (e.g. Hall, 1983; Koselleck, 1985; Levine, 1997). This necessarily extends to the dominant conceptions or valorizations of the future, or 'futurity', whose evolution merits closer scrutiny when thinking about the capacity for strategic control of and planning for the future.

In ancient and medieval societies, the future was widely understood as controlled and pre-articulated by the weight of the past and tradition, or governed by the influence of Christian eschatology—or both simultaneously (Carvounas, 2002). According to the dominant cosmology, every earthly event and the fate of every individual was understood as predetermined according to divine providence; an individual's position within the social hierarchy was likewise 'established by God, continued by heredity, and backed by tradition', thus 'utterly inflexible' (Reith, 2004, p. 387). Likewise, the future is central to the Christian imperative to bear one's earthly cross humbly in life, and to always turn the other cheek in exchange for eternal future reward in the afterlife. This is what Boyd and Zombardo (1997) have categorized as the 'transcendental future orientation', one which Karl Marx famously derided as the 'opiate of the masses', and which he blamed for stonewalling the working-class revolution.

In the late seventeenth century, the future determinism of the Middle Ages started to give way to a new dominant temporal orientation, paving the way for what has been called 'colonization of the future' (Hagerstrand 1985 cited in Reith, 2004, p. 388). In economics, the rise of the new merchant class encouraged a new, more active engagement with the future's uncertainties since the idea that divine providence would oversee the unfolding of events was no longer satisfactory to those whose goods might be at stake. The 'creation of profits depended on foresight and planning, which in turn demanded consideration of a future that was neither fixed nor beyond human control' (Reith, 2004, p. 388). As noted by Tony Porter and Liam Stockdale in their contribution to this issue, a significant milestone in the capitalist endeavour to colonize time in line with its imperatives was achieved in the late nineteenth century with the implementation of world standard time, thanks to the efforts of a small economic elite with a vested interest in accelerating capital's global flows.

In addition to shifts in the political-economic context, on the social and cultural plane, the advent of the Enlightenment also helped to advance the radical reorientation in the dominant future time perspective. First, the 'grand narrative' of progress and the perfectibility of human-kind that emerged with the Enlightenment replaced the idea of nature's cycles or Christian salvation in the afterlife. Instead, it promised better things to come on earth, as encapsulated by the Enlightenment's idea of the progressive movement of history, which made the past seem largely supercedeable and no longer continuous with the present or constraining of the future (Carvounas, 2002).

The cultural sense of human control over the future grew along with the progress of the Industrial Revolution. On the one hand, the accelerated technological progress of the nineteenth century, involving the spread of railways, the first instantaneous media of communication (the telegraph and telephone), and the bicycle and the automobile, gave rise to widespread concern about the quickening pace of life; on the other hand, humanity continued to hold onto a strong sense of control of the future. Eloquent and impassioned evidence of confidence in what Koselleck (1985) famously called the specifically modern concept of an 'open future' is easily recognizable in the cultural texts of the era (see Kern, 1983).

In Praise of Speed

The modernist faith in the ability of accelerating transportation and communication technologies to bring about a more progressive world—a key part of what has been termed the technological sublime—reappeared at the turn of the twenty-first century as the discourse of the 'digital sublime' (Mosco, 2004). This period saw a proliferation of scholarly and popular accounts celebrating the emancipatory potential of the Internet as a decentralized and instantaneous global communication technology. According to these commentators, including Dyer-Witheford (1999), Hardt and Negri (2004), Shirky (2010), and Castells (2012), to name just a few, digital media provide an unprecedented opportunity for marginalized and dispersed political actors to connect instantly, cheaply, and 'rhizomatically'. For Shirky, moreover, part of this emancipatory potential proceeds precisely from the speed-up that digital media encourage and facilitate, insofar as this in turn frees up 'cognitive surplus' and spare time in which people might choose to engage in civic pursuits.

Yet, while it is certainly true that the Internet and related technologies are centrally instrumental to much if not most contemporary political activism, at least in technologically advanced parts of the world, the argument that faster media merely promote social movement engagement overlooks the 'dark side of the digital'. A few noted scholars including speed theorist or, to use his own terminology, '*dromologist*' Virilio (2005) as well others including Habermas (1962/1991), Scheuerman (2009), and Sunstein (2007) have shed light on some elements of this dark side by pointing out that while communication and information technologies can empower the citizen, they can also serve to fragment the public sphere and potentially hinder citizen engagement. In this paper, the aim is to add to this literature by highlighting the important ways in which our ways of thinking, particularly ways of thinking about time, are being reshaped by the predominant communication technologies, and the disturbing implications of the temporal dimensions of 'dark side of the digital' for the capabilities of social actors to engage in long-term thinking and strategic planning. Already having been weakened by several decades of neo-liberal restructuring, these capacities, I contend, are being eroded further in the context of the most recent wave of the ongoing process of social acceleration, rooted in the fundamental dynamics of capitalism, and facilitated by ubiquitous, instantaneous communication devices.

The Collapse of the Future

The nexus between the emergence of neo-liberalism and the digital revolution has meant that two centuries past the replacement of the past orientation with a future one, the dominant temporal orientation shifted yet again—this time, away from the future and towards what Nowotny (1994) has termed 'the extended present'. As before, a number of significant developments helped to bring about this development. On the cultural plane, the idea of progress that had permeated Western culture since the Enlightenment diminished significantly in the wake of famine, genocide, and two devastating world wars. Then, starting in the 1970s and 1980s, the advent of postmodernism and the associated 'linguistic turn' in literature and philosophy dealt a further blow to the twinned 'grand narratives' of *telos* and progress. The close of the century subsequently saw the proliferation of texts proclaiming the 'end' of things—the end of ideology, the end of work, and, perhaps most provocatively, the end of history, as posited famously by the neo-liberal ideologue Francis Fukuyama.

Crucially from the temporal perspective, the 1970s also saw two key developments that transformed how many societies conceptualize and organize the future, namely the rise of neo-liberalism and a revolution in information and transportation technology. The nexus between the two facilitated the shift from the Fordist mode of capitalist production to faster, more flexible, and globally coordinated economic paradigm dubbed famously by David Harvey (1989) as the post-Fordist 'mode of flexible accumulation'. The innovations associated with this shift include so-called just-in-time production, outsourcing, and importantly, as Porter and Stockdale point out in this volume, the financialization of capital, thanks to high-speed online trading, which has significantly accelerated capitalism's inherent tendency towards crisis.

Combined with the sociocultural developments outlined above, the vast improvements to the speed and spatial reach of information and transportation technologies initiated in the 1970s have resulted in a qualitative shift in the dominant structure of temporal relations in advanced capitalist countries like Canada. A growing body of interdisciplinary scholarship (e.g. Hassan, 2003, 2009; Leccardi, 2003, 2007; Scheuerman, 2004, 2009) demonstrates that this shift can be properly understood as the latest wave of the quintessentially modern 'general process of social acceleration' (Rosa, 2003). Although this process is not in itself new, as demonstrated above, in recent years, the ongoing penetration of everyday life by instant, global communication has helped to usher in a qualitative shift from the supremacy of so-called clock time of the industrial age, to 'network time', characterized by high-speed, short-term perspectives, and the imperative for immediate responses (Hassan, 2009).

In this political-economic and cultural milieu, then, existence is increasingly 'marked by high rates of change and oriented to short-run time horizons' (Rosa, 2013, p. 138). The need for instantaneous responses permitted by ever-expanding, instantaneous and increasingly inescapable communication technologies means that, as John Urry put it, echoing Nowotny, 'the future dissolves into an extended present' (2009, p. 191). As a result, the future has largely ceased to be a controllable dimension in our collective consciousness. The profound and disturbing implications of this temporal contraction for individual and organizational capacity to think and plan long term have not escaped Rosa's analysis. As he notes in his recent book,

> the need for planning in late modernity increases to the same extent that the range of what can be planned decreases. As a result, fewer and fewer things can be provided with regulations once and for all or at least for the period of one or more generations; the limit of the foreseeable moves steadily closer to the present, and politics has to shift over to a mode of muddling through where the urgency of the fixed-term reigns and temporary and provisional solutions take the place of larger political designs. (2013, p. 264)

What has been society's reaction to the hectic pace of life, perpetual state of uncertainty and pervasive sense of futurelessness? As Susie O'Brien elucidates in this issue, the response of industry, government and other organizations has been to embrace the practice of scenario planning. However, the fashion in which organizations go about this practice has little to do with radical efforts to reimagine and prefigure a more equitable world: instead, they are more properly understood as constitutive of imperialist capitalist temporality and related attempts to assert control over all possible futures. Moreover, as O'Brien's contribution makes clear, community stakeholders and social movements tend to be shut out from such planning sessions. Where does this leave contemporary oppositional social movements like the alter-globalization movement? How are their efforts to create a brighter, more just and equitable future for all affected by the pervasive short-termism and the sense of futurelessness? A brief glance at today's anti-status quo political terrain makes one wont to wonder, following Turpey (2001), whatever happened to those early twentieth-century expressions of optimism in the socialist future trumpeted in the Italian socialists' *Avanti!* or the German Social Democrats' *Vorwärts*—and where do we find their analogues today?

Anti-systemic Slowness

There are two contemporary social trends that seem to offer the most hope for challenging contemporary temporalities. The first is an upswing of enthusiasm for slowness, and the second is the alter-globalization movements. I comment on each in turn.

One of the areas in which we can observe recognition and some resistance to the frenetic pace of life in contemporary comes from the self-help sector. In recent years, a number of popular titles have appeared such as *In praise of slowness, the slow fix* (Honoré, 2004, 2013), and *Focus: A simplicity manifesto in the age of distraction* (Babauta, n.d.). These texts offer advice on decelerating one's life, including recommendations for 'digital detox', yoga, meditation, and the rejection of multitasking in favour of dedicated 'quality' time for deep reflection and interaction with loved ones.

Such individual-level solutions can certainly provide some respite from the imperatives of speed and by extension, a useful starting point for resistance to the capitalist speed imperative; however, they are inherently limited in their wider transformative potential to the extent that, in targeting the individual, they leave intact larger social structures and systemic imperatives towards acceleration. Indeed, these 'restorative' practices arguably help to maintain the status quo by recuperating the individual's ability to be 'a productive member of society'.

On the collective level, several counter-cultural movements have emerged to promote various aspects of social deceleration. Notable examples include the 'slow cities' and 'slow food' movements (though the latter in particular is not immune from a class-based critique) as well proposals to implement a 30-hour work week (see Knox, 2005; Pink, 2008). However, accounts of these movements are limited, and a gap remains when it comes to the literature on temporality and activism. More importantly, the integration of temporal themes into social movements in response to social acceleration has tended to ignore the issue of reclaiming the future.

According to some scholars, the answer to the futurelessness of global, high-speed society lies with radical social movements. Enter the alter-globalization movement, which the Italian scholar of time Leccardi has identified as

> capable of escaping from the shrinking of the global present (the time of cosmopolitan capitalism) in order to look equally at the past, by shedding light on the roots of contemporary social inequalities, and at the future, by underlying the responsibilities to unborn generations. (2007, p. 33)

This was the movement whose meteoric rise at the turn of the century prompted the aforementioned flurry of celebratory scholarship on the emancipatory power of the Internet for the emergent 'global civil society'.

What makes the alter-globalization movement particularly interesting and relevant as a case study for our present purposes is the strong, unifying desire on behalf of alter-globalization movement activists to envision and enact a future radically different from the neo-liberal status quo. One of the main themes of the alter-globalization movement is resistance to the Thatcherite dogma that 'there is no alternative'. Indeed, perhaps the key slogan of the alter-globalization movement is 'Another World Is Possible', the motto of its ongoing annual activist gathering known as the World Social Forum.

When it comes to studying the alter-globalization movement, however, a methodological challenge immediately presents itself in that the movement is far too diverse, loose and amorphous to be studied in its entirety—such a task would exceed the scope of a monograph, let alone a single journal article. For the purposes of this paper, then (and those of the larger research project upon which this article is based), in what follows, the focus falls on the temporal orientation and in particular, the future orientation among activists affiliated with the alter-globalization movement in Canada.

A focus on the Canadian alter-globalization movement is productive for several reasons. First of all, Canadian global justice activists played a key part in many of the campaigns that are commonly understood to have inaugurated the movement on the international plane, notably the 1997–1998 campaign against the Multilateral Agreement on Investment, characterized as the first successful international social movement campaign to take advantage of the internet (Ayers, 2001). Relatedly, in light of Canada's status as a highly networked, high-speed capitalist society, results of research on the role of temporal shifts in shaping the tendencies of contemporary Canadian activism can easily be generalized to manifestations of the alter-globalization movement—and to contemporary, globally networked cases of 'new media activism'—in other high-speed, industrial democracies more generally.

So, has the Canadian movement lived up to Leccardi's optimistic assessment expressed above? Has it succeeded in expanding the hegemonic temporal horizons and redesigning the future 'as a potentially controllable dimension' (Ayers, 2001)? Having mapped the changes in the hegemonic conception of the future, it is to this empirical query, then, that we now turn.[1]

Strategic Planning in the Network and in Organizations

In this section, I examine the impact of accelerated temporalities on the capacity for strategic planning in the alter-globalization movement, starting with the network which focuses on particular actions, and then looking at more formal organizations. While formal organizations might be expected to have greater capacity for strategic planning, it will become evident that they too are negatively affected by the factors that create serious difficulties for the type of longer range strategic planning that is needed for the alter-globalization movement to imagine and bring about alternative futures. I focus on strategic planning since it is crucial if an alternative future is to be imagined and brought into existence. If activists focus too exclusively on the moment, then the future will fade from view and hegemonic temporalities will continue to keep us in our extended present.

Strategic Planning in the Network

Interviews with activists revealed three ways that the influence of hegemonic temporalities undermined strategic planning. First, events are organized with no plans for follow-up. Second, there is inadequate advance planning for unexpected developments during the preparation for the events, and such developments can then add to the time pressures of the event, precluding strategic thinking. Third, there is a kind of 'addiction to urgency'. After discussing each of these in turn I show that these problems associated with a lack of strategic planning are recognized by many activists.

A discussion of long-term strategic planning in the context of the alter-globalization movement itself must begin with a recognition of the movement's networked, 'rhizomatic', and typically ephemeral structure. When individuals and groups come together during 'moments of convergence' to organize a Day of Action or a People's Summit, they do not, in most cases, intend to keep organizing together in the same formation after the action is over. The network/coalition is intentionally forged for a limited time and dissolves as soon as it has served its short-term purpose. As summed up by one activist, Benoit Renaud, who was active in the Halifax organization Mobilization for Global Justice,

> with the global justice movement, the planning was usually: what is the next big mobilization that we're building and the planning was going all the way there, and that was it. You could go as far as planning some kind of debrief after the mobilization and that was all.

As noted by several activists interviewed in this study, in the aftermath of large mobilizations, what remains in place, hopefully, are strengthened ties among the various activists who had taken part; however, how meaningful or durable these ties prove to be over time is questionable. Moreover, while short-lived, one-off actions and events are not intrinsically a bad thing (and can sometimes have powerful and lasting effects), another significant downside to becoming absorbed in the logistics of organizing a large one-off mobilization (such as the protests against the G20 in 2010 in Toronto, examined below) is that the sheer extent of the task absorbs all the time and energy of the organizers, leaving little time for reflection and long-term thinking and planning.

To give a concrete example, the chosen end point on the Toronto Community Mobilization Network's (TCMN) G20 planning timeline was the final day of the protest, and more specifically, the clean-up of the 'convergence space'. My interviews with the TCMN activists a year after the protests revealed some critical reflection on this point. Noting the urgency of the compressed organizing time frame, one TCMN member stated that the group 'did not have the time to think about the time after'.

Unexpected developments can create further time pressures. When a number of core organizers were suddenly arrested on charges of conspiracy in the lead-up to the protests (in some cases at night and at gunpoint), jail support had to be organized spontaneously and 'on the fly'. This not only presented a severe logistical challenge, but also placed additional strain on the already traumatized activists who managed to escape arrest. Earlier internal challenges had contributed to the postponement of earnest protest mobilization on behalf of the TCMN network. I wish to suggest, however, that the cultural neglect of the future and long-term thinking was also revealed in the priority placed upon mobilizing for the summit without equal effort or energy being directed to thinking longer term beyond the summit. The TCMN's planning time frame ended with cleaning out the convergence space; little forethought was given to figuring out ways of maintaining the momentum that typically follows in the wake of mass street protests.

A number of activists commented on the problem of 'addiction to urgency'. It was evident in the strategic planning brochure (2012) co-authored by Jessica Bell and other seasoned activists. In it, the authors warn against placing too much emphasis on short-term tactics at the expense of long-term strategy. They argue that

> many small groups swallow the pill of urgency-addiction and dedicate their time to doing action, action, action. As a consequence, some groups fail to address group health, address power-imbalances within the group, recruit and train new members, and build friendships. Members then burn out and leave. It's useful to occasionally ask if doing an action is the best thing the group could be doing right now. (Bell, Russell, Lungo, & Swoboda, 2012, p. 6)

This insight was likewise conveyed in a 2007 interview by Dave Bleakney, then national organizer of the Canadian Union of Postal Workers (CUPW) and member of the now-defunct alter-globalization network called People's Global Action (PGA). To Bleakney's mind, the predominant 'addiction to urgency' is profoundly inimical to long-term thinking and planning:

> there's not a lot of strategic discussions because the urgency, of course, of completing an action and taking it on and doing it can take a lot of energy out of people and often we don't debrief afterwards ... The whole notion of strategy is quite avoided, because we just go through this repetition of action to action and repeating ourselves ...

The sense of urgency identified above cannot be separated from the sense of perpetual crisis taking place in the 'extended present'. In the minds of social actors, including activists, this sense of crisis militates against the ability to think long term, an insight reiterated time and again during the interviews. Insofar as *strategy* entails forging a long-term plan involving *multiple short-term tactics*, the capacity to craft strategy becomes inevitably reduced.

Many activists recognize the problems associated with lack of time for strategic planning. While more research is necessary to ascertain the extent to which this critical assessment is shared among other TCMN organizers, the above comments by three TCMN organizers do suggest that temporal pressures linked to the sense of urgency and abbreviated organizational time frame limited the amount of time, energy, and effort dedicated to planning for the long term. The TCMN 'totally failed to foresee ... this upsurge of young activists who had nowhere to go', recalled a TCMN organizer. 'So had we been thinking better, if we were thinking beyond just the campaign, we would have had something waiting.' Another group member noted similarly that

> there was not enough done beforehand to carry the momentum from G20 into anything. I think that was a big failure. So, on the one hand we didn't have support for the people arrested pre-figured out well enough, but also, actually, how do we carry on relationships and the momentum? We hadn't done that, and because of the crackdown we lost the space to do it afterwards. So one of the lessons is, you have to do it before.

Echoing this sentiment while reflecting on the reactive character of much contemporary activism, another key TCMN member, Joanna Adamiak, remarked that 'a lot of organizing seems to happen in relation to governmental shifts, in Canada at least. So the plans that you make for protesting, it's kind of like union work, you only really talk about this bargaining round'.

The lack of capacity for strategic planning has not escaped the attention of the activists; indeed, it was recognized by many of those I interviewed. For instance, when asked for her thoughts on social movement activists' ability to create strategy, movement trainer and co-author of the aforementioned brochure Jessica Bell did not mince words: 'they suck at it'. In confirmation of this article's main argument, she attributed this shortcoming to the uncertainty and volatility impacting on activists' personal lives. Given unstable life circumstances and the perceived inability to predict even the relatively near future, strategic planning within movements is limited to one year, 'because we know we can all commit *to a year*'. A one-year plan is a short-term one, and as such, it cannot but be considered tactical rather than strategic; nevertheless, it was easily the most commonly identified strategic planning time frame among the organizers interviewed in this study.

A number of activists affirmed strategic planning while also insisting on the need to remain flexible. Paraphrasing an old adage about military campaigns, Fairley and Balkwill (2011) made a related point in their campaign planning handbook authored for the Toronto and York Region District Labour Council, by stating that '[no campaign plan survives first contact with the opponent'.[2] Adjustments to the plan should be expected, but if the plan is well conceived, the overall framework will likely stand the test of conflict, they insist. The adoption of the 'plan, act, evaluate' as a continuous practice can help activists to adjust their plans under changing conditions.

Having considered the challenges pertaining to strategic planning on the broad level of the alterglobalization movement and its network-based 'moments of convergence', the following section examines strategic planning on the meso level, by tracing the relevant practices and difficulties in relation to the groups and organizations comprising the movement. While the more structured character of these organizations might be expected to allow them to engage more in strategic planning, it will be apparent that they experience similar problems to the ones discussed above.

Strategic Planning in Social Movement Organizations

Our discussion begins with the Ontario Coalition Against Poverty (OCAP), a twenty-year-old Toronto-based community organization well known for its direct action approach to activism. Based on interviews with several long-time OCAP organizers, it appears that when it comes to strategic planning, there is significant room for improvement. According to one of its staff organizers, a strategic planning session takes place at OCAP's annual general meetings in the form of a general discussion, guided by a set of recommendations advanced by the (elected) executive committee, and open to new campaign proposals from the floor. All members are invited to take part, with the aim of reviewing and interrogating ongoing campaigns and time lines, to see if they fit into what the members think is going to be happening down the road— 'nothing more formal than that', she said.

Similarly, 'kind of ad hoc' is how fellow long-time OCAP organizer Mac Scott characterized the organization's strategic planning practices. While it boasts many experienced organizers who are 'good at learning their lessons every year' and who put a lot of thought into the alter-globalization movement, OCAP has been struggling with strategic planning for a number of years, he added. This is partly because of the lack of any kind of concrete strategic planning model. More to the point, OCAP, and arguably many other social movement organizations, struggles with strategic planning because they are always responding to the attacks on their constituencies while also trying to promote more revolutionary social change. 'We often get caught up in a crisis mentality which plays against the idea of strategic planning', Scott explained.

> At the same time, if you don't do a certain amount of strategic thinking about how you deal with crisis, you'll just be caught like everyday dealing with crises because the communities we deal with are dying everyday, there's multiple crises everyday.

Scott's insights bear out the by-now familiar argument about the pervasive addiction to urgency; they also help us to understand why strategic planning and evaluation rarely come up during regularly scheduled OCAP meetings—as confirmed by Liisa Schofield, 'in theory our meetings are supposed to be spaces for that, but often we're so focused on the immediate task list of getting through the next two weeks that it's hard to think beyond that'.

According to the organization's founding member, John Clarke, OCAP's shortcomings vis-à-vis strategic planning are part and parcel of the challenges imposed by the historical conjuncture of neo-liberalism. When asked about the activist Left's capacity to plan for the long-term future, Clarke found it lacking, as did most of the activists interviewed in this study. Attesting indirectly to the fact that the sense of disorientation experienced by individuals today has intensified, John Clarke further confirmed that

> it's genuinely difficult to have an assessment of the way forward. If you were organized in the beginnings of the post-war boom, you might make mistakes but there seemed to be clear ways forward. Today, it's much less clear. Movements that existed have been weakened massively and there's so little to draw from and so few examples. I think in OCAP we have a clearer perspective than many people but who doesn't today have more questions than answers?

Thus, it appears that even though OCAP fares comparatively well with respect to its collective memory practices (as also disclosed by the interviews for the purposes of the larger project), it is less immune to temporal pressures when it comes to forging long-term strategy. Its strategic planning sessions take place but briefly and only once a year; moreover, they are not subject to regular and systematic revision. In short, despite the organizational stability, OCAP is not entirely unlike the ad hoc networks of the alter-globalization movement insofar as it tends to operate primarily on a reactive, short-term basis.

How about strategic planning capacity in the labour movement? Here we have a relatively well-resourced sector of the Canadian left: Might we expect more long-term planning capacity than reported by grass-roots activists? The answer, in short, is no: the interviews with a number of seasoned labour activists disclosed that, by and large, Canadian unions tend to operate without a strategic plan. 'I don't think five years in the future, ever, no. Maybe a year?' said Denise Hammond, president of CUPE Local 1281 and an alter-globalization movement veteran:

> I don't think there is a long-term strategy because people in many ways are trying to survive and get through today. And it takes more time and energy to think about what we'll do for the next year than just focusing on: next June, we're going to build for a rally.

Echoing the often-repeated argument about the general state of social volatility, Denise Hammond further observed that

> within CUPE, there is an effort to do some strategic planning, but the reality is that at least at this current moment there's so many battles being waged on workers and public services that even at our convention we sort of adopt a plan of action that we're going to work on for the year, and it's constantly changing because there's just so much is happening and you have to be able to respond.

To be sure, it is important to acknowledge that the reasons for the paucity of strategic planning in labour unions suggested by the above comment are multiple and complex. It is certainly true that the 'post-war compromise' between labour and capital, followed a few decades later by the onset of neo-liberalism, that has played a key part in the foreclosing of the progressive left's long-term radical imaginary. The related shift within the labour movement has been away from efforts to create a different kind of society and towards a focus on what a retired Canadian Auto Workers (CAW) educator Steve Watson termed 'babysitting the membership'. Watson elaborated by explaining that the day-to-day reality of the union is still more like a business than a social movement. And like a business, it's just thinking about the next quarter, like, what are the next quarter's results going to be? What are we going to report to our shareholders this quarter so they don't dump all their shares? There's that kind of mentality, that's the business way of operating. I think corporations are doing more strategic planning than we do, when we should be doing the strategic planning about how we organize ... Nobody seems to have an industry-wide campaign: OK, here's our plan to union-ize all the auto parts plants in Canada, which are only about forty percent unionized at best, lucky if it's thirty percent ... We're the Canadian Auto Workers! Where's the plan to unionize the auto industry?!

In light of these comments, it becomes clear that the short-termist orientation driven by social acceleration and inimical to long-term thinking is prevalent across the alter-globalization move-ment, not only within the ephemeral-by-design counter-summit coalitions but also within the relatively well-resourced and durable organizations of the Canadian labour movement.

Speaking from his extensive experience within the CAW, Watson continued to attest to the inimical consequences of the propensity of unions to prioritize the immediate at the expense of the long term:

I think one of the faults of our union, and it's a real downfall of the union, is that we're great at start-ing something—do we ever finish it? Look at all the different campaigns we'll initiate, go to our website on any particular day and you'll see: oh, today's campaign is this, we're gonna save the ship-yards in Halifax, tomorrow it will be this, something else, we go from one thing to the next, and everything is important that day, but the next day it's something else, so what did we do yesterday? Well, I can't remember, we're doing this today! But where's the strategic plan when you can't remember what you did last week, and you're doing something else this week that you weren't doing last week? I'm not saying reacting to new challenges isn't important, but I'm saying we could do a little bit better than the purely reactive. Think about this: would we have medicare in this country if Tommy Douglas thought it was a three-month campaign?

Similarly, when asked whether uncertainty bears the blame for the lack of long-term strategic plan-ning within unions, labour strategist Rob Fairley shot back: 'Is the world constantly shifting and shifting dramatically? Absolutely! Have other people worked under changing circumstances with wars and invasions and economic collapses and all of that? Sure. You still have to have a plan.'

Fairley has extensive experience with strategic planning within the labour movement; as men-tioned above, he is co-author of the Toronto and York Region Labour Council's *Campaign plan-ning handbook.* From his perspective, the key to successful strategic planning is making it a participatory process; however, this happens very rarely, he noted, for reasons for this get to the very heart of union democracy, as well as the need to accept change.

Echoing fellow labour activists, Fairley also confirmed a troubling absence of strategic plan-ning within unions. Asked whether there are any exceptions, he was able to identify only one, namely CUPE Local 4400, Toronto Education Workers. This particular local employs a variety of strategic planning practices, he explained, including an out-of-town annual executive board strategic planning session that lasts several days, and involves a comprehensive planning process which yields a final report as well as a 'user-friendly' single-sheet report summary. Work planning is subsequently carried out with the help of the local's vice-presidents in order to implement the handful of key strategic priorities identified in the report. Furthermore, an annual 'committee day' involves the members of all the various committees in reviewing the strategic plan in order to figure out how the committees can advance that plan. Finally, there is an annual stewards' assembly of about 150 individuals, which also takes place out of town over a weekend out of town, and is focused on the role of stewards in moving forward the strategic plan. 'It's a pretty good model', said Rob Fairley, 'and I think it's pretty rare within the union movement'.

Strategic Planning in Comparative Perspective

Despite the critical tone of our assessment so far, in assessing the effects of social acceleration on individual and collective capacities, it is important to keep in mind that this process has not penetrated all parts of the globe to the same extent. The growing 'time studies' literature offers a number of cross-cultural analyses of different temporal orientations (e.g. Hall, 1983; Levine, 1997). The important point is that the relatively 'underdeveloped' or 'developing' countries of the global South, as well as a number of localities in the advanced capitalist world, including some regions of Europe, retain a relatively greater emphasis on tradition, history, and the importance of sustained, intimate relations with one's extended family and community members. In such places, the cultural influence of time-annihilating media has been relatively constrained, supporting qualitatively different cultural and intellectual habits and capacities and relationships than those pervasive in the North.

In light of this, it seems reasonable to assume that the capacity for long-term planning might be stronger among activists in those places. Indeed, this hypothesis was confirmed by several activists. For instance, long-time CUPW organizer and former North American PGA convener Dave Bleakney noted that

> it'd be interesting to compare some of the Southern movements around this 'cause I find they're a little more 'stewed' at long-term strategies and that one action must build towards something else. They're not 'one-offs', so if you're doing something in the street, it is tied to something else.

In working alongside some Southern activists within the networks of the alter-globalization movement, Bleakney came to believe that although they may be somewhat bureaucratic, 'there's still some sense of—you don't just do actions 'cause you're angry. You do actions because you're trying to build something'.

Likewise, Elsa Beaulieu, an organizer with Marche Mondial des Femmes (Women's World March) and veteran of the alter-globalization movement in Québec, expressed admiration for the strategic orientation evidenced by the Latin American activists within her organization. 'Every meeting they have in Latin America there's analysis of *coyuntura*, context and its evolution, local, national and international', she stated. 'They use it all the time, always thinking about the situation evolving and how we're going to create strategy for ourselves within it ... I find it so inspiring.' Echoing Dave Bleakney, she contrasted the Latin American activists' propensity towards strategic analysis with that of Canadian or North American activists, who, to her mind, tend to focus their energies on event publicity and public relations rather than on seriously thinking through the systemic problems facing them and long-term plans for addressing them.

As Bleakney and Beaulieu's comments illustrate, temporal biases influencing cultural tendencies, habits, and intellectual capacities are not an automatic outcome of technology or its use. Rather, they are shaped by the given configuration of pre-existing political-economic and cultural conditions. To be sure, further research is necessary in order to permit a comparison of the sense of the future and the associated ability for long-term thinking and planning across the global North and South. While an initial effort in this direction was elucidated above, a fuller comparison is beyond the scope of this paper and constitutes a worthwhile goal for future research. For the time being, it may be asserted with confidence that the predominance of the hegemonic 'space bias' of modern capitalist media whose implications for activism we have been examining in this study is not a universal, worldwide condition—it is specific to those parts of the globe that have undergone capitalist technological modernization to an advanced degree. To reiterate, then, rather than *creating* biases, communication media, structured by vested interests, serve to intensify or deepen pre-existing tendencies.

Concluding Remarks: The Need for Reflection

In this article, I have argued that the dominant cultural sense of future precariousness militates against the individual and collective capacity to create plans for the long-term future; what is more, the shift away from building lasting movement infrastructure in favour of a loose and amorphous, networked mode of political engagement that I am calling 'fast activism' likewise impacts on the capacity for strategic planning evident among alter-globalization activists.

By way of conclusion, it is important to acknowledge that a sense of urgency can be a powerful motivational factor, and it is not my intention to discount or discourage it altogether. Nonetheless, in the contemporary capitalist society reeling from social acceleration, the tendency to attend only to what is on the immediate temporal horizon has resulted in excessive tendency towards short-term reaction on the activist left. Confirming a lack of planning capacity on the left, activist and author David McNally noted in our interview that

> the ruling class thinks long term even though it can get obsessed with the momentary and the short term ... but all the time it uses institutions to shape long-term strategic visions and there's no meaningful left organizing without that. You have to be able to do it.

Many other activists I spoke with felt similarly. Indigenous solidarity activist Alex Hundert summed it up well in insisting, in my opinion correctly, that 'things are rarely as urgent as we think they are ... there is always more urgent things happening than we can possibly deal with. So strategic planning is about disrupting the cycles of crisis that create the urgency'.

In short, although the temporal horizon of the future has been foreshortened, activists can learn to become better strategic thinkers and planners by reflecting upon their unconscious biases and learning new heuristic planning tools. Preliminary evidence from the interviews suggests that there exists percolating awareness of the need to develop strategic planning capacity among Canadian activists. Philippe Duhamel, for one, who works today as a movement trainer and consultant, noted that in recent years, he has observed growing interest in learning 'how to do strategic planning' among young activists, as 'more and more of 20s generation know that they live in a complex world, one that their elders from 70s or 80s couldn't fathom ... '. Along similar lines, after commenting on the failure of the Toronto Community Mobilization Network to plan beyond the last day of the G20 protests, a young TCMN activist who earlier despaired about the lack of planning in the group revealed that she had joined a new group

> which in order be a core member you have to submit a one year work plan, which I think is kind of amazing cause they're actually trying to start doing that, like, thinking beyond the end of the next action.

At the time of our interview, the group did not yet have a name, but the expressed enthusiasm for long-term planning was both infectious and inspiring. Similarly, according to Alain Savard, one of its activists, the student movement in Quebec has been honing its capacity for strategic planning, with the 2012 student strike against drastic tuition fee increases involving a time frame of two years—the movement's most radical organization is currently in the midst of figuring out whether a long-term strategic plan for free education is feasible.

Admittedly, deep reflection on the future or any other subject is increasingly a luxury in our turbo times; nonetheless, it must be stressed that just like capitalism, the way in which time is structured is historically contingent, hence subject to critical reflection and radical transformation. In striving towards radical change to the social order that compels acceleration, intermediate steps could address how time is distributed as an aspect of power. As noted by Panitch, these efforts can include the implementation of radical proposals for a statutory reduction in the working day, which would not only ameliorate the 'maldistribution of employment in contemporary capitalism', but also 'establish the conditions for the extension and deepening of democracy by providing the time for extensive involvement in community and workplace decision making' (1994, p. 88). France has been leading the way in this regard, recently implementing a law that clamps down on workplace-related communication after 6 pm. The ability of the state to reduce the working day is significant in that it represents a potential to 'slow down' the tempo of life in capitalism, and to provide people with more time to develop critical intellectual and creative capacities. Whatever the intermediate steps taken in this direction, from the radical perspective, the long-term goal involves the eventual emergence of a post-capitalist society wherein the equation 'time is money' will no longer obtain.

Disclosure Statement

No potential conflict of interest was reported by the author.

Funding

This work was supported by the Social Sciences and Humanities Research Council of Canada through the Joseph-Armand Bombardier Canada Graduate Scholarship.

Notes

1   In terms of methodology, I examine the practice of strategic planning within Canadian activism by drawing upon interviews with activists of different ages and backgrounds who have engaged, in a leadership capacity, in the various movements comprising in the alter-globalization movement. The interviews were semi-structured and secured using the snowball method, starting with the author's own contacts in Canadian social movements. The transcribed interview data were coded using the Nvivo software on themes related both to the history of this movement in Canada over the past 15 years and to its temporal orientations, values, and practices, particularly those related to movement building, collective memory—and long-term strategic planning. Together, these make up the contents of the author's doctoral dissertation (Pietrzyk, 2013).
2   Drawing on the work of many people, the handbook was 'written for unions, but the principles of campaign planning apply to all social movements', according to the authors (Fairley & Balkwill, 2011, p. 2). Inside the handbook the reader can find advice on creating, implementing, and evaluating campaigns, as well as a number of planning tools, such as Force Field Analysis, Spectrum of Member Support, and Power Mapping.

References

Ayers, J. M. (2001). Transnational political processes and contention against the global economy. *Mobilization: An International Journal, 6*(1), 55–68.
Babauta, L. (n.d.). *Focus: A simplicity manifesto in the age of distraction*. Retrieved March 12, 2013, from http://zenhabits.net/focus-book/
Bell, J., Russell, J. K., Lungo, S., & Swoboda, M. (2012). *Action strategy: A how-to guide*. Retrieved March 20, 2012, from http://www.toolsforchange.net/wp-content/uploads/2012/03/RuckusActionStratGuidedraft7.pdf
Boyd, J. N., & Zombardo, P. G. (1997). Constructing time after death: The transcendental-future time perspective. *Time & Society, 6*(1), 35–54.
Carvounas, D. (2002). *Diverging time: The politics of modernity in Kant, Hegel, and Marx*. Langham, MD: Lexington Books.
Castells, M. (2012). *Networks of outrage and hope: Social movements in the internet age*. Cambridge: Polity Press.

Dyer-Witheford, N. (1999). *CyberMarx: The circuits of struggle*. Urbana, IL: The University of Illinois Press.

Fairley, R., & Balkwill, M. (2011). *Campaign planning handbook*. Toronto: Toronto & York Region Labour Council.

Habermas, J. (1962/1991). *The structural transformation of the public sphere: An inquiry into a category of bourgeois society*. Cambridge, MA: The MIT Press.

Hall, E. T. (1983). *Dance of life: The other dimension of time*. Garden City, NY: Anchor/Double day.

Hardt, M., & Negri, A. (2004). *Multitude: War and democracy in the Age of Empire*. New York, NY: Penguin Press.

Harvey, D. (1989). *The condition of postmodernity: An enquiry into the origins of cultural change*. Oxford: Blackwell.

Hassan, R. (2003). *The chronoscopic society: Globalization, time and knowledge in the network economy*. New York, NY: Peter Lang.

Hassan, R. (2009). *Empires of speed: Time and the acceleration of politics and society*. Leiden: Brill.

Honoré, C. (2004). *In praise of slowness: How a worldwide movement is challenging the cult of speed*. New York, NY: Harper.

Honoré, C. (2013). *The slow fix: Solve problems, work smarter, and live better in a world addicted to speed*. New York, NY: Harper.

Kern, S. (1983). *The culture of time and space, 1880–1918*. Cambridge, MA: Harvard University Press.

Knox, P. L. (2005). Creating ordinary places: Slow cities in a fast world. *Journal of Urban Design, 10*(1), 1–11.

Koselleck, R. (1985). *Futures past: On the semantics of historical time*. Cambridge, MA: MIT Press.

Leccardi, C. (2003). Resisting the acceleration society. *Constellations, 10* (1), 34–41.

Leccardi, C. (2007). New temporal perspectives in the 'high-speed society'. In R. Hassan & R. E. Purser (Eds.), *24/7: Time and temporality in the network society* (pp. 25–36). Stanford, CA: Stanford University Press.

Levine, R. (1997). *A geography of time: The temporal misadventures of a social psychologist; or how every culture keeps time just a little bit differently*. New York, NY: Basic Books.

Mosco, V. (2004). *The digital sublime: Myth, power, and cyberspace*. Cambridge, MA: MIT Press.

Nowotny, H. (1994). *Time: The modern and postmodern experience* (Neville Plaice, Trans.). Cambridge: Polity Press.

Panitch, L. (1994). Globalisation and the state. In R. Miliband & L. Panitch (Eds.), *The socialist register* (pp. 60–93). London: The Merlin Press.

Pietrzyk, K. (2013). *Time, technology, and troublemakers: 'Fast activism' and the alter-globalization movement in Canada* (Unpublished PhD dissertation). Toronto, ON: York University.

Pink, S. (2008). Sense and sustainability: The case of the slow cities movement. *Local Environment, 13*(2), 95–106.

Reith, G. (2004). Uncertain times: The notion of 'risk' and the development of modernity. *Time & Society, 13*(2/3), 383–402.

Rosa, H. (2003). Social acceleration: Ethical and political consequences of a desynchronized high-speed society. *Constellations, 10*(1), 3–33.

Rosa, H. (2013). *Social acceleration: A new theory of modernity* (J. Trejo-Mathys, Trans.). New York, NY: Columbia University Press.

Scheuerman, W. E. (2004). *Liberal democracy and the social acceleration of time*. Baltimore, MD: John Hopkins University Press.

Scheuerman, W. E. (2009). Citizenship and speed. In H. Rosa & W.E. Scheuerman (Eds.), *High speed society: Social acceleration, power, and modernity* (pp. 287–306). University Park: Pennsylvania State University Press.

Shirky, C. (2010). *Cognitive surplus*. New York, NY: Penguin.

Sunstein, C. R. (2007). *Republic.com 2.0*. Princeton, NJ: Princeton University Press.

Turpey, J. (2001). The past after the future. *Open Democracy*. Retrieved May 11, 2012, from http://www.opendemocracy.net/faith-globaljustice/article_222.jsp

Urry, J. (2009). Speeding up and slowing down. In H. Rosa & W. E. Scheuerman (Eds.), *High-speed society: Social acceleration, power, and modernity* (pp. 179–201). University Park: Pennsylvania State University.

Virilio, P. (2005). *The information bomb*. London: Verso.

Index

24/7 time 14–18, 20
9/11 8, 93–4, 99n9

Abacus CDOs 33
acceleration: capitalism's trajectory of 13–14, 18, 21, 24, 44; circle of 43–4; and health risks 43, 50–2; and ICTs 9, 59–60, 64; *see also* social acceleration
accidents, normal 94
Adamiak, Joanna 109
adaptability, rapid 5
Africa: inevitability of suffering in 82n2; temporal narrative of 69–70, 76–7
aid, international 4–5, 68–9, 73–5
air travel, spread of disease through 6, 44, 46–7
alter-globalization movement 10–11, 103, 106–8, 110–14, 115n1
anachronism 14, 18–20, 24–5, 26n6, 77, 82
ANC (African National Congress) 91–2
Animal's People 10, 86–8, 94–6, 98, 99n3
apartheid 92, 95
Apple 37, 64, 65n4
asymmetry 23
atemporality 21, 23
avian flu 43

Bangladesh, e-waste recycling in 61–3
Bank for International Settlements 21, 35
Barthes, Roland 72, 77
Basel Action Network 58, 61–2
BBC 74–5, 78, 82–3n4
Beaulieu, Elsa 113
Bhabha, Homi 79
Bhopal gas leak 10, 53, 86, 94–5, 99n1
Bilderberg group 99n6
biological time 44
biopolitical globalitarianism 22
Birhan Woldu 76–7, 79–82, 83n5
Blackberry 37
black swans 8
body, as untimely 20–4
Bollywood 71, 73

border control 43–4, 49–50; *see also* cross-border movement
boundaries, erosion of 44
British Columbia Cancer Agency 51

cadmium 62–3
Canada: alter-globalization movement in 102–3, 107; infectious disease responses in 49–51; labour movement in 111–12
capitalism: Eurocentric account of 69; financial flows of *see* financial markets; globalized production under *see* global production; historical process of 10; lack of alternative to 8, 98; mode of flexible accumulation 105; and scenario planning 86, 88, 93; temporality of 13–18, 20–1, 31, 103; and waste 64–5
Cartesianism 16
catastrophe 90, 94
CAW (Canadian Auto Workers) 111–12
CBC (Canadian Broadcasting Corporation) 76, 78, 83nn5–6
CDOs (collateralized-debt obligation) 33
celebrity humanitarianism 68, 76
Centers for Disease Control (CDC) 51
ceremonial politics 79
Chakrabarty, Dipesh 15, 68–9, 71, 75
China: response to SARS in 48, 50; spread of SARS from 46–7, 49
Christian eschatology 103
chronopolitics 4–5, 9, 64, 69
Clarke, John 111
clichés 75, 77–8
climate change 2, 8, 93
clocks, as technical artefacts 30, 39n1
clock time: accelerating 18; in globalization and colonization 3, 15; shift from 10, 102
Club of Rome 90
cognitive surplus 104
Cold War 86, 88–91
colonialism: and anthropology 70; and capitalism 86, 88; and development 95; and globalisation 10; legacy of 87–8, 97; and time 3–5, 15

117